Security Integration in Europe

Security Integration in Europe

HOW KNOWLEDGE-BASED NETWORKS ARE TRANSFORMING THE EUROPEAN UNION

Mai'a K. Davis Cross

The University of Michigan Press
Ann Arbor

First paperback edition 2013
Copyright © by the University of Michigan 2011

Published in the United States of America by
The University of Michigan Press
Manufactured in the United States of America
⊗ Printed on acid-free paper

2016 2015 2014 2013   5 4 3 2

A CIP catalog record for this book is available from the British Library.

Library of Congress Cataloging-in-Publication Data

Cross, Mai'a K. Davis, 1977–
    Security integration in Europe : how knowledge-based networks are
    transforming the European Union / Mai'a K. Davis Cross.
        p. cm.
    Includes bibliographical references and index.
    ISBN 978-0-472-11789-5 (cloth : alk. paper) —
    ISBN 978-0-472-02768-2 (e-book)
        1. Security, International—European Union countries—Planning.
    2. Policy networks—European Union countries.   3. National
    security—European Union countries—Planning—International
    cooperation.   4. Internal security—European Union
    countries—Planning—International cooperation.   I. Title.
    JZ6009.E94C76   2011
    355'.03354—dc22   2011014830

ISBN 978-0-472-03531-1 (pbk. : alk. paper)

For Murphy

Acknowledgments

THE FIELD RESEARCH for this project was possible in large part because of a fellowship from the Fulbright Foundation and because of the cooperation of the nearly eighty ambassadors, military generals, crisis management experts, Commission officials, and think-tank analysts who kindly granted me interviews in 2009. The opportunity to spend so much time talking with these individuals one on one about the work they do opened up an entire world of dialogue, interaction, and persuasion that I have tried to convey in these pages. I also received generous research support from the University of Southern California's School of International Relations, the Von Kleidsmid Center, the Center for International Studies, the Center on Public Diplomacy, and the Dornsife College of Letters, Arts, and Sciences. The EU Institute for Security Studies (EUISS) also hosted me as a visiting fellow for three months in 2009.

I especially appreciate the feedback I received from Giovanni Grevi while visiting EUISS. Daniel Keohane and Marcin Zaborowski were also very kind to offer their comments on parts of this work. Many other colleagues gave me their opinions on various aspects of this research, including Thomas Christiansen, Costas Constantinou, Magnus Ekengren, Jolyon Howorth, Vincent Pouliot, Mark Rhinhard, and four anonymous reviewers. This research has been especially influenced by the work of Jeffrey Checkel, Simon Duke, Martha Finnemore, Peter Haas, Jolyon Howorth, Peter Katzenstein, Margaret Keck, Kathleen McNamara, Andrew Moravcsik, Thomas Risse, John Ruggie, Paul Sharp, Kathryn Sikkink, David Spence, Ezra Suleiman, Alexander Wendt, and Geoffrey Wiseman. Ezra Suleiman has been an excellent mentor and has advised me on my career and research both during and after my time at Princeton.

My wonderful editor at the University of Michigan Press, Melody Herr, provided me with excellent advice in the final stages of revision and took very good care of the manuscript through the whole publication process. Mary Child worked with me on the title of the book and made suggestions for the introduction. Kathryn Simons was of great help with the index. Two students at Colgate University, T. J. Gunerman and Sarah Tilley, performed some of the preliminary research, and at USC, Christina Gray was invaluable in helping me set up interviews and doing some last-minute background research. Maya Swisa carefully read over the proofs.

I began this research while I was an assistant professor at Colgate University, and thus I am grateful to Colgate University's Research Council and to the school's political science and international relations departments. While at Colgate, I had the opportunity to lead a faculty seminar on epistemic communities and was able to invite Peter Haas to come to campus. These discussions helped me shape the framework of this book. At Colgate, I especially thank Stanley Brubaker, Tim Byrnes, Fred Chernoff, Bob Kraynak, Lyle Roelofs, and Al Yee.

My father, Michael C. Davis, a professor himself, has read all of my work in one form or another and is always the first to point out how I can sharpen my arguments. The ability to brainstorm my ideas with him has been invaluable. My mother, Pamela Davis-Lee, has inspired me with her ideas, efficiency, and passion for what she does, even though it has nothing to do with European security or epistemic communities. Most important, my husband, Robert Cross, has taken care of so much on his own to enable me to go to Europe and write this book. He did everything one could imagine—including caring for Murphy and then raising Bailey (our puppy) while recovering from two major surgeries and writing his dissertation—so that I could focus on my work without any burdens. He was the first person to read this manuscript cover to cover, and he edited my writing with close attention to detail.

This book is dedicated to Murphy, my dear golden retriever, who was a constant fixture in my life from my days in high school until May 3, 2009. Murphy flew to Hong Kong twice and lived with me in New York City, Princeton, Washington, D.C., Upstate New York, and the Los Angeles area. He was the best dog one could imagine. I was in Europe conducting interviews for this book during his last few months, but my heart was unfailingly with him.

Contents

Introduction   I

CHAPTER 1. Why Do Epistemic Communities Matter?   13

CHAPTER 2. Toward European Security Integration   42

CHAPTER 3. Diplomats and Internal Security   77

CHAPTER 4. Diplomats and External Security   122

CHAPTER 5. The Military Community   145

CHAPTER 6. Loose and Nascent Communities   186

Conclusion   214

Notes   229
Bibliography   251
Index   265

Introduction

THE EUROPEAN UNION is quietly emerging as a significant security actor. It is perhaps a little-known fact that the EU has thousands of troops deployed around the world under its blue-and-gold-starred flag. In the past decade, it has engaged in 24 civilian and military operations in unstable and conflict-ridden regions.[1] Member states altogether spend nearly €200 billion annually on defense in support of around 1.7 million active service members.[2] More often than not, the EU speaks and acts with one voice in the international community. Such instances include imposing international sanctions, condemning external actions that violate the rule of law, and offering high levels of development assistance.

But these activities are just the beginning. Security is a broader concept than it once was. Traditional aspects of security such as national defense spending, sanctions, and boots on the ground are no longer necessarily central to power in the international security realm. New threats arise from nonstate actors, the integrity of borders is more vulnerable to transnational flows, and attacks are increasingly perpetrated from within states. The EU is addressing these new challenges through common approaches to police protection, border defense, intelligence sharing, legal guidelines, and so on. It has even created agencies in these fields, thereby assuring coordination, integration, and follow-through. In many ways, the EU is uniquely able to adapt to these developments as an evolving actor in its own right. But at the same time, such successful and rapid adaptation has been highly unexpected. After all, integration in the security realm affects the very core of traditional state sovereignty.

The EU comprises 27 member states, all with strong claims to national sovereignty, especially with regard to security and defense. Nonetheless, the EU has adapted and continues to do so in ways that reflect a strong understanding of the new complexities in today's globalized world. European member state militaries are being reformed, transformed, and streamlined so that they are more amenable to engaging in crisis response abroad rather than simply in conventional defense on European soil. They are also becoming interoperable vis-à-vis each other, a process that is gradually leading to increasing common capacity. Over the past few years, influential EU officials have realized that integration across and within various security sectors means that member states can maintain or even decrease defense spending while still augmenting common capabilities. To support this effort, member states have established the European Defence Agency and are willingly abiding by the norms it sets forth, including a common program of security research and development. The EU continues to find ways to take advantage of economies of scale in its increasingly integrated approach to security.

A similar process is unfolding on the internal security front. Since the EU is largely internally borderless, member states tackle protection of the European "homeland" in common; for the most part, this is a highly integrated area of security policy. Member states have harmonized their approaches to police, intelligence, and border protection—everything from European evidence and arrest warrants to common procedures on immigration and asylum. Collectively, they deal with nonconventional weapons threats in the form of chemical, biological, and radiological attacks and address environmental, food, and energy security concerns alongside crime, drugs, and human trafficking. The line between internal and external security is virtually nonexistent; the EU's remarkable progress in both dimensions thus contributes to its power as a global security actor.

Because the EU operates and acts according to an expansive definition of security, it is quite distinctive from the other major security actor in the region, the North Atlantic Treaty Organization (NATO). In contrast to the EU, NATO still applies a relatively narrow definition of security and tends to reflect vestiges of the Cold War approach to conflict. NATO is also heavily reliant on the United States and its military resources. While the EU constitutes an important pillar of NATO—only six EU member states are not part of NATO—the EU increasingly encompasses much more. It reaches into the daily lives of its citizens through internal security protections and exercises various forms of external power. Civilian power has been quite evident, but military power is on the rise. Compared to nation-states, the EU is an actor in flux; it is continuously defining and redefining what it can do and what it is. Security integration is unexpected, but it provides an important window into understanding the EU's nature, its future trajectory, and how governance works in this hybrid organization that has many statelike qualities.

This book primarily explains why the EU is becoming a security actor and shows how this process has already affected security outcomes in international relations. While security integration was never inevitable, the European project has always been about security. In 1951, with the inception of the European Coal and Steel Community, forward-looking leaders launched a grand, idealistic experiment to try to end the possibility of future war on the continent. The leaders of France, Germany, Italy, and the Benelux countries (the Six) agreed to pool production and allow the free movement of coal and steel, precisely the resources behind France and Germany's military power. From the beginning, the Six wanted more for Europe than just economic integration. They also called for the creation of a common European defense policy and a European political community, and many even spoke of federalism—a United States of Europe. While progress in the security area has endured several setbacks over the past half century, the EU's track record began to improve in the wake of the 1992 Maastricht Treaty and has evolved remarkably in the past ten years.

As security issues have become increasingly technical—involving border control, migration, justice, common arrest and evidence warrants, cross-border crime, and civil-military operations in third countries, among others—the number of different types of actors contributing to policy shaping and decision making has grown in tandem. These actors include professional diplomats, top-level military officers, technology experts, police officers, defense experts, defense industry professionals, scientists, and think-tank researchers.

This book examines the role of these actors in crafting security and defense policy, devoting special attention to the transnational and expertise-driven nature of their interaction. It addresses the broad questions of how diplomatic processes influence policy and the nature of the connection between expertise and outcomes in the context of the EU. European security integration is occurring largely through the diplomatic dialogue and agency of key transnational knowledge-based networks, known as epistemic communities. While most research on the topic of EU security tends to focus on the influence of member states, this arena is really only part of the picture. Member states tend to pull toward maintaining national sovereignty in the security area, but security integration is nevertheless occurring. Understanding this phenomenon requires looking at the main actors who pull in the opposite direction. Through a better understanding of the dynamics within these epistemic communities, I offer a compelling explanation for the emerging process of security integration in Europe.

THE BEGINNING AND END OF INTEGRATION

Predicting the end point of integration requires redefining the beginning point. Given that integration is a result of dialogue, the first stages of integration actually take place in the mind when a certain number of decision makers are persuaded by transnational consensus and their worldviews begin to shift. When those who take on these worldviews persuade a critical mass of others, the impact of diplomatic dialogue shifts from shared norms to concrete policy and finally to actual output.

Since outcomes of international relations arise from human interaction and choices, integration begins with normative diffusion, persuasion, and dialogue well before member states start changing their behavior and achieving more formal integration.[3] Taking issue with international relations research that focuses only on policy outcomes while ignoring prior processes, Andrew Cortell and James Davis argue that it is not possible to decipher the strength of a norm simply by investigating whether it is institutionalized into a state's legal systems.[4] They write, "A focus on observable behavior may be inappropriate for explaining situations where an actor did not choose a particular course of action, or did not exploit an opportunity for gain."[5] Similarly, I argue that the process of integration involves many more steps prior to the adoption of new laws or taking of common action. Such steps may include consensus building in Brussels, gradual persuasion of officials in the capitals, ongoing deliberation, and subtle shifts in worldview. While these processes may not be readily observable from the outside, they are essential to the strengthening of political will among policy actors that allows integration to move forward in practice. If political will for integration is present, lasting changes in behavior will usually follow. Anticipating or predicting future areas of integration in the EU early on requires investigating the transnational dialogue, looking for evidence of successful persuasion, and gauging shifts in worldviews in the member states' capitals. Then a solid foundation is set for the examination of observable policy creation and its significance on the path toward further integration.

What about the end point of integration? A rich scholarly debate concerns why EU member states have willingly given up sovereignty in certain policy areas to the supranational level of governance.[6] At one end of the spectrum, some intergovernmentalists argue that member states give up sovereignty only insofar as it benefits their economic self-interest.[7] At the other end, some constructivists argue that as long as European citizens continue to identify themselves increasingly with the idea of Europe, integration will continue indefinitely.[8] Implied in many of these arguments is the idea that this process of integration will have an end point. But much ambiguity has persisted about what this end point will look like and why it will be reached. When will the European project be declared essentially accomplished? When will officials in Brussels simply maintain the status quo and capitals cease debating the merits and demerits of new levels of integration?

Of course, a natural stopping point would seemingly be the achievement of a federalist model of governance in which the EU ceases to be an international organization and starts to resemble a federal nation-state.[9] After all, nation-states have been the end point of political evolution for some time. But for many reasons, this development has seemed on the surface to be impossible in the case of the EU. First, the many member states have vastly different languages, cultures, customs, and identities, all of which pose significant obstacles to shifting national and political allegiances to Brussels. Second, the member states have entrenched constitutional and judicial traditions that they are not willing to give up. Finally, and perhaps most commonly cited, EU member states do not seem to be able to work together when it comes to foreign and security policy, thus preventing the EU from projecting itself as a coherent international player.[10]

This book challenges these assumptions about the obstacles to EU integration by arguing that the second and third of these claims are not insurmountable. Rather, security integration—in both its internal and external dimensions—is advancing quite well and successfully, thanks in no small part to the strength of the diplomatic dialogue and degree of normative persuasion that has been achieved. The beginnings of integration in the security area are robust, and some of the outcomes are surprising. Of course, since security is the ultimate bastion of sovereignty, as long as Europe remains a collection of nation-states, the expectation should be that each state will fight to maintain its jurisdiction over security issues and resist security integration. As chapter 2 discusses, although security integration is still in its nascence, progress in overcoming these obstacles has included everything from harmonization of visa and asylum measures to common arrest warrants to cross-border collaboration on weapons procurement. Transnational actors can and do supersede member states in driving these outcomes, and as a result, the EU is beginning to emerge as a viable security player.

What, then, about the why? A significant reason why security integration is occurring despite some member states' resistance is the influence of important epistemic communities in the EU setting. Peter Haas defines an epistemic community as "a network of professionals with recognized expertise and competence in a particular domain and an authoritative claim to policy-relevant knowledge within that domain or issue area."[11] These groups of elite and expert actors serve in crucial roles as what might also be called knowledge-based networks. Each of the book's five case studies focuses on a specific knowledge-based community of actors; examines from a sociological perspective how decision making occurs within this community; and then illustrates with a specific policy example how the dynamics of decision making within that epistemic group have influenced and shaped security outcomes.

The networks of actors examined in this study exert varying degrees of power over outcomes. Comparing the most likely groups of actors involved in the security policy area, variations in the qualities they possess, and their ability to persuade enables the formulation of some real conclusions about what makes certain transnational groups more influential than others and why. Thus, I not only argue that security integration is under way but also explain why it is happening.

I leave aside the question of whether a common identity is possible in Europe and do not closely examine the evidence for shifting political loyalties among European citizens, a discussion that would be well beyond the scope of a single book.[12] To be sure, popular perceptions alone can easily mean that EU integration will stop short of federalism, at least in the short to medium term. I focus instead on the issue of security policy and how it is unlikely to be the obstacle to integration that it is often envisioned to be by those who emphasize the strong pull of sovereignty, national self-interest, and constitutional traditions.

THE INTERNAL AND EXTERNAL DIMENSIONS OF SECURITY

This study is unique in that it addresses both internal and external security in the same body of research and sees them as closely related phenomena.[13] Internal security includes such priorities as counterterrorism, upholding fundamental human rights, finding common approaches to legal and illegal immigration, harmonizing asylum procedures, protecting the EU's external borders, sharing law enforcement information, agreeing on minimum standards of justice, and fighting cross-border crime, drugs, and illegal trafficking in humans.[14] External security policy refers to member states' commitment to come to each other's aid in the event of an attack, the sanctions or restrictive measures that the EU imposes on third countries in an effort to prevent human rights abuses and violations of democratic norms, and crisis management and conflict prevention operations under the Common Security and Defence Policy (CSDP). More broadly, for both the Council of the European Union and the European Commission, external security also involves member states' efforts to speak with one voice in response to a variety of international issues and challenges, such as environmental protection, weapons of mass destruction, inter- and intrastate conflict, poverty, food security, and education. The Commission has more than 130 delegations around the globe whose work is to accurately convey the EU's external image through public diplomacy.[15] Chapter 2 elaborates on the progress and shortcomings of both of these dimensions of security in Europe and gives a comprehensive overview of where the EU stands as a security actor.

With the implementation of the Lisbon Treaty, internal security is now almost fully merged into community policy, coming under the jurisdiction of the Community Method.[16] This change leaves external security—the Common Foreign and Security Policy (CFSP)—as the main policy holdout in the intergovernmental domain. But the Lisbon Treaty creates inroads here as well, making significant progress in enabling the EU to have a stronger, more unified external voice. In particular, the High Representative for CFSP gains the added role of vice president of the Commission and is supported by a new European External Action Service.

It is valuable to study the internal and external sides of security in parallel for a variety of reasons. First, more generally, the ability to distinguish between internal and external security has become difficult with increasing transnationalism worldwide.[17] In the EU in particular, this process has been taken even further.[18] Member states' national borders have now become internal EU borders, redefining the whole concept of boundaries and formally blurring the internal-external distinction. Each member state must now think of internal security as including territory outside of its borders.

Second, a very clear external dimension to internal security, and vice versa, is involved in decision making both in Brussels and in the capitals. Especially since 9/11, a concerted effort has taken place to treat internal and external security as two sides of the same coin. The 2003 European Security Strategy (ESS) in particular sharpened this approach with its explicit linking of the two.[19] The ESS stipulates that the key threats to Europe in the twenty-first century are terrorism, the proliferation of weapons of mass destruction, chemical and biological attacks, illegal migration, and cross-border trafficking of humans, drugs, and weapons.

To combat these threats effectively, the ESS calls for more involvement in helping weakened or failed states, preventing or resolving regional conflicts, increasing defenses at common borders, and standing up against nuclear proliferation through support of the International Atomic Energy Agency (IAEA). The ESS reflects the belief that internal threats require external strategies and that external threats in turn require the tools of internal security, such as police, intelligence officers, judicial officials, and others. Thus, addressing both dimensions side by side more accurately captures how member states deal with security issues in practice. This process holds increasingly true as Europeans strive to overcome the remaining barriers to the common market and to expand the Schengen zone—Europe's passport-free area, in which internal borders have been dismantled.

A third reason why it is useful to approach the two dimensions of security alongside each other is methodological: Doing so increases the types of groups available to study and thus the variety of possible outcomes, making theorizing more robust. Since internal security has progressed more rapidly than its external counterpart, looking at internal security provides a window onto the future of external security. And while distinct differences exist between internal and external security, both encroach on core functions of national sovereignty.

I explicitly seek to expose the degree to which security integration already has occurred by focusing on the inroads that have been made rather than fully detailing the ways in which the EU has fallen short of full and complete integration. This task is in many ways more difficult than simply outlining the litany of criticisms that have been directed at the EU's progress toward security integration. Since security is the last bastion of state sovereignty, it is valuable systematically to explore the extent to which security has opened up to nonstate governance, whether transnational or supranational. Ultimately, only through examining the most difficult cases of integration might the end point of integration be found.

MEMBER STATES, TRANSNATIONAL ACTORS, AND SUPRANATIONAL GOVERNANCE

The role of member state governments as actors in EU integration has been researched extensively and thus will not be covered in much depth here. Rather, this book shows that while member states' preferences are crucial, they are only a part of the story. Member state influence tends to pull toward maintaining national sovereignty in the security area, so any study that focuses exclusively on the states misses the crucial role played by nonstate actors with influence of their own. In contrast, my work isolates the key actors pulling in the opposite direction—that is, toward integration. Such actors, who make up the epistemic communities discussed here, have with some degree of success engaged in a dialogue about how to combine resources, power, and decision making regarding security and about how to persuade member states to transcend cooperation to achieve integration. Many of these actors both are connected to nation states and operate beyond strict state control in carrying out their European functions. Of course, member states are typically these actors' target audience and thus still play a part in the analysis insofar as they are persuaded (or not) by the activities of these nonstate actors.

At the same time, member states remain fully invested in their foreign and security policies, whether such policies involve decisions about common action under CSDP, determinations about defense budget allocations, or national agreements with third parties. On the external security side, unanimous support is required, with every member state holding the power to veto any dossiers on the table. On the internal security side, member states are less dominant, as dossiers are increasingly determined through qualified majority voting. Rather than seeing the two as a dichotomy of influence in which member states have either ceded their sovereignty over certain policies or have not, I see the distinction as more a matter of degree. As the following chapters describe, the requirement of unanimity does not mean that a simple vote is the final arbiter of out-comes, and the fact that an issue is subject to qualified majority voting does not mean that only a certain number of votes are necessary. The modus operandi nearly always is to reach consensus, whether the policy area is in-ternal or external or said to be integrated or not. This example shows why exploring prior processes of cooperation or integration sheds light on the real significance of outcomes and provides a good indication of what is in store for the future.

The actors on whom this study focuses are typically organized into groups or networks, whether they are behind the scenes, formal, or infor-mal. According to Elisabeth Clemens and James Cook, networks "may gen-erate durable ties and practices through constitutive processes of social in-teraction or by shaping the opportunities and obstacles to exchange and cooperation."[20] As a multistate, quasi-federal entity, the EU is a natural breeding ground for network formation. It provides a multilevel gover-nance structure that encourages and facilitates people with varying inter-ests to come together across national boundaries to accomplish common goals. I focus on networks for two main reasons. First, individual, nonstate actors in Europe rarely can single-handedly change state preferences (with perhaps the exception of the top EU diplomatic official, the high represen-tative, Catherine Ashton).[21] Second, group dynamics are enduring and im-portant because new generations of security actors are typically socialized into groups, thus making it easier to generalize about networks.

The key qualities that define these networks include selection and train-ing, shared professional norms, meeting frequency, and common culture. Such qualities, in turn, determine the strength of each network's influence. Successful influence is a demonstrated ability to persuade others of the need for more security integration—and more tangibly, policy change in this direction. In the new external security area, the power to persuade is considerable and not only shows the significance of current outcomes of integration but also promises significant future developments. For internal security, successful persuasion has been even more visible and has already resulted in a substantial number of effective policy outcomes, proving that security integration is increasing over time.

Networks are always involved in shaping policy, regardless of whether capitals fully control the issue area. Though member states matter enor-mously in the determination of security policy, there are some limits to what capitals can do. Transnational networks based in Brussels obviously have the advantage of being able to meet frequently, receive regular updates, and discuss issues with all 27 member states. It is thus important to find evidence for actors' agency beyond structural constraints. Strong epistemic communities in particular may take a baseline consensus further or operationalize vague political agreements. Consequently, the end result may not necessarily be what member states had anticipated. Consequently, the case studies presented in this volume trace how and why these networks accomplish these results.

OUTLINE OF THE BOOK

Chapter 1 introduces some key concepts and debates about transnational networks and epistemic communities and lays out more fully the book's argument, thereby providing the foundation for the analysis that follows. Chapter 2 provides a definitive overview of the state of security cooperation and integration in Europe, giving the reader an idea of the breadth and depth of security areas in which the EU is involved as a coherent actor. In particular, chapter 2 describes how far security integration has come, which policy goals are still in the process of being achieved, and where a lack of cooperation among member states continues.

The subsequent chapters are devoted to the case studies: the epistemic communities of diplomats (chapters 3 and 4), high-level military officers (chapter 5), and scientists and civilian crisis experts (chapter 6). While chapter 2 surveys the wide spectrum of security outcomes, the case study chapters address specific aspects of security integration to show how a particular outcome came about through the influence of that epistemic community. Through process tracing, I show how the ambassadors dealing with internal security integration shaped the Strategy on Radicalization and Recruitment, leading to a host of common actions to tackle the problem of terrorism and extremism. Similarly, I show how the network of three-star military generals and admirals crafted the Long-Term Vision for European Defence, which triggered outcomes of interoperability, consolidation, and increasing common investment by member states. In the case of the scientists in security research, I trace their influence on the Preparatory Action on Security Research, which launched dozens of multicountry research projects that required a Europeanized implementation of security technology. And in the case of civilian crisis experts, a more nascent epistemic community, I trace how the persuasive processes in this network enabled certain CSDP missions to reach fruition. The Political and Security Committee (PSC) is an epistemic community of moderate strength, and its outcomes fall short of providing strong evidence for security integration although it often facilitates security cooperation. The case shows what happens when an epistemic community is not quite as cohesive or persuasive as a whole and thus provides a means of testing for variation in the composition of a knowledge-based network.

Although all of these chapters ultimately address concrete outcomes of security integration, the processes of socialization, deliberation, and persuasion within networks and between networks and other actors truly indicate the strength of these trends. They put in place lasting normative or legal structures that bind together member states, making it far more likely that the EU will increasingly speak with one voice in world politics, respond to crises as a single actor, and seamlessly defend its borders. Still, security integration is clearly a work in progress, and it may be closer to the beginning than the end. Thus, chapter 7 concludes with a prognosis for EU security integration and returns to the question of when and in what form security integration will reach its end point. Taken together, these case studies illustrate how knowledge-based networks are transforming the EU's prospects for integration. They put into place various pieces of a puzzle to explain why European states are increasingly willing to test a new kind of supranational order and to commit even their security to it.

CHAPTER I

Why Do Epistemic Communities Matter?

A RICH DEBATE within EU studies focuses specifically on explaining integration and the nature of EU power. Scholars come at the question from many different angles, drawing on a variety of policy areas to craft nuanced arguments. But most agree that the social context of Europe has been an important variable in explaining nearly all aspects of integration since the EU's inception.[1] Social context is defined as the processes of learning, persuasion, deliberation, and socialization that shape how actors assign meaning to things and form preferences.[2] The process of ongoing enlargement of EU membership, for example, cannot simply be reduced to a calculation of the economic benefits that come with accession; it also reflects a history of social interaction shaped by the Cold War.[3] Central and Eastern European countries have not only adopted EU rules to satisfy formal membership criteria (*acquis communautaire*) but have also willingly internalized existing EU norms and values.[4] The same is true in the area of security policy.[5] Actors' preferences are usually defined through lifelong processes of social interaction and filtered through frames of reference, perception, and interpretation.[6] Identity and interests change over time, making the social context of EU governance crucial to understanding how the EU is evolving and what it is becoming.

Research into the history and processes of EU integration has led scholars who take a more intergovernmental perspective to conclude that the EU has indeed achieved the status of a "quiet superpower."[7] Andrew Moravcsik, who argues that integration is driven primarily by national economic incentives and interstate bargaining, nonetheless consistently reminds us that the EU is significantly ahead of China, India, and other "rising powers" in terms of economic, civilian, normative, and to some extent military power.[8] Indeed, he argues that Europe's hard, soft, and civilian power is so significant that it has become a superpower to rival the United States. To be clear, contention arises regarding what drives processes of integration, and not everyone is optimistic about the EU's future. However, the research presented here supports the arguments that social interaction matters and that the EU has emerged as a quiet superpower on the world stage. The bipolarity of the international system results largely from the EU's vibrant and multidimensional social context, in which the pursuit of national interest is only one part.[9]

In addition to contributing to this growing body of EU literature, I engage with broader international relations theories to develop an argument that might apply to other regions of the world. After all, similar though much more embryonic processes of regional integration are occurring in Africa, Latin America, Asia, and the Middle East. Moreover, globalization has created an environment rich with nonstate actors that often span the globe, influencing such areas as environmentalism, human rights, nuclear proliferation, drug trafficking, and so on. Within the academic field of international relations, several approaches contribute to a fuller understanding of integration, and transnationalism is chief among them. Transnationalism gained momentum in the literature in the 1970s. It added another dimension to the structural realist approach, which assumes that state behavior is exogenously given by the international system, and to rationalism, which assumes that all actors have fixed, profit-maximizing preferences. Like much of the EU literature, transnationalism recognizes that nonstate actors affect world politics and have evolving preferences. Transnationalism's contribution has been particularly important because these actors are involved in norm formation—the creation of implicit or explicit rules about what is appropriate behavior—at the systemic level as well as at the intersection between the systemic and domestic levels. As Jeffrey Checkel points out, too many questions remain unanswered unless we consider social norms as explanatory variables.[10] Social norms can have just as much impact as formal rules or laws and carry social sanction if violated.

A variety of transnational actors seek to change state behavior, domestic preferences, and international norms. Transnational actors can be as broad as informal networks of people with shared ideas and identity or as narrow as specific international nongovernmental organizations (NGOs), human rights advocacy networks,[11] transgovernmental networks of legislators,[12] and epistemic communities, among others. Much evidence suggests that in the context of Europe, transnational communities of communication are becoming increasingly robust.[13] Before getting to a more detailed analysis of the scope of conditions surrounding security epistemic communities and the framework put forward in this book, it is helpful to specify what epistemic communities are not.

First, epistemic communities are distinct from informal networks, which are defined as webs of personal, social, or professional relationships among groups of people that enable them to share various kinds of information and resources. Epistemic communities are much more directed than informal networks in that they seek less to gain benefit for themselves and more to share a group policy goal. An example of an informal network is an old boys' network, in which businessmen keep up contacts with others in their profession to exchange favors and contacts. Closely related to this idea is the concept of issue network, which should also not be confused with an epistemic community. Issue networks comprise people who are in contact with one another to discuss or debate similar issues.[14] People in an issue network may be from the same or different professions, but they do not share norms, causal beliefs, or validity tests. They simply possess some degree of overlapping knowledge.[15] A casual observation of a group discussing a single policy issue should not lead to the assumption that it comprises an epistemic community.

International NGOs and transnational advocacy networks are a second category of transnational networks. They have more in common with epistemic communities than informal networks in that they have specific policy goals that are based on shared causal beliefs about what actions will result in the achievement of their aims. However, their goals typically derive from idealistic interests such as human rights, environmental protection, and social change.[16] They tend to target causes that require external influence to change domestic patterns. NGOs are more centralized than advocacy networks, with those officially employed in the NGOs responsible for determining projects, actions, statements, and day-to-day operations. Transnational advocacy networks include NGOs but are also much broader. As Margaret Keck and Kathryn Sikkink define them, "these networks are similar in several important respects: the centrality of values or principled ideas, the belief that individuals can make a difference, the creative use of information, and the employment of nongovernmental actors of sophisticated political strategies in targeting their campaigns."[17] The key way in which they differ from epistemic communities is that professional norms and expertise are not a major part of their operation. They are values driven and thus seek to change both policy outcomes and the terms of the debate. Their emphasis is more on grassroots participation and persuasion than on elite discourses.

A third category of transnational actors includes transgovernmental networks. More broadly speaking, Robert Keohane and Joseph S. Nye define transgovernmental cooperation as the process through which sub-units of governments engage in direct and autonomous interaction separate from nation-states.[18] Possible configurations of this concept of cooperation include transgovernmental networks, coalitions, and committees.[19] Although committees have a degree of autonomy, they are characterized as limited in membership with an official mandate to carry out the broader instructions of higher political bodies. Networks are typically more informal, while coalitions have more specific agendas that may even go against what national authorities had in mind.[20] Epistemic communities may or may not be governmental, so the concept of transgovernmental community is too narrow to encompass them. It is also important to distinguish between an ordinary governmental committee and an epistemic community. Most committees will have a level of esprit de corps, regardless of their place in the hierarchy and level of expertise. However, an epistemic community is more than its formal label. Indeed, epistemic communities might not and often do not exist within structures of government.[21] It is typically easier to identify and study nongovernmental epistemic communities, such as environmentalists, doctors, and economists. However, since epistemic communities exist regardless of whether they have a formal place in institutional structures, it is necessary to look broadly to find them, to peel back structures to find the real dynamics. Without this careful look at processes of influence and decision making, a big piece of the puzzle could be missing.

There are numerous ways in which it is possible to recognize an epistemic community even if it is part of a formal structure. Is a particular committee more than the sum of its parts? Does it produce outcomes that go beyond the expectations of its formal functions? Did the committee's members possess a high level of expertise before taking up their institutional positions? Did they perhaps even know each other or work with each other in previous settings? Might they, as a collective, wield influence by virtue of their expertise and high status even without the existence of the committee? A look into the emergence and historical development of the expert network is useful in this regard. Do the members of the committee often meet informally, outside of work? Do they share a particular culture and professional norms that are independent of the committee? These factors are helpful in distinguishing not only between strong and weak epistemic communities but also between weak epistemic communities and ordinary governmental committees.

A fourth category that should be distinguished from epistemic communities is the concept of security communities. In 1957, Karl W. Deutsch, Sidney A. Burrell, and Robert A. Kahn first discussed the idea that states that form an alliance often become a security community in that over time they begin to define their interests in common, share a social identity, and develop altruism, trust, and reciprocity toward each other.[22] Scholars such as Emanuel Adler, Michael Barnett, Glynn Snyder, and to some extent Charles Tilly subsequently took the argument further, operationalizing the concept of security communities to test whether states develop a collective identity and begin to empathize with each other once they are part of an alliance.[23] Research on security communities initially focused at the level of states in the international system rather than specific transnational communities of nonstate actors. Many studies started with the question of which systemic conditions trigger the rise of security communities and the accompanying process of state socialization. Subsequent contributions to this body of literature have acknowledged the internal dimension of security communities and the fact that they rest on the prior existence of communities of practice and epistemic communities at the individual and group levels of analysis.[24] Security communities are thus broader than epistemic communities, and a focus on the latter helps to shed light on the former.

In sum, epistemic communities are not simply issue networks whose members use personal contacts in the community to exchange services and information or debate issues; rather, they have a much tighter membership. They are also not advocacy networks with idealistic goals for change. Instead, epistemic communities are driven by their expert knowledge, whether or not it lends itself to social or environmental advocacy. They may exist within transgovernmental structures such as institutional committees, but they would have to possess certain qualities beyond their formal structure to act as epistemic communities. Finally, the concept of security communities may seem similar to security epistemic communities, but the latter is more appropriately subsumed within the former. These similar and somewhat related concepts are easily confused with epistemic communities, but they play a different theoretical function. Epistemic communities may certainly overlap with these other concepts, but the key to their power and influence is their authoritative claim on knowledge.[25]

EPISTEMIC COMMUNITIES: DEVELOPMENT OF A CONCEPT

The concept of epistemic communities traces its origins to Thomas Kuhn's *The Structure of Scientific Revolutions*.[26] Kuhn's notion of scientific community stipulates that students of a particular discipline are bound together through a shared paradigm. This paradigm entails a set of common beliefs and methodological standards for the pursuit of scientific inquiry. Although Kuhn did not use the term *epistemic* to define these scientific communities, it is clear that they have much in common with our current understanding of epistemic communities. Kuhn also famously developed the idea of a paradigm as the set of norms, values, and processes shared and practiced within a particular community.[27] His concept of a paradigm is directly applicable to the internal dynamics within epistemic communities.

Following on the earlier works of Kuhn and others, John Gerard Ruggie coined the term *epistemic community* in 1975, borrowing Michel Foucault's notion of *episteme*.[28] The rapid growth of technological development, especially in the post–World War II era, prompted Ruggie to argue that international responses to technology would all but require a collective response on the part of states because "technological, ecological, political, economic, and social environments are becoming so globally enmeshed that changes taking place in one segment of international society will have consequential repercussions in all others."[29] International collaboration among states would enable economies of scale and better management of the increasing complexity of science and technology. Thus, states would benefit more from working together on science and technology than from working separately. Deriving such material benefit would entail sacrificing a degree of control as a consequence of what Ruggie described as "the tension between the need of states to respond collectively to problems and opportunities such situations contain, and their desire to maintain national autonomy and flexibility in so doing."[30] The collective response to this collective situation, as he described it, would take the form of institutionalization.

One type of relationship that would emerge from the need to represent national interests internationally, according to Ruggie, was that of epistemic communities. Although his initial analysis of the concept was somewhat limited, certain key properties emerge. Epistemic communities can arise from "bureaucratic position, technocratic training, similarities in scientific outlook and shared disciplinary paradigms."[31] They share symbols, points of reference, behavioral rules, expectations, and intentions. The *episteme*, binding an epistemic community together, "delimits . . . *the* proper construction of social reality" for its members and, if successful, for international society.[32] He advanced two preliminary arguments: (1) epistemic communities are more likely to have an impact if the issue is of low political concern; and (2) in the case of several epistemic communities, each seems to find its own niche rather than competing with others over the same issue area.

Citing Kuhn and Ruggie, among others, Peter Haas was influential in bringing the idea of epistemic community into the mainstream of international relations literature in the 1990s, operationalizing the concept much further. He defined the concept as "a network of professionals with recognized expertise and competence in a particular domain and an authoritative claim to policy-relevant knowledge within that domain or issue area."[33] Epistemic communities are transnational networks of individuals with shared professional expertise. According to Haas, epistemic communities must have an authoritative claim on knowledge to affect policy outcomes. This feature differentiates the membership of an epistemic community from others who interact transnationally in international society. The knowledge itself may or may not be socially constructed, but it is based on common validity tests within the community. Epistemic communities must share norms or beliefs about cause and effect. Therefore, an epistemic community is rarely so broad as to include an entire discipline. It must be narrow enough that all members have the expertise necessary not only to understand the issue at stake but also to interpret the information similarly and to form the same goals about what should be done. At the same time, members of an epistemic community may come from different professional backgrounds as long as they put forward consensual knowledge. Haas writes,

> Although an epistemic community may consist of professionals from a variety of disciplines and backgrounds, they have (1) a shared set of normative and principled beliefs, which provide a value-based rationale for the social action of community members; (2) shared causal beliefs, which are derived from their analysis of practices leading or contributing to a central set of

problems in their domain and which then serve as the basis for elucidating the multiple linkages between possible policy actions and desired outcomes; (3) shared notions of validity—that is, intersubjective, internally-defined criteria for weighing and validating knowledge in the domain of their expertise; and (4) a common policy enterprise—that is, a set of common practices associated with a set of problems to which their professional competence is directed, presumably out of the conviction that human welfare will be enhanced as a consequence.[34]

An epistemic community is primarily knowledge-based in that its members share beliefs about cause-and-effect relationships, usually of a technical nature. Within the community, members have tested and validated beliefs about causality. The epistemic community is then held together by values, which manifest as shared policy objectives. Members of an epistemic community wish to affect outcomes in their issue area. In the end, an epistemic community should agree on policy goals based on members' interpretation of data or evidence. Their policy aims have to reflect their expert knowledge, not some other motivation, or they lose authority with their target audience, which usually is made up of elite decision makers. Community members thus must have a reputation for recognized expertise in their domain and must have common validity tests that support their shared causal beliefs.

Epistemic Communities Applied

Several scholars, including Haas, have applied the concept of epistemic communities to empirical case studies of environmentalists, economists, and scientists. Amy Verdun argues that knowledge and expertise are critical to understanding the creation of the European Monetary Union (EMU).[35] Her study shows that the Delors Committee, a group of monetary experts, constituted an epistemic community, and its role has been underrecognized in studies explaining the Maastricht Treaty. In support of Ruggie's earlier hypothesis, Verdun's argument rests on the idea that the process of EU integration has for the most part been more technocratic and expert-driven than political. The Delors Report, which launched the European Monetary Union, was crafted by central bankers—monetary experts—and the Maastricht Treaty closely paralleled the contents of the report. Verdun, Haas, and others argue that uncertainty is a major precondition for epistemic communities to have an impact. If decision makers encounter a new problem or if new information has been brought to light, they are more likely to call on and trust experts to interpret the information and recommend a new policy approach. Epistemic communities may exist prior to being "called" to action, but their impact is contingent on this uncertainty.

Claudio Radaelli further supports this approach, adding that epistemic communities often compete with other types of actors, all striving to impact policy outcomes. He writes, "It may well be that in a certain policy area there are two competing coalitions and one coalition is assisted by an underlying epistemic community."[36] To determine when epistemic communities will likely have the most influence, Radaelli argues that it is important to find "conditions of radical uncertainty and political visibility."[37] In these scenarios, epistemic communities can both provide and interpret expert knowledge, triggering a learning process that enables decision makers to act. Haas argues that the main exception to epistemic community influence, given these conditions, occurs when the available data do not support previously held causal beliefs.[38] In cases where the epistemic community itself cannot agree about how to interpret data, it abstains from offering policy advice.

Craig Thomas also applies the concept to a specific empirical case study but argues that epistemic communities can be adapted to explain domestic rather than international cooperation.[39] To test this idea at the domestic level, Thomas examines cooperation among ecologists within the United States, finding that interagency committees are less effective at promoting cooperation than are interagency epistemic communities. His research finds that actors must want to work together to find compromise. It is not enough for them to simply be assigned to formal committees created by those at the top. Like other authors, Thomas emphasizes the contextual element of uncertainty needed for the epistemic community to gain influence.

Anthony Zito applies Haas's framework to the EU's acid rain policy in an effort to select an easy test for epistemic communities.[40] He seeks to find out the extent to which the EU's structural context restricts epistemic communities' ability to influence policy outcomes. In general, he argues that the EU is a favorable environment for policy change since it has so many access points into decision-making processes. Innovation is regarded positively, and norm entrepreneurs can try to put forward their ideas in numerous ways. At the same time, Zito argues, the fact that there are so many access points means that there are also many veto points. Decision making in the EU is often fragmented and complicated, and for an actor such as an epistemic community to influence outcomes, it must achieve consensus across a number of institutions. Zito's study concludes that epistemic communities can be influential, especially at early stages in the policy process, when the policy costs are not clear, when a crisis has caused a variety of actors to let go of previously held norms, and when the epistemic community controls numerous EU veto points.[41] But even in an easy test for epistemic communities, Zito concludes that numerous constraints affect their influence in the EU setting.

Thus, Haas, Verdun, Thomas, Radaelli, and Zito, among others, apply the idea of epistemic communities to real case studies, refining the idea beyond its beginnings. All of these authors seem to agree that epistemic communities can exercise agency only when a kind of contextual gap—uncertainty—allows them to do so.[42] They pay careful attention to context as well, whether in the EU setting, within the domestic level of governance, or when epistemic communities must compete with other actors. Overall, several useful additions have occurred to the epistemic community concept since Haas's 1992 article. To some extent, all of the studies address the critical questions of when and why epistemic communities matter. Zito nicely brings together twelve conditions from various studies, indicating when each of the scholars say epistemic communities are likely to be more persuasive (table 1).

Despite these important advances in the literature, however, researchers of epistemic communities have engaged in little debate about the concept itself. Claire Dunlop noticed this phenomenon back in 2000, claiming that "the approach as it stood in [1992] remains largely the same today."[43] Scholars have more or less uniformly accepted Haas's definition and criteria. There are numerous responses to the literature by scholars who have pointed out some of the weaknesses of the epistemic community concept, but generally one finds either supporters or detractors.

Criticisms of the Epistemic Communities Concept

Those who dismiss the importance of epistemic communities argue either that their role has been exaggerated or that too many other factors have been left unexplained. Some of those who believe that the role of epistemic communities has been exaggerated argue that the epistemic community

TABLE 1. When Epistemic Communities Are Persuasive: Summary of the Literature

Epistemic Communities Are More Likely to Be Persuasive When:	Scholars
1. they have access to all necessary top decision makers	Haas; Drake and Nicolaidis
2. there is uncertainty surrounding the issue because it is complex, new, or uncertain	Haas; Radaelli
3. they anticipate other actors' preferences and actions despite fluidity in the system (as in the EU)	Richardson
4. there is respected quantitative data instead of very subjective qualitative data	Sabatier and Jenkins-Smith
5. the issue involves natural systems (i.e., the environment) instead of social systems	Sabatier and Jenkins-Smith
6. they share a high level of professional norms and status	Sabatier and Jenkins-Smith
7. they deal with subsystemic, technocratic decisions	Peterson and Bomberg
8. they seek to influence the terms of the initial debate instead of the decision itself	Raustiala
9. the networks they are competing against are not as cohesive or certain of their aims	Peterson
10. their norms and policy goals are compatible with existing institutional norms	Jordan and Greenway; Sabatier
11. the decision makers they are trying to persuade are unhappy with past policies and present problems	Hall
12. the issue is surrounded by uncertainty and it is politically salient	Radaelli

Note: This table only summarizes Zito's analysis (Anthony Zito, "Epistemic Communities, Collective Entrepreneurship and European Integration," Journal of European Public Policy 8 [2001]: 588–90). Zito cites the following: Peter Haas, Saving the Mediterranean (New York: Columbia University Press, 1990); William Drake and Kalypso Nicolaidis, "Ideas, Interests, and Institutionalization: 'Trade in Services' and the Uruguay Round," International Organization 46 (1992): 37–100; Claudio M. Radaelli, Technocracy in the European Union (London and New York: Longman, 1999); Jeremy Richardson, "Actor-Based Models of National and EU Policy Making," in The European Union and National Industrial Policy, ed. Hussein Kassim and Anand Menon (London: Routledge, 1996), 26–51; Paul A. Sabatier and Hank C. Jenkins-Smith, "The Advocacy Coalition Framework: An Assessment," in Theories of the Policy Process, ed. Paul A. Sabatier (Oxford: Westview Press, 1999), 117–68; John Peterson and Elizabeth Bomberg, Decision-Making in the European Union (Basingstoke: Macmillan, 1999); Kal Raustiala, "Domestic Institutions and International Regulatory Cooperation: Comparative Responses to the Convention on Biological Diversity," World Politics 49 (1997): 482–509; John Peterson, "Decision-Making in the European Union: Towards a Framework for Analysis," Journal of European Public Policy 2 (1995): 69–93; Andrew Jordan and John Greenway, "Shifting Agendas, Changing Regulatory Structures and the 'New' Politics of Environmental Pollution: British Coastal Water Policy, 1955–1995," Public Administration 76 (1998): 669–94; Peter A. Hall, "Policy Paradigms, Social Learning, and the State: The Case of Economic Policymaking in Britain," Comparative Politics 25 (1993): 275–96; Paul A. Sabatier, "The Advocacy Coalition Framework: Revisions and Relevance for Europe," Journal of European Public Policy 5 (1998): 98–130.

literature tends to assume that these groups have direct access to top decision makers without competition from other voices.[44] In other words, pro-
ponents of this view believe that research about epistemic communities
tends to underplay or ignore the role of other actors. A second reason why
epistemic communities' impact might be exaggerated is that scholars tend
to assume that they are in the best position (even better than states themselves) to help governments sort out complex technical problems.[45] Third,
scholars of epistemic communities have been criticized for seemingly ignoring the possibility that members of epistemic communities might pursue personal or professional goals and are affected by their domestic cultures, norms, and strategic interests.[46] Fourth, skeptics argue that to be
heard, epistemic communities need to be political or to form a coalition
with those who are engaged in political activism (a winning coalition). This
process entails effective political bargaining to empower the epistemic
communities' consensual knowledge.[47] Finally, detractors criticize Haas's
analysis in particular for glossing over which of the four factors that describe epistemic communities—(1) shared principled beliefs, (2) shared
causal beliefs, (3) shared notions of validity, and (4) a common policy enterprise—lies at the true core of their belief systems.[48]

To resolve some of these shortcomings, several of these critics have suggested ways to improve the viability of the concept: (1) a strong theory of
domestic politics to explain why certain ideas win out over others;[49] (2) a
theory of competition among epistemic communities and other actors;[50]
(3) a careful consideration of the real political stakes that provide the context within which epistemic communities act;[51] (4) an explanation for the
degree of power epistemic communities might have by virtue of their
knowledge; and (5) a clarification of the ways in which scientific knowledge might simply reinforce political preferences.[52] In general, critics of the
concept generally seek to define epistemic communities in looser terms. To
grapple with each of these factors is a tall order, and this book thus addresses these points only insofar as they apply to the case of EU security
policy. It is important to take seriously these criticisms and suggestions, as
the concept of epistemic community thus far has been relatively marginal-
ized in the international relations literature, even among studies of transnational networks. However, for processes of decision making in the EU, it
is critical that the influence of epistemic communities be recognized and
understood, since they define a crucial aspect of how governance really
works.

REFINING EPISTEMIC COMMUNITIES: A FRAMEWORK

In the context of the EU, the concept of epistemic communities can be made more precise in some ways and broadened in others. It can be more precise through (1) a prioritization of Haas's four properties of epistemic communities, (2) a recognition of the importance of professionalism and professionalization at the heart of epistemic community cohesion, and (3) an understanding that epistemic communities do not simply exist or not exist but can be characterized as strong or weak. At the same time, the concept can be broadened with regard to both the current empirical emphasis on scientific knowledge and the assumption in the literature that uncertainty or a triggering crisis event is a necessary prerequisite for epistemic community influence.

The Core of Epistemic Communities: Professionalism

How should one prioritize Haas's four-part definition of epistemic communities? How do the parts fit together? What is really at the core of each epistemic community? Of the four characteristics—(1) shared normative and principled beliefs, (2) shared causal beliefs, (3) shared notions of validity, and (4) a common policy enterprise—Haas argues that shared causal beliefs and notions of validity most distinguish epistemic communities from other groups. Between these two, he seems to prioritize shared notions of validity, arguing that more than for other groups, "truth-tests" enable epistemic communities to strive to be "politically untainted, and thus more likely 'to work,' in the political sense that [they] will be embraced and followed by political authorities concerned about the need for appearing impartial."[53]

By contrast, I emphasize the importance of shared causal beliefs and a common policy enterprise over shared notions of validity. These two characteristics are distinctive from the other two in that they are intimately related to the professional competence, practices, and expertise of epistemic community members. Specifically, the core of an epistemic community is how its members are socialized and embedded into their profession. A shared set of normative beliefs and common notions of validity naturally follow from professionalism and are somewhat secondary as they are derived from professional practices. Between shared causal beliefs and a common policy enterprise, I prioritize the former, which is ultimately central to the expertise of an epistemic community. Shared causal beliefs reflect the long-term analytical capabilities of a profession, the basis of their knowledge, while a common policy enterprise is more focused on the policy outcomes that an epistemic community seeks to accomplish with its expertise. Of course, the end result of policy creation lies at the heart of the importance of studying epistemic communities, but policies are the final phase of their impact and depend on shared causal beliefs. Thus, an emphasis on shared causal beliefs ultimately maximizes our ability to understand an epistemic community's common policy enterprise.

In sum, I agree with Haas that the appearance of being politically untainted and impartial is critical to an epistemic community's ability to be persuasive. However, professionalism sits at the core of an epistemic community, more central than the academic practices of truth tests and peer-reviewed publications. This approach provides a broader criterion for measuring what holds together an epistemic community.

At the same time, this interpretation of the concept of epistemic communities problematizes Haas's contention that an epistemic community can comprise members from multiple disciplines. I agree that this phenomenon is certainly possible, but my case study evidence shows that a professionally diverse epistemic community is less cohesive and thus weaker than a community whose members come from the same discipline. A group of experts pushing for the same policy goals but with different types of expertise can likely advance a variety of justifications for their common policy enterprise. Ultimately, however, this heterogeneity is to the detriment of the longer-term cohesiveness of internal group dynamics, as illustrated in the case studies described in chapter 6. Along with my hypothesis that internal cohesiveness is a key component of external persuasiveness, I argue that an epistemic community is stronger if professional, procedural, and social commonalities are easier to find. Numerous actors compete for influence in the EU's thick landscape of interaction, and to have an impact without crossing the line into advocacy or lobbying, an epistemic community must be highly cohesive despite the possibility that its members represent different interests. As a result, epistemic communities rarely encompass an entire discipline. Cohesiveness within the epistemic community is critical to the strength of its influence.

A Continuum of Influence

Another way in which the concept of epistemic communities could be more precise is in the recognition that they do not simply exist or not ex-

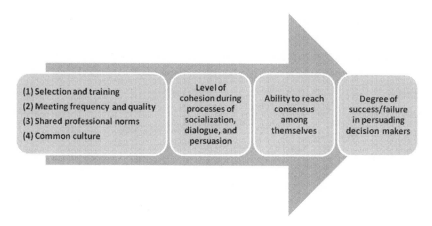

Fig. 1. Epistemic communities framework of analysis

ist. They can be strong or weak and have a varying impact depending on their internal cohesiveness, authoritative claim on knowledge, and ability to persuade. Epistemic communities might be fully fledged, or they might be nascent. The case studies in this book qualitatively measure epistemic communities' strength through an analysis of four key independent variables, as shown in figure 1: selection and training, meeting frequency and quality, shared professional norms, and common culture. This book addresses the extent to which these internal qualities and the resultant processes indicate epistemic communities' success or failure in reaching compromise and subsequently influencing policy outcomes.

Selection and training are very much part of the origins of an epistemic community as well as reasons for its continuity. Professional selection begins when individuals embark on their careers and is repeated when they are promoted or assigned to positions in their professions. These periods of selection set the stage for an individual eventually to acquire enough expertise to join or be a part of an epistemic community. During the course of professional development, training can be formal, informal, or on the job. The more the members of an epistemic community have consistent standards across national borders, the more cohesive the epistemic community will be. Selection and training determine the status of a profession to a great extent. If it is competitive to become a high-level expert in a certain field and the training is rigorous and lengthy, outsiders are more likely to respect those who have achieved success in that field and to trust their expertise. If little effort is required to embark on such a career and to move up in the ranks, outsiders are far less likely to believe that those at the top have valuable authoritative knowledge in that area.

Meeting frequency and quality enable and reinforce common culture and shared professional norms within an epistemic community. Meetings are also where working and personal relationships are formed. Critics of sociological approaches that rest on the idea that interaction leads to mutual understanding—the so-called contact hypothesis—argue that as often as not, when individuals or groups come into contact with each other, they find they have less in common than they thought and like each other less as a result. Ronald Krebs argues, for example, that it is impossible to know when contact will result in more cooperation or more confrontation.[54] Krebs may be right, but in the case of epistemic communities whose members come from the same profession, undergo similar selection and training processes, and share a similar level of expertise, contact is unlikely to repel them. If they find that it does and both parties seek policy influence, they may ultimately form competing epistemic communities within the same profession.

Shared professional norms are defined as the practices that govern interaction formally and informally within an epistemic community. They consist of shared protocol, procedure, and norms of consensus building, which vary across different groups, as well as a kind of inarticulate or even subconscious knowledge of day-to-day practices that comprise their way of life. These qualities smooth interactions and give members a common basis of understanding that is both tangible and intangible. Epistemic communities are in essence a subcategory of communities of practice, but the nature of their practice is distinctive in that it is tied to their professionalism and expertise.[55] Shared professional norms differ from shared causal beliefs, which refer to the substantive norms derived from the epistemic community's knowledge. Indeed, shared professional norms enable the development of shared causal beliefs about the way the world works and foster agreement on the appropriate policy goals.

Common culture is an encompassing concept that is typically a key part of the identity, heritage, symbolism, and sense of purpose shared by a group of individuals. It includes esprit de corps—a sense of camaraderie and devotion to the goals of the group—but is also more. Some transnational networks, bureaucratic committees, or nascent epistemic communities rest only on esprit de corps, but a strong epistemic community is also characterized by a shared culture. Camaraderie is a natural development that arises within any group, no matter how diverse or even discordant, simply as its members spend time together. Group members may be in competition with each other and face scenarios with zero-sum outcomes, yet because they are in the same situation, they develop an esprit de corps. When members of a group begin to identify other members as being on the same team, they share a strong common culture. They find they have such similar worldviews that when they tackle problems, they tend to have the same overarching goals.

The strength of these four variables determines the overall cohesiveness of an epistemic community. Cohesiveness, in turn, has a significant impact on the ability of an epistemic community to reach a strong consensus on particular issues and subsequently to persuade decision makers of that consensus. Indeed, when a high-status professional group shares a strong consensus and exercises collective agency to pursue certain policy goals, it can be very persuasive. The group's strength lies in its collectivity and ability to advance a common perspective. Thus, the processes within and qualities of an epistemic community determine its potential for success—defined as acceptance of its norms and then achievement of shared policy goals.

The outward face of an epistemic community begins with its ability to shift the worldviews of its target audience. Security integration is cognitive before it is concrete. This is true especially when the issue at stake involves a very different approach, as is true in the security realm, where decision makers begin to shift their worldviews before this change is manifested in policy. During this process, actors within epistemic communities frequently interact with decision makers at home, a process that works both ways. Community members seek simultaneously to persuade those at home and those in the network until common ground is reached. A hub and spokes analogy comes to mind (figure 2).

It might be relatively straightforward to look for a norm's presence in domestic political discourse, but that norm often develops quite late in the process of an epistemic community's influence. Andrew Cortell and James Davis argue that one might also look for a norm's emergence in national institutions and see if policy changes occur beyond those that directly relate to the norm. This development could foreshadow that a norm is starting to gain real salience. They argue that "it would be easy, and wrong, to code a norm as salient merely because state behavior is observed to be consistent with an existing international norm."[56] A state or an actor might also have changed a policy just as a one-off. Thus, end results are not the only mea-

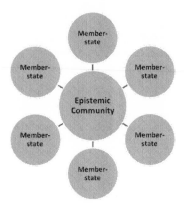

Fig. 2. Hub and spokes: epistemic communities and member-states

sure of the success or failure of an epistemic community. Changes in world-views, especially at elite levels, are often more indicative of fundamental and long-lasting shifts in behavior.

The Nature of Knowledge

What kind of expertise is necessary for a group to be defined as an epistemic community? Whether coincidental or not, the empirical focus of the literature on epistemic communities has been on scientific knowledge. Perhaps this focus results from the concept's origins, which emphasize technological development. However, it also arises from a kind of subtle partiality in the original definition of the concept. Haas's emphasis that truth tests are central to what differentiates epistemic communities from other actors and stress that the final output of tested knowledge should be its publication in peer-reviewed journals have led to a rather narrow interpretation of what qualifies as an epistemic community.

Clair Gough and Simon Shackley argue that "scientific knowledge is the 'glue' that helps to keep policy actors committed and can be used as a trump card against opponents to the epistemic coalition."[57] This statement is certainly true, but there is no reason to assume that nonscientific knowledge does not work the same way. Exploring the idea that an authoritative claim on knowledge need not be confined to scientific expertise would render the concept more useful to understanding international cooperation.

At the same time, we need to be careful not to take this idea too far. One should not assume that nearly any transnational grouping of people who share some kind of interest are an epistemic community. Professional expertise still lies at the heart of why epistemic communities come together and seek policy influence.

But scientific knowledge should not be held in some kind of privileged position. Science is often contested, and the line between what is scientific and what is nonscientific is often blurred. Diplomats, judges, defense experts, and international lawyers can be just as much defined by their expertise and knowledge as are scientists. They are not less expert because of the "softer" nature of their knowledge, nor are their shared causal beliefs less reliable. Although the literature has focused nearly exclusively on epistemic communities of scientists, even Haas seems to find this focus too narrow, writing in a footnote in his original article on the subject, "We stress that epistemic communities need not be made up of natural scientists or of professionals applying the same methodology that natural scientists do."[58] He continues with the argument that people are often bound together even in the face of "diverse interpretations of ambiguous data."[59] What matters is that community members share a means of assessing and interpreting the data.

Andreas Antoniades observes that authoritative claims on knowledge are embedded in social contexts.[60] Thus, it is not so important whether the knowledge is correct. The knowledge espoused by an epistemic community must be "socially recognized," which is its source of power—its ability to persuade, to get people to use particular language, to control worldviews and identity. Disagreements within a professional or expert group about what constitutes true knowledge do not undermine the epistemic community but can lead to multiple epistemic communities or the prominence of a single community with the most support.

Is Uncertainty Necessary?

Another way that the idea of epistemic community influence has been taken too narrowly in the literature is in terms of the prerequisite of post-crisis periods of uncertainty. Rather than focusing on specific critical junctures, I argue that epistemic communities are always at work because uncertainty is a built-in feature of the international system. This idea especially holds true in the EU, which by its nature is a work in progress with no agreed upon end goal. Moreover, security policy tends to be quite technical and requires the knowledge of experts. While crises may provide the space for epistemic communities to be heard as decision makers search for new answers to problems, crises are not necessary.

For a variety of reasons, very strong actors can influence policy outcomes even when the issue is relatively certain. For example, they might have new and compelling evidence that calls for a shift in policy orientation. Or they might reach a new level of consensus about previously contested knowledge that enables them to push more convincingly for policy change. Epistemic communities often accomplish gradual change through step-by-step persuasion. This approach rests on their desire to exercise independent agency. Although it is sometimes less dramatic, gradual change is often more difficult to achieve than filling gaps of uncertainty during postcrisis situations.

Some critics of the epistemic communities approach have embraced the more limited characterization of the role of epistemic communities, arguing that they really matter only when the issue is of low salience or of low political impact. High salience, by contrast, is defined as an issue that is very controversial because it is fundamental to the definition of the EU. Thus, the argument is that politicians are willing to grant epistemic communities authority in a more bureaucratic or technical domain since the politicians lack the time to deal with such matters themselves.[61] In the EU security domain, epistemic communities regularly determine both high- and low-salience issues. Moreover, the entire area of security integration is arguably high politics, even if a particular issue has a more technical flavor. To assume that the role of epistemic communities is reserved only for issues of low salience is to presuppose that their influence is highly contingent and circumscribed. The case studies in this volume show why such is not the case, even when an epistemic community is only moderately influential. Politicians rarely come to Brussels to guide the policy process directly. When they do come, they are often unable to figure out the right course of action without the close guidance of their experts. These experts not only advise their policymakers on what to do—advice that is usually followed precisely—but remain loyal members of their transnational, knowledge-based networks.

In sum, the concept of epistemic communities has value for the field of international relations. The literature that provides support for what they do and how they influence has in some ways been too cautious, consigning epistemic community agency to very narrow circumstances. Whether the argument is that epistemic communities must be scientists or that they can operate only in postcrisis periods of uncertainty, the end result is an approach that fails to capture the full range of epistemic community activity. By broadening some of these assumptions while following a more specified framework of analysis, the concept of epistemic communities can add real value to our understanding of international cooperation.

A NOTE ON METHODOLOGY

Epistemic communities play a powerful role in EU decision making, and careful analysis of this role will help us to appreciate and anticipate the trajectory of future EU security arrangements. Understanding why epistemic communities of various kinds play such a role requires an examination of the socialization of members within each community as well as their socializing effect on those outside, and their consequent actions must be traced to policy outcomes. Security experts and scientists do not simply happen to agree on the outcomes they want to achieve. Shared beliefs in cause-and-effect relationships do not automatically lead to homogenous policy goals. For example, Haas writes that all members of the ecological epistemic community agreed that chlorofluorocarbons have a detrimental impact on the environment, but they initially disagreed about the appropriate policy response.[62] Some wanted to initiate legislation that would protect against all kinds of atmospheric pollution, whereas others were more focused on limiting the specific impact of chlorofluorocarbons. Some were motivated by cost-benefit calculations, and others believed that the environmental crisis was so critical that it had to be corrected no matter the cost.[63] Community members ultimately reached a compromise policy goal despite initially diverging values because of their common acceptance of their scientific knowledge and desire to address the problem.

It is important to examine the internal qualities of an epistemic community—such as selection and training, shared professional norms, common culture, and meeting frequency—to understand why members of an epistemic community might engage in productive dialogue and convince each other of common policy goals. The processes that result in consensual knowledge (deriving from how expertise generates ideas) are important to understanding how and why epistemic communities resolve initially diverging opinions and interests.[64]

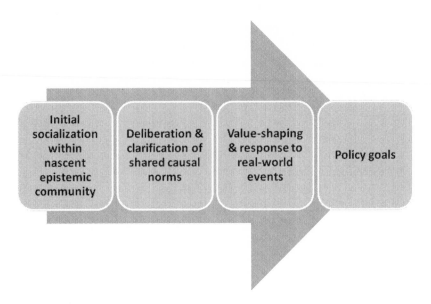

Fig. 3. Mechanisms for socialization within epistemic communities. (Based on Mai'a K. Davis Cross, "An EU Homeland Security? Sovereignty vs. Supranational Order," *European Security* 16 (2007): 83.)

I follow a methodology of historical process-tracing, beginning with the creation of the epistemic community and including its evolution over time, to examine the impact of these transnational actors on security integration. I argue that membership in an epistemic community entails (1) a process of initial socialization, followed by (2) continued deliberation and clarification of norms, (3) shaping of values over time, and finally (4) development of coherent policy goals. The value-shaping phase allows members to reshape their knowledge in light of learning, real-world events, and shifting expectations. Epistemic communities sometimes espouse policy goals after the first or second stages and then reevaluate these goals if an event causes them to do so. Figure 3 clarifies the processes that occur within epistemic communities, illustrating the mechanisms for socialization over time.

Mechanisms are defined as "what happens between a cause and its effect."[65] The mechanisms for socialization in epistemic communities are not unlike those in any kind of organization or institution. As Liesbet Hooghe explains, such mechanisms "may range from the self-conscious (for example, normative suasion) to the sub-conscious (for example, social mimicking or role-playing), and from the instrumental (for example, shaming) to the noninstrumental (for example, communication)."[66] Hooghe points out that the longer an individual is exposed to a particular social context, the more likely it is that he or she will become socialized. Thus, socialization is affected by meeting frequency.[67]

After these internal qualities are understood, it is then possible to investigate the expected external impact of an epistemic community. Transnational actors are significant because of their ability to shape domestic preferences and norms through persuasion. Indeed, there is a body of literature devoted to the international-domestic nexus—specifically, how international norms affect domestic ones (sometimes described as second image reversed).[68] The domestic level of analysis is typically defined as local populations, policies, and institutions. Research questions in this literature investigate processes of normative persuasion, adaptation, and change to explain why certain international norms gain salience at the domestic level. Amitav Acharya, for example, sheds light on "the contestation between emerging transnational norms and preexisting regional normative and social orders." He argues that in Southeast Asia, local populations sometimes borrow foreign ideas and adapt them to fit into indigenous cultures and practices.[69] Perhaps more specifically, Matthew Evangelista argues that the domestic structure of states determines their level of openness to the influence of transnational actors. He contends that a closed domestic structure that is centralized and statecentric may be more likely to listen to transnational actors if leaders find their proposals convincing.[70] Conversely, in a more open society that values pluralism, there may be so many competing transnational actors that none is a strong competitor. Thomas Risse, Jeffrey Checkel, and Jeffrey Legro similarly explore the domestic structural or political cultural contexts within which international norms sometimes operate and compete.[71]

As a rule, theorizing about the domestic salience of international norms is important if the goal is to understand changes in domestic behavior, but it is also necessary to specify the target audience. Cortell and Davis argue that "not all international rules and norms will resonate in domestic debates."[72] That is, not all international rules and norms need to resonate in domestic debates at large to have an impact. Certain norms may affect only certain sectors of domestic audiences. The norms promulgated by transnational security actors often need only to convince high-level decision makers and are targeted as such. Many norms—especially those dealing with fundamental human rights, democracy, and the rule of law—matter to the domestic audience as a whole. However, not all norms resonate with a domestic population at the grassroots level even if transnational actors attempt to grab their attention. This proposition holds particularly true in technical areas such as the distribution of public utilities (which is important in some countries but not others) or with issues that deal with a particular economic sector, (for example, tire manufacturers). As long as life continues as usual, there may be no reason for the domestic audience as a whole to care about what transnational actors are debating; thus, it would appear at first glance that the domestic salience of certain norms is low. This assumption would be misleading, however, because for those involved in providing electricity or selling cars, norms about the distribution of public utilities and standards for tire manufacturing are quite important. Thus, it is necessary to specify the target audience before measuring the domestic salience of a norm; otherwise, vital discourse could be overlooked or underrecognized. Whose behavior stands to change as a result of normative persuasion? Whose values are in direct competition with the outside norm? Who has the ability to effectuate real change? And who are transnational norm entrepreneurs trying to persuade at the domestic level?

In the case of EU security policy, the target audience of security epistemic communities typically comprises officials in the ministries of defense, foreign affairs, interior, and justice, depending on the specific policy. The security epistemic communities in this study tend not to target grassroots groups or the general public directly, which means that the audience is usually quite narrow. The epistemic communities leave broader democratic processes to domestic actors, leading to a kind of nested target audience model (figure 4), in which ministry officials ensure that elected government officials are persuaded and they in turn ensure that the will of the citizens is adequately represented.

Research Design

This book brings together nearly 80 personal interviews and a host of recent government documents important to five separate case studies to provide an account of how governance works in practice in today's EU. I engage in process tracing of each epistemic community to determine the

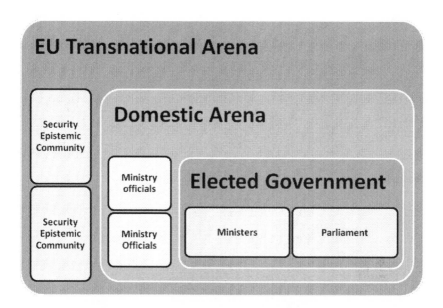

Fig. 4. Target audience of security epistemic communities. For very important issues, security epistemic communities may deal directly with elected government ministers. But in general, members of security epistemic communities are in frequent dialogue with only a limited number of domestic actors in specific ministries.

origins of its allegiance, the social background of its membership, the creation and evolution of norms, and the subsequent success or failure of efforts to persuade and socialize others. In particular, I seek to determine the degree of impact these norms have had on member states' political will to move toward more security integration.

The study of EU integration requires looking beyond the limited analysis of member states' interests to consider the role played by and the political culture of the individuals who make up these transnational epistemic communities. By comparing epistemic communities operating in the same policy realm and time period, I make generalizations about how norms within epistemic communities translate into policy goals despite different motivations and causal beliefs. A shortcoming of the current epistemic community literature is that it tends to assume that each epistemic community is operating in a transnational vacuum.

This study investigates what is usually considered to be unobservable. For this reason alone, many scholars have shied away from such research designs, arguing that it is nearly impossible to get at the actual dynamics of decision making and thus is better to focus on what is readily observable from the outside. Indeed, Dunlop argues that the study of epistemic communities is very difficult methodologically because of the necessity of operationalizing a microlevel approach:

> It seems likely that the practical obstacles entailed in the approach, such as identifying, locating and gaining access to those believed to be members of any epistemic community (this is before any attempt can be made to discern their importance), may have frustrated some scholars' attempts to use and test the thesis effectively, if at all.[73]

Despite these difficulties, the evidence presented in this study comes mainly from personal interviews and analysis of primary documents. The interviews took place in Brussels, Lisbon, Paris, the Hague, and London between January and June 2009 and lasted an average of 45 minutes each, although many were over an hour. While primary documents are uncontroversial as a source of evidence, interviewing has often been criticized for potentially introducing biases. Interviewing, however, is invaluable to any study of epistemic communities as there is typically no other way to establish motives and preferences. As Brian Rathbun argues, "Without an understanding of desires, even the most rigorous rationalist argument will not be falsifiable if it simply infers preferences from observable behavior and a posited set of situational constraints."[74] While it may often be possible to decipher the sequence of events, there is no way to find out motivations without speaking to the people involved.

Interviewees might exaggerate their role or mischaracterize other people and processes. How do we know if what they are describing is true?[75] As Rathbun argues, "When a consensus appears among those in a best position to know, it should be taken very seriously."[76] In other words, extensive interviewing also allows the researcher to "weigh conflicting evidence and offer the best interpretation possible supported by the evidence."[77] For policy areas that are still works in progress, including EU security, interviewing enables a far more timely analysis, since it also captures processes that may not yet have manifested as concrete policy outcomes. In the case of the EU, primary documents also provide this benefit. To promote transparency, the Council of the European Union strives to make documents available as soon as possible rather than strictly following a 30-year rule for declassification.

Case Selection

The literature on epistemic communities has been criticized for lacking scope conditions.[78] Risse argues that most of the research on the topic focuses on single-case success stories. Indeed, most publications on epistemic communities are articles and thus do not compare potential epistemic communities to test what makes them strong or weak. This lacuna makes it difficult to say something about the role of epistemic communities more generally and to determine when they are expected to be successful. At the same time, large-N studies on epistemic communities are difficult if not impossible because of the need for extensive interviewing and the fact that it is difficult to determine which actors might comprise an epistemic community.

This book analyzes multiple epistemic communities in the same time frame (1) to test for collaboration or competition across potential epistemic communities dealing with similar issues at the same time and (2) to look for variation across independent variables that characterize processes within epistemic communities. The specific methodology was first to select groups prominently involved in security policy then to test whether they comprised epistemic communities. In some cases, they did; in others they did not. Moreover, the strength of their influence varies. Chapter 2 indicates the range of security policy processes within which I looked for epistemic community influence.[79]

The cases were not selected randomly. Rather, I sought the most likely actors to be involved in security integration. Certain cases that would seem likely candidates were discarded after initial research. For example, one case that is not included here is the network of security think tanks across Europe. This arena would seem promising since there are a plethora of organizations that seem to share the same function: the European Union Institute for Security Studies, Security and Defence Agenda, the Centre for Studies in Security and Diplomacy, the Centre for European Security Studies, the Center for Strategic and International Studies, the Royal Institute for International Relations, and many more. However, after conducting numerous interviews of think-tank leaders in Europe, I determined that the findings were not robust enough to establish these think tanks as an epistemic community (or epistemic communities). This finding might be surprising in that think tanks quite visibly host numerous meetings, seminars, and conferences on the topic of EU security, bringing hundreds of people together to discuss important security topics. But the interviews revealed that think tanks do not have close ties with one another, tend to not advance shared policy goals, and generally serve more as forums for other professionals to meet. Think tanks do not act as policy leaders in their own right. Even the individuals who come together at think-tank events are more properly understood as an epistemic coalition because the nature of their expertise is typically quite diverse. Think tanks certainly play a useful role in encouraging and providing exposure to important policy debates, but they do not constitute an epistemic community.

Because I conducted a broad exploration of possible cases before eliminating noncases, the sample selected here is likely close to the full universe of cases. I selected the most likely rather than the least likely cases because security integration itself has typically been regarded as unlikely. Thus, the challenge is to find any evidence at all for epistemic community influence in this policy area. In many ways, it is an issue area in which epistemic communities are least likely to succeed. In addition, epistemic community research has focused on issue areas where it is relatively easy for the communities to have an impact: economic and environmental integration.[80] Thus, the goal here is to make any inroads in debunking the assumption that epistemic communities cannot influence a difficult issue area—security integration. On the external security side, the groups are the Political and Security Committee (PSC), the EU Military Committee (EUMC), and the Civilian Crisis Management Committee (Civcom). On the internal security side, the groups are the Committee of Permanent Representatives (Coreper) and the Group of Personalities in the Field of Security Research (GofP).

The epistemic community literature brings together a remarkable blend of philosophy, sociology, economics, and politics, making it an incredibly fruitful avenue for research. Knowledge is a source of soft power, and soft power influences international relations in profound ways, especially in the European context. But if knowledge is not organized in some way beyond the individual level and is not shaped into some kind of coherent consensus, it is likely to have little impact. Thus, epistemic communities can help us understand when and why knowledge translates into power. Processes of persuasion and deliberation triggered by epistemic communities bring to light larger trends and lend greater visibility of the future. Since the case study chapters are devoted to a close analysis of each of the five epistemic communities and their impact on specific policy examples, the next chapter puts these examples into the greater context, providing a picture of the overall state of security integration.[81]

CHAPTER 2

Toward European Security Integration

"It is impossible to separate the internal and external dimensions of counter-terrorism. The most serious challenges we face outside the EU, all have complex connections inside the EU."

—GILLES DE KERCHOVE, EU COUNTERTERRORISM COORDINATOR,
NOVEMBER 19, 2008[1]

TRANSCENDING COOPERATION

Security integration involves much more than counterterrorism, but in many ways, 9/11 and the subsequent 2004 and 2005 attacks in Madrid and London served as critical junctures in the intensification of integration in this area. How did these events affect EU security policy? One argument is that "the reframing of terrorism as a transnational, networked phenomenon has infused the need for international co-operation" as "catastrophic events in the USA formed a pretext for the acceleration of the legislative process."[2] In other words, the terrorist attacks created such a sense of urgency that agreements in the pipeline were pushed through quickly and rubber-stamped if necessary. Even members of the European Parliament were more willing to fast-track security policy dossiers that came to their table. Shortly after 9/11, cooperation and information sharing across the Atlantic flourished, but then the vast divide that separated the American and European worldviews became more apparent. Even in spite of the outward cooling of this relationship, the opportunity for the EU to define itself against the United States further jump-started Europe's efforts to gain an autonomous capacity to protect itself and to be an active player outside of its own geographic sphere.[3]

Such was the climate at the very beginning of the twenty-first century. This atmosphere triggered a large number of new initiatives, including the

Declaration on Combating Terrorism, the European Security Strategy (ESS, also known as the Solana document), and the Solidarity Clause, which promised that if one member state was the victim of a terrorist attack or other natural or human-created disaster, the others would come to its aid. But short-run exigency is not enough when it comes to the long-run difficulties of constructing an untested supranational order. Security is too fundamental to national sovereignty.[4] Indeed, terrorism as an impetus to move European integration forward is much less often invoked only a decade after 9/11. These critical junctures have certainly provided some momentum for a reevaluation of EU security among its leaders, but more important are the longer-term processes, incentives, and obstacles that have been shaping the new order for decades. Some even refer to this era as "post-Westphalian" in that the old rules and structures that have more or less governed the state system since the 1648 Treaty of Westphalia are giving way to something entirely different.[5]

SECURITY AND THE INTERNAL-EXTERNAL NEXUS

The traditional definition of security, as exemplified in neorealist theory, is quite basic: the ability to use military force to protect one's state against external invaders and ensure its survival. The problem with this definition is that it neglects the other components of security that are just as critical to the survival of a state. Threats to security can arise in the form of organized crime, drug addiction, terrorism, corruption, illegal immigration, money laundering, and human trafficking, and these problems can attack the integrity of a state from within. While the EU is not a state, it is largely internally borderless, and security thus poses many of the same challenges. Moreover, the EU has not faced any real threat to its security from the outside, in the traditional sense, since the fall of the Soviet Union. This is not to say that traditional military security is irrelevant to the definition but rather that a more expansive view is required.

No clear dividing line separates internal and external security. With the exception of the UK and Ireland, internal security for each member state includes territory outside of its national borders. In addition, a major part of the EU's strategy for providing internal security is to engage in third-country humanitarian and peacekeeping operations. The means of engaging in external security operations often involve the tools of internal security, such as police, intelligence, rule of law, and state building.

In the past, the internal and external dimensions of security have been treated as two distinct spheres of action. In a democratic system of governance, the same rules of conduct that apply to external wars must not be applied to securing the safety of citizens within a state. In the process occurring now, the rules and means of conduct that typically provide internal security are increasingly being applied to external security practices. Largely for this reason, Markus Ekengren argues, "the internal-external divide has to a large extent lost its importance as an analytical concept and as a political guideline for EU security action."[6] Thus, both dimensions are part of a broad rubric of what constitutes security in a way that is consistent with democracy. In fact, security as "the perception of guarding against a seamless web of threats" is not unlike conceptions of security found at least as far back as the Reformation and the rise of states in Europe.[7]

The next section provides a brief overview of the development of both internal and external security policy over the past few decades. I subsequently define the concepts of cooperation and integration and differentiate between hard and soft integration. I then provide an overview of the main security issue areas, highlighting the extent to which EU member states are integrated in their ability to deal with those issues. Finally, I address the challenges for security integration and the role of expertise in overcoming these challenges. This chapter sets the stage for examining the impact of epistemic communities by showing what has been accomplished or is in the process of being accomplished. The EU has achieved a degree of security integration that is quite unexpected, and knowledge-based networks have played an important role in getting the EU on its current path. While each of the case studies in the following chapters focuses on a particular policy example as a window into the role of each epistemic community, this chapter paints the bigger picture of security integration.

Historical Background

Despite the current seamlessness of internal and external security, cooperation and eventually some degree of integration in these areas did not always develop in a way that reflected the close relationship between the two aspects of security. The specific roots of the European Union's external security cooperation can be found during the Cold War.[8] In the 1950s, when the European Coal and Steel Community (ECSC) was still in its early years, the six member states hoped to achieve cooperation or at least coordination of their foreign policies. Two failed attempts—the European Defence Community (EDC) and European Political Community (EPC)—seemed to portend purely economic cooperation, and during the following decade, another attempt fell through. The Fouchet Plan, a French proposal to restructure the European Community and give it military independence from the United States, was too ambitious in some ways and flawed in others.

In 1970, the six nations finally put into place a new institutional framework: European Political Cooperation. While the framework stuck, it was from all perspectives underwhelming, separated as it was from European Community structures and not backed by treaty agreement. As one scholar has put it, "Not only was EPC's scope of action so indeterminate that it threatened to invite more conflict than cooperation, but its mechanisms to induce such cooperation were feeble and peculiar."[9] Nevertheless, the EPC enabled more progress in political cooperation than might have been expected given its shortcomings. It made possible some major diplomatic initiatives, among them the Euro-Arab Dialogue and the Conference on Security and Cooperation in Europe, and served as more than simply a forum for discussion. Perhaps most important, the EPC enabled Europeans to overcome their initial hesitations about security cooperation and provided a venue for the expression of their desire to turn the EPC into something more.[10] But security cooperation did not really take off until after the Cold War.

The 1992 Maastricht Treaty on European Union transformed the EPC into the Common Foreign and Security Policy (CFSP), for the first time enshrining political and security cooperation in a treaty. The advent of CFSP set the stage for possible progress in this area. It called for the EU

> to assert its identity on the international scene . . . including the eventual framing of a common defence policy, which might in time lead to a common defence. . . . The Member States shall support the Union's external and security policy actively and unreservedly in a spirit of loyalty and mutual solidarity. They shall refrain from any action which is contrary to the interests of the Union or likely to impair its effectiveness as a cohesive force in international relations.[11]

One drawback of the Maastricht Treaty in terms of its prospects for eventual integration of foreign and security policy is that it clearly separated supranational areas from intergovernmental areas. It put all the pre-Maastricht areas of integration into the first pillar (the single market, the Schengen Agreement, environmental law, and so forth) and made external security the second pillar and internal security the third. In effect, the Treaty on European Union introduced a cognitive and practical tool for conceiving of security differently and, most important, separately from the general process of EU integration. Moreover, this system psychologically separated internal from external security by giving each a distinct pillar despite the fact that both were intergovernmental issue areas and subject to decisions based on unanimity. Over the past few years, however, these pillars have gradually merged as the lines between their areas of focus have become blurred.

As part of the quest to instill a European security and defense identity, member states, meeting under the Western European Union (WEU) format, agreed on the 1992 Petersberg Tasks. They stipulated that member states might use force if a crisis called for "humanitarian and rescue tasks; peacekeeping tasks; and tasks of combat forces in crisis management, including peace-making."[12] Jolyon Howorth argues that the Petersberg Tasks "implied radical transformation of the EU's existing capacity to provide deployable, professional intervention forces geared to 'out of area' crisis management."[13] But during the first few years after Maastricht and the Petersberg Declaration, CFSP was relatively empty. According to Wyn Rees, "CFSP remained weak and represented little more than a loose amalgam of the national foreign policies of the fifteen members."[14] It needed some kind of enabler, a way for it to become concrete. This opportunity came during a December 1998 summit in St. Malo, France, when French president Jacques Chirac and British prime minister Tony Blair agreed that the EU needed a true defense capability.[15] In other words, the two main security actors wanted the EU to "have the capacity for autonomous action, backed up by credible military forces."[16] Blair and Chirac were witnessing Europe's utter inability to act in the midst of the crisis in Kosovo and the collapse of Yugoslavia. The St. Malo Declaration represented a big shift in British policy, as the UK had for decades resisted the idea.[17] The European Security and Defence Policy (ESDP), reflecting the goals of St. Malo, was approved by member states in 1999 and was launched in 2003.

CFSP is no longer a loose political promise among states that fear what real security cooperation would mean. Instead, CFSP demonstrates a clear willingness to work together in areas such as imposing economic sanctions on third countries to achieve foreign policy aims, researching and manufacturing weaponry, building up military power, and engaging in third-country operations under the ESDP framework. In an extensive study of these issues, Seth G. Jones discovers that member states now choose to impose sanctions through the EU rather than unilaterally around 78 percent of the time, compared to 12 percent of the time during the Cold War. In arms production, Jones finds that member states and their defense industry corporations largely engage jointly in research and development and that in some areas, such engagement occurs completely at the European level.[18] Most recently, the implementation of the Lisbon Treaty brought about a name change from European Security and Defence Policy to Common Security and Defence Policy (CSDP) as an indication of the EU's serious commitment.

Alongside the advent of the 2003 European Security Strategy and the operationalization of CSDP, EU leaders and diplomats increasingly emphasized the external dimension of internal security—the extent to which external threats could harm the integrity of the European "homeland." But this was not the first major point of internal-external convergence. In 1985, France, Germany, and the Benelux countries established Schengen I, agreeing to have only visual surveillance of vehicles as they crossed borders at a reduced speed while gradually dismantling border checkpoints altogether. Five years later, Schengen II fully implemented the agreement, effectively creating an internally borderless zone. Since then, the Schengen zone has enlarged dramatically, with only the UK and Ireland opting out among EU members and several non-EU states also taking part. This new freedom of movement meant that domestic security had to be understood more broadly. National borders became internal EU borders, thereby redefining the concept of boundaries. Consequently, each member state had to conceive of internal security as including territory outside of its borders. Both Schengen and CSDP made clear in practice and in the minds of decision makers that internal and external security were inextricably intertwined. By this point, internal security had already evolved rather quickly, surpassing the external dimension in terms of cooperation across member states.

So what of the prior evolution of internal security? Internal security has been the focus of much less academic attention than external security, although internal security is undeniably more fundamental to the daily lives of European citizens. Early in EU history, leaders expressed an interest in pursuing both external and internal security, but the latter was less visible.[19] The Maastricht Treaty, however, included Justice and Home Affairs (JHA) an an important component. The third pillar (synonymous with JHA) was subsequently and rapidly communitarized—that is, increasingly subject to the Community Method of decision making—despite its intergovernmental starting point. In fact, the Committee of Permanent Representatives, comprised of member states' ambassadors, was so quickly and intensively caught up in JHA that on January 14, 2004, the Presidency issued a Council memo warning committee members against overtasking themselves.[20]

Despite the third pillar's intergovernmental label, many of the original JHA issues have been relocated to the community (first) pillar over the past few years.[21] The 1997 Amsterdam Treaty transferred immigration, border controls, visas, and asylum to the first pillar, reducing the third pillar to "Police and Judicial Cooperation in Criminal Matters." Amsterdam also enabled the EU to sign international agreements pertaining to the third pillar, giving it an unambiguous external dimension. This aspect was not superfluous to the core of internal security but was necessary so that common approaches to immigration, border controls, and asylum would work at the EU level. These three areas directly affect citizens of non-EU countries and their ability to enter the EU as well as move within it.[22] With Amsterdam, JHA was also promoted to an "area of freedom, security, and justice." The French word *espace* not only means *area* but also *space* and denotes something as integrated and coherent as the Schengen area.[23] Overall, the internal security sector has experienced the largest growth of all EU policies in the past fifteen years, in some ways comparable to the advent of the European economic and monetary union of the 1990s.[24]

An ongoing process of review continues gradually to chip away at the remaining collection of intergovernmental JHA policies. The 2005 treaty establishing a constitution for Europe attempted to give the EU a single legal personality, shared competencies on issues pertaining to territorial cohesion, and new areas of cooperation for criminal justice proceedings on terrorism and illegal trafficking of arms, humans, and drugs. Although the Constitutional Treaty never passed, the June 2007 Council meeting ended with the unanimous belief among member states that JHA no longer belonged in the intergovernmentalist framework. The revised Constitutional Treaty, the Lisbon Treaty, is the capstone to this historical development, dissolving what remains of the pillar system and what it represents for internal security integration. It also formally gives the EU a single legal personality in its dealings with external parties. An important process is clearly under way, and although it was not wholly anticipated, it has important implications for what Europe is going to become.

What used to be the third pillar is now a hybrid of intergovernmental and supranational approaches. Immigration and external border controls, for example, are now more or less integrated, while police and judicial cooperation remain more intergovernmental. At the same time, the emphasis on the external dimension of internal security is growing. The recent three-presidency agenda on JHA stipulates that "the artificial distinction between internal and external dimensions of the fight against terrorism is to be reconsidered in order to carry out more efficient and global actions."[25] The 2005–10 Hague Programme reflects this belief: It has ten internal security priorities, and all of them have key ramifications for how the EU deals with its neighbors and third countries.[26]

Thus, over the past few decades, member states have made great progress in working together when it comes to matters of security. Not only has a remarkable degree of cooperation been achieved, but integration is also marching steadily forward. Some questions remain: Who is spearheading this process? And why have they been so convincing? Knowledge-based networks are steadily persuading member states and gradually reshaping their worldviews and have a unique ability to inculcate new norms about security.

Cooperation versus Integration

In the context of the EU, security cooperation is quite significant.[27] Cooperation occurs when states decide to work together on a particular issue and act in common to the degree that they are all willing to participate. There are many ways in which states can fall short of cooperation. A weaker form of cooperation is coordination, which involves information sharing and a common desire to take into account what others are doing in a similar vein. Coordination at times benefits from the help of an agency that can oversee joint operations or facilitate the exchange of information, such as the EU's Joint Situation Centre (Sitcen), which helps share intelligence across member states. Cooperation is clearly more complicated, but it is also not unique to the EU. The Concert of Europe and League of Nations are examples of previous attempts to build security cooperation. The United States and Europe have also collaborated and cooperated on military security since the end of World War II, although the relationship has been unequal. The North Atlantic Treaty Organization (NATO) has been a significant example of security cooperation; others include the Western European Union, the Council of Europe, the Organization for Security and Cooperation in Europe (OSCE), and the Commonwealth of Independent States.[28]

Security cooperation is not entirely novel, but integration takes cooperation much further. While cooperation is intergovernmental and is determined on a case-by-case basis, integration occurs when cooperation becomes automatic and irrevocable. The relationship between cooperation and integration is not dichotomous, and more or less advanced stages of integration can exist (figure 5). Such stages begin with consensus building in Brussels and then emanate outward to include persuasion of decision makers in the capitals as well as ongoing deliberation in Brussels and between Brussels and the capitals. If persuasion is successful, gradual shifts in worldview occur, paving the way for formal integration.

For the purposes of drawing out and simplifying these distinctions, I differentiate between hard and soft integration. *Hard integration* is the formal process of transferring authority from the national to supranational level until individual member states can no longer veto outcomes. The financing of civilian crisis missions overseas is an example of hard integration, as such financing falls entirely under the purview of the Community budget. The advent of EU battle groups with rapid-reaction capability is also a good example, even though they have yet to be deployed. Hard integration reflects a standard definition but does not capture levels of integration that have been achieved in practice but may not be codified in treaties or EU regulation. I define *soft integration* as the development of a strongly held norm among actors to always deal with particular issues collectively and interdependently. This norm can be held by member states' decision makers as well as by nonstate transnational actors. The issue is then Europeanized or assumed to be a European issue, even if it is not mandated as such.[29] For example, a decade ago, Burkhard Schmitt carefully documented transnational integration among defense and aerospace technology firms across Europe.[30] After a certain degree of transnational collaboration was achieved, it became institutionalized in the defense market. By default, member states ended up with a common manufacturer of certain military technologies, even though only two years earlier, the traditional production model—national manufacturers serving national defense needs—remained in place. If transnational nonstate actors change the way states operate from the inside, governments may find that they are de facto integrated.

In addition, *harmonization* of member states' policies over time is a form

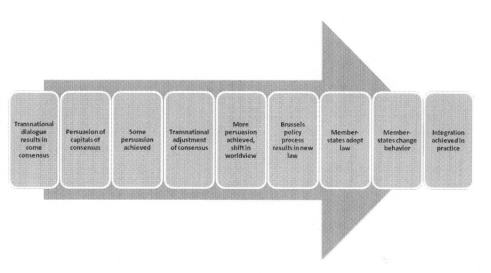

Fig. 5. Stages of integration

of soft integration. As is the case with transnational processes of integration, harmonization is not necessarily accomplished through supranational mandate but relies on all member states agreeing to bring their laws in line with each other. Implementation of such agreements does not involve punishment for noncompliance but relies entirely on member states believing that it is appropriate for them to change their national legislation. A key example is the current process of harmonizing external border regulations. The EU's external borders are gradually becoming fully integrated in that they are increasingly treated as one continuous border subject to the same visa rules, security measures, and record keeping of individuals who have entered the EU.

The Common Foreign and Security Policy, along with its CSDP component, is nearly always described as being limited to cooperation. The main reasons often cited are that the EU cannot consistently speak with one voice, its common foreign policy decisions are still made in capitals, it does not seem to be forming some kind of superstate, and there is apparently no European army in the making.[31] But a strict dichotomy between cooperation and integration misses areas that are in the process of becoming supranational or that have achieved transnational integration in the absence of formal obligations (soft integration). Permanent cooperation that is required by EU law may not even be as significant as permanent cooperation that is voluntary or based on strongly held norms. The former may become tangled up in bureaucratic red tape, while the latter might evolve into soft integration.

Many scholars also tend to conflate integration with an end point that is synonymous with the qualities of a unitary state. For example, they assume that military integration means the advent of a European army or that foreign policy integration means that all decision-making authority must rest with the European Commission. But these results may not be the end point of integration. The EU can be a security actor with significant military power even without a European army. Member states' governments can consistently speak with one voice on foreign policy without formally giving up national sovereignty in this area. Even in the most intergovernmental security sectors, decisions are not made solely in the capitals, and processes under way encompass both soft and hard integration.

Even the achievement of some level of security cooperation is significant, although not so unexpected. This process began with the founding of the European Coal and Steel Community and has often rested on the preferences of political leaders responding to the various crises of a given time period. Some observers argue that security cooperation has simply been a response to changes in power in the international system.[32] By contrast, others offer more constructivist or institutionalist explanations.[33] However, the move from security cooperation to integration is more difficult to explain, requiring an examination of various patterns of influence in the EU. Europe's decision makers could have stopped with economic integration but were determined from the beginning to accomplish more. Given that member states hold varying—often opposing—security positions and perspectives, this approach presents an important puzzle.

Member states have a history of different aspirations, traditions, and worldviews when it comes to protecting their own citizens and grappling with the need to balance security and civil liberties. Even more fundamental is the significant differences in nations' legal cultures—with some based on civil law and others based on common law—that lead to a host of other distinctions in terms of court systems and criminal proceedings.[34] The member states are also very dissimilar when it comes to choices about engaging in external action and the type of action they favor. The British, for example, have traditionally backed U.S. foreign policy, while the French have preferred to act much more autonomously. Some countries stress the military aspect of their capabilities, while others pride themselves on civilian power contributions. Member states such as Germany, Poland, France, the UK, Spain, and Italy have many more military personnel at their disposal than do Malta, Cyprus, Luxembourg, Latvia, Slovenia, and Estonia.[35] Certain member states—Sweden, Finland, France, Germany, Slovenia, Hungary, and Belgium, for example—consistently emphasize the importance of CSDP as a tool for influence, while others, including some of the newest member states, emphasize NATO's role.[36] Despite these fundamental differences, EU member states as a whole continue to strive for and achieve new levels of cooperation and even integration.

This book explains this puzzle through a focus on the key role of epistemic communities. To understand how epistemic communities work and to show what is being explained, it is first important to lay out the state of security policy more generally and the trends in each sector. Knowledge-based networks have been instrumental in shaping policies in all of these security sectors. In the following chapters, I draw out a few of these examples to show specifically how policies came about through the influence of these networks.[37]

THE STATE OF SECURITY POLICY BY SECTOR

This section provides a brief overview of each major security policy area in turn: terrorism and organized crime; internal and external border security; migration, immigration, and asylum; privacy and civil and criminal justice; military research, capabilities, and procurement; and finally Common Security and Defence Policy and interoperability. I do not attempt to give a full and detailed account of the ongoing struggles to craft each policy area but rather to show broadly which issues benefit from coordination, cooperation, or integration.

Terrorism and Organized Crime

Some analysts of EU internal security policy see terrorism and organized crime as its key components.[38] To what extent do member states deal with these twin challenges at the European level? Police and judicial authorities across member states work together in a number of ways and are bringing national justice systems and penal laws in line with each other.[39] The European Arrest Warrant, for example, allows police to issue warrants that apply across the EU for the arrest of individuals suspected of terrorism or other serious crimes, even if offenses are defined differently. Thus police in any other member state can arrest and detain suspects, regardless of their national origin. In effect, this ability goes well beyond the principle of mutual recognition of laws to legal harmonization across member states,[40] and in 2005, 7,000 arrests occurred as a result of the European Arrest Warrant.[41] Similarly, the European Evidence Warrant gives national courts the power to mandate that other member states provide evidence relevant to particular cases. In this area, mutual recognition of judicial orders enables authorities to freeze and confiscate assets. Finally, policies such as the freezing of terrorist finances and prevention of money laundering are already first pillar concerns. These areas, as well as others, represent hard integration.

One of the key areas of rapid soft integration is in the realm of police activity. Europol plays a central part as a supranational police office dedicated to addressing all serious crimes involving more than one member state as well as any issue related to counterterrorism. Europol has a staff of more than 600 and a budget of over €80 million from the EU.[42] While Europol does not conduct investigations on its own, it does prepare strategic analyses and threat assessments, facilitates the exchange of information with the United States, and maintains several extensive databases.[43] It also facilitates coordination between various national police and justice authorities. Within Europol are the Police Chiefs Operational Task Force, which discusses best practices, crime trends, and operations planning, and joint investigation teams (there are currently six) made up of police and judicial authorities from multiple member states and even the United States who are working on the same crime. The EU's European Police College brings together senior police officers from across Europe to further develop their networks, organize training initiatives, and conduct research.

In addition to working through Europol, police can also share information about crimes or criminals through various networks. One is the Schengen Information System, effectively a common law enforcement tool that enables member states to integrate their efforts to stop cross-border crime. It has a database of more than 14 million records on the movement of individuals wanted for crimes, vehicle registration records, and residence permits. Another such network is the Counterterrorist Group, which brings together heads of national intelligence agencies. Member states have adopted the availability principle, which means that they agree to provide law enforcement information to other agencies across the EU according to the same standards that are applied within individual member states. Many other more specific measures address the sharing of information on suspicious financial transactions, lost or stolen passports, asylum seekers, fingerprints or photographs of possible criminals, and illegal immigrants. However, not all areas are showing signs of harmonization or integration. Europol does not have the authority to "stop, search, and arrest,"[44] and national intelligence chiefs still prefer to share information directly with each other, through the Counterterrorist Group, rather than through Europol.[45]

Both Europol and the European Judicial Cooperation Unit (Eurojust) have units dedicated to counterterrorism, and the Council has a counterterrorism coordinator (CTC), who oversees all aspects of counterterrorism policy, especially those that fall under the Action Plan on Combating Terrorism and the EU Counterterrorism Strategy. The CTC relies on member state ambassadors (the Committee of Permanent Representatives) to monitor the strategy's progress, provide updates, and follow up on implementation as well as on the European Council to provide political oversight. The Commission, Parliament, and Council also meet once every six months to ensure coherence across institutions.[46] The Strategy on Radicalization and Recruitment (chapter 3) is a major component of the Action Plan on Combating Terrorism and includes a number of initiatives in response to experts' advice that the EU faces a threat from its own Muslim communities. The Strategy on Radicalization and Recruitment receives input from both the second pillar's CFSP working group on terrorism and the third pillar's Terrorism Working Group before going to member states' ambassadors for final discussions and guidance. In fact, many counterterrorism policies rest on multiple EU pillars, showing that integration is occurring in a very complex way.[47]

These community-level institutions, like the antiterrorism units and CTC, perform their roles because EU member states have agreed to common definitions of terrorist offenses. These practices include a list of individuals or groups considered terrorists and minimum sentences for certain acts of terrorism. Agreeing to an overarching definition of terrorism is quite significant given that only Spain, Portugal, France, and the UK had even defined terrorism in a satisfactory way a few years ago. Belgium had not even made it a crime to belong to a terrorist organization, and several countries, including both Belgium and the Netherlands, had no counterterrorist legislation on their books.[48] Now, member states continuously share information on terrorist-related convictions, abide by the same standards, and agree that these activities are crimes.[49] Common definitions and punishments for terrorist activities embody a path toward hard integration and are crucial prerequisites for the development of a European security space.

The EU also has common methods for dealing with the consequences of terrorist attacks. Several institutional bureaus have been created with the aim of setting up a framework for an integrated response. These bureaus include the Civil Protection Working Party of the Council, the Civil Protection Unit within the Environment Directorate General, the Commission's Monitoring and Information Centre, the Common Emergency and Communication and Information System, and the Health Security Committee, among others.[50] In particular, special attention has been paid to scenarios involving nonconventional weapons attacks. The EU's Community Mechanism for Civil Protection, an institution that stands ready to respond in the event of an emergency, maintains a database of experts on chemical, biological, radiological, and nuclear weapons and of teams of available emergency workers. At the core of the Community Mechanism is the Monitoring and Information Center, which is available at all times in the event of a major disaster. These various common provisions—representing hard integration—are backed up by the Solidarity Clause, which is essentially the EU's version of NATO's Article V. The clause's main shortcoming is that it is fundamentally reactive, not proactive. There is a promise of help, but only after an attack has occurred.

The EU also has in place some proactive provisions signaling hard integration. The main preventive group, the Health Security Committee, makes sure that an attack never happens. Its Health Security Program includes information exchange, detection and identification of chemical, biological, and radiological agents, building a medicine supply, and providing rules for how the EU will respond in the event of an attack.[51] A second major proactive area is the security of air transportation. EU member states are fully integrated when it comes to international safety regulations. Thus, all EU airports follow the same aviation security standards, passenger screening, staff training, and aircraft inspection procedures.[52]

The external component of the fight against terrorism and organized crime is also quite developed.[53] The 2003 European Security Strategy laid out Europe's threats and common strategies in the post-9/11 environment, emphasizing in particular the inseparability of internal and external security. A common definition on terrorism has been important in enabling the

EU to cooperate with third countries as a coherent actor.[54] As part of the Action Plan, the EU has provided funding to third countries committed to combating terrorism and has entered into numerous bilateral cooperative initiatives with North America, including the appointment of liaison officers and the transfer of data from Europol. The EU has also signed international agreements against terrorism, such as an international policy on weapons of mass destruction, and established a central system of information exchange that enables sharing of data about visas. Finally, through the Action Plan, member states have agreed on international causes and solutions to international and EU terrorist recruitment.[55] Most of these areas are governed by first pillar legislation, meaning that they reflect hard integration and not simply cooperation. Implementation at the national level has been slower in some areas than in others, but progress has been steady.

Internal and External Border Security

The EU is close to achieving a fully integrated system of border management with a single set of rules. EU member states are working together to protect their common external borders from illegal immigration and threats posed by terrorism and organized crime. This effort has required the introduction of a significant amount of new legislation in all member states. As with all areas pertaining to security, member states have their own traditions and laws, but any disparity risks encouraging asylum seekers and others to search for the weakest point of entry. To facilitate a common system of dealing with asylum seekers and immigrants in a way that protects internal security, the EU has put into place the European Automated Fingerprints Identification System (EURODAC) to share information and keep track of all those who have tried or are trying to enter the EU. The Schengen Information System also stores data about the movement of illegal immigrants. In addition, all travel documents and passports issued by member states have biometric identifiers, a feature that has drawn criticism from some human rights groups for encroaching on privacy rights.

The external dimension of border security is no exception to this ongoing process of hard integration. It includes common customs controls in the form of new legislation and the Visa Information System, which enables border agencies to share information about visa applications and check them against terrorist watch lists. In addition, the European Agency for Management of the External Borders (Frontex) ensures certain high standards of surveillance along all external borders, helps member states with training, and manages joint border control activities. Frontex has focused on interception at sea and deportation of illegal immigrants, among other areas.[56] Although the existence of Frontex makes integrated border management possible, member states still formally retain the power to determine how they want to control external borders. While Frontex facilitates joint operations, they must be initiated by member states. The agency's management board is made up of member state officials and representatives from the Commission.[57] Thus, while member states have integrated their approach to some policies, other policies merely rest on voluntary cooperation. A natural extension of Frontex, for example, would be the creation and training of a common corps of border guards to assist national guards, but some member states have resisted this idea.[58] As integration moves forward, this resistance may dissipate.

The European Commission is also involved in border security with a system of security monitoring at airports and harbors across the EU. One of its chief initiatives is the Research Framework Program, which offers funding for multistate projects that aim to produce new technology for the protection of harbors, airports, and other types of cross-border transportation. The Commission now maintains a catalog that details all the measures in place intended to provide common border security: surveillance, intelligence, investigations of cross-border crime, agreements with third countries, and cooperation between national police and border agencies.[59] Any issue controlled by the Commission naturally falls within first pillar competences, meaning that member states have given up their ability to intervene in decision making.

Migration, Immigration, and Asylum

Policies involving the free movement of persons were communitarized with the implementation of the 1997 Amsterdam Treaty. Consequently, the EU has supranational competence over migration, immigration, asylum, visas, and related areas of border control. At the same time, there is no clear way to separate these communitarized areas from a number of other areas of EU policy, and together they tend to reinforce Community competences.[60] For example, illegal immigration or migration is linked to the Schengen Agreement and thus to criminal legislation and border protection. Likewise, the free movement of people directly affects policies on immigration, crime, commerce, and tourism. Moreover, although migration, immigration, and asylum policies tend to dictate what people cannot do, these policies inevitably enable other activities that are fundamental to the daily EU operations. Visa policy, for example, is designed to prevent illegal immigration but also encourages interaction between EU citizens and people from third countries. Over time, the right to free movement within the EU has pulled a host of other policies toward more integration.

More generally, external border control is harmonized when it comes to the movement of goods and people. Since internal border controls between member states are virtually nonexistent, it would make sense that external border controls, including visa policy, should converge across member states. The Amsterdam Treaty did just that; it was designed to supranationalize external borders.[61] The process of harmonization, however, is still not totally complete. It has been very successful in terms of short-term visa policy (pertaining to stays not exceeding three months), but long-term visa policy has achieved harmonization only in some areas. For example, Community legislation allows third-country citizens to enter the EU for research, student exchanges, training, or voluntary services but not for the purposes of economic migration, paid employment, or self-employment.[62]

Immigration legislation is intimately tied to the EU's external association agreements with third countries.[63] In effect, immigration serves as an opportunity to engage with outside countries and create legal channels to enable the protection and movement of refugees. The EU has the Common European Asylum System, established in two phases and based on the Geneva Refugee Convention. Certain minimum standards are in place for enacting asylum law across the EU. Member states have harmonized their approach to situations of mass influx, standards for the reception of asylum seekers, qualifications for refugee status, methods for processing claims, and instruments for distributing asylum claims across member states. In addition, member states recognize the external dimension of such a common asylum system. They work together with third countries based on previously established partnerships with policies that enable the safe return of asylum seekers to their countries of origin and that prevent illegal immigration through the use of common information systems and visa rules.[64]

Overall, migration and asylum policies as well as their accompanying strategies reflect hard integration among member states. External borders are all the more critical given the absence of internal border checks to control the movement of people. Consequently, alongside the dissolution of internal borders, the EU has put into place certain compensatory measures, such as police cooperation, harmonized visa policy, and common strategies, to combat threats in the form of terrorism and organized crime and to make external borders even more secure.[65] To resolve the ongoing challenges associated with this policy area, member states also cooperate to investigate the common causes of migration, encourage legal immigration, and help third countries manage their migration flows.

Privacy and Civil and Criminal Justice

In every democratic society, there is always the risk that rights to privacy and liberty could be sacrificed in the name of security. With so many new security initiatives that affect EU citizens' daily lives, many scholars and commentators have criticized the EU for not balancing rights and security in policies concerning immigration and asylum.[66] Indeed, EU security agreements and legislation have been far more weighted toward security than toward democratic transparency or protection of rights. Tellingly, Frontex does not even deal with the protection of refugees or their rights. The integration of such rights protections across member states could improve and ensure that the right balance is upheld, but integration has been relatively slow in this area.

The existence of the European Court of Justice (ECJ) is the primary means for private individuals within the EU to seek redress. They can take their cases directly to the ECJ or go to local courts where they can get preliminary rulings from the ECJ—the mechanism by which local courts ask the ECJ for a recommended ruling. More often than not, local courts follow through with these preliminary rulings. Over time, the ECJ's powerful role has resulted in a body of Community law that has superseded expectations and even treaty stipulations in many respects. In addition, the ECJ plays a strong role in enforcing its rulings and imposes fines on member states or other entities that do not comply with EU law. Much work remains to be done, however, especially with regard to upholding the rights of foreign nationals. Integration of privacy and justice regulation is necessary precisely because of the integration achieved in areas such as border security, immigration, asylum, organized crime, and counterterrorism.

Some of the items of greatest concern in terms of privacy rights have been data retention initiatives, biometric passports, and the transfer of data regarding travelers entering the United States.[67] Data retention in particular has been a hot-button issue. The Schengen Information System, for example, contains information gathered for the purposes of tracking illegal immigration, but that same data can be used to track criminal activity. Much depends on what safeguards are in place, how the data are collected, and whether there is transparency in what is happening with the information.[68] The EU has a privacy directive as well as a data protection policy to ensure that this information is not misused. This minimal level of harmonization is necessary because all member states must comply for the policies to work.

One big challenge is safeguarding the rights of foreign citizens. Third-country nationals cannot appeal to the ECJ for rights claims, and EU common policy is a bit lacking with regard to respecting the international rights of asylum seekers and refugees. Both the European Convention on Human Rights and the Schengen Borders Code ensure a certain level of common standards.[69] The latter stipulates that the European Parliament can play a key role in protecting individual rights. But the EU focuses more on integration of border security than on achieving a comprehensive approach that balances the need to protect EU citizens with the need to respect foreign nationals' rights.[70]

Member states are increasingly cooperating to ensure that citizens' rights are protected with respect to major anticrime operations. Cooperative links have been forged between member states' judiciary and prosecutory branches. Eurojust brings member states' magistrates and prosecutors together to better enable coordination across the EU. It often works with Europol, both to solve crimes and to resolve criminal issues. Eurojust enables member states to cooperate on investigations, prosecutions, international extradition, and mutual legal assistance pertaining to cross-border crime. But since Eurojust cannot initiate investigations but can only ask member states to do so, it does not represent integration among member states. The European Judicial Network regularly brings together around 200 magistrates and prosecutors to share problems they face in their work, compare differences in legal cultures, and provide ideas regarding best practices. This kind of informal forum for networking has gone a long way in enhancing cooperation, especially considering that the main ingredient missing in this area of integration is a high degree of trust in other legal systems.[71] At minimum, trust will be necessary to enable integration and harmonization.

The European Union has the power to draft binding legal instruments. For example, the Mutual Legal Assistance Convention not only enables the formation of joint investigation teams but also harmonizes how member states spontaneously exchange information, transfer individuals in custody to investigators in other member states, hold hearings by video or teleconferencing, and intercept communications among suspects.[72] Nearly all member states have ratified the convention, and it represents the soft integration of special investigative techniques that at the same time respect the rights of individuals. The European Arrest Warrant is similar in this respect, requiring that member states integrate acts of surrender requests while respecting due process.

The EU's overarching principle is that it grants citizens certain freedoms: free movement of people, goods, services, and capital. The Charter of Fundamental Rights of the European Union, part of the Lisbon Treaty, provides an EU-wide guarantee that these common freedoms will be upheld. A European legal space that addresses security issues is emerging as a result of judicial cooperation.[73] Research into federal systems suggests that the more individual rights are safeguarded at the federal level, the more state governments are drawn into conforming to these regulations. Citizens will naturally fight for the recognition of their federal-level rights, thereby enhancing federal law.[74] In the case of the EU, the same dynamic has taken place, with individuals presenting their cases directly to the ECJ. However, the process has only begun and remains a patchwork of noncooperation, cooperation, and integration.

Military Research, Capabilities, and Procurement

Since the end of the Cold War, militaries in Europe have been undergoing a gradual process of reform. Instead of being used primarily to protect European soil, they are being transformed into more streamlined forces capable of undertaking expeditionary missions to deal with crises worldwide.[75] Indeed, Europe's militaries recently have been deployed from the Balkans to Africa and from the Middle East to Asia. In 2009, the EU member states spent a combined €194 billion on defense and had nearly 1.7 million active service members in the armed forces, of which nearly 68,000 were deployed.[76]

The fact that the EU has 27 member states and that this policy area is the least integrated to date makes the reform process very difficult. Policymakers must devise recommendations that take into account the reality that most post–Cold War threats are nontraditional—involving an unknown battlefield and nonstate actors—and that there is a need for interoperability, given that most modern operations use multinational forces. Uncertainty consequently arises surrounding precisely how to reform the armed forces and regarding the extent to which integration or even cooperation is possible. Each member state has its own national military agenda and will define its threat and defense priorities differently. The UK and France, for example, have more political will and ability to get involved in third-country operations than do other countries. CSDP provides a context under which member states can recognize their common goals with regard to international crisis response, regardless of their level of ambition and capability. As Giovanni Grevi argues, "Both political convergence and policy coherence remain inescapable conditions for generating effective action at the EU level."[77]

Member states must continue to find pathways toward military reform and integration, since various studies of threats over the past ten years have indicated that the future need for the use of force could very well be greater than it is today. European countries cannot afford to decrease military investment now that the nature of security threats has moved away from conventional warfare. Nearly all European countries have made it a national objective to increase their ability to participate militarily in international missions by training flexible forces and striving to increase capacity.[78]

Although the ownership of Europe's militaries rests in the hands of individual nations, the EU's hard power capability is not simply the sum of its parts. Each member state's army is designed to stand on its own, and a high level of duplication thus exists if militaries are considered as a whole. Plus, not all of the capabilities are available to the EU at any given point. For example, if a member state has already committed a helicopter to a NATO operation, that helicopter is no longer available for an EU operation. Finally, member states must have the ambition and political will to contribute to an operation.

To deal with these concerns, in 1999 the EU agreed to the Helsinki Headline Goal of bringing together 50,000–60,000 troops by 2003. These forces would be deployable within 60 days and would be able to remain active for at least one year. While the original deadline of 2003 was not met, significant progress has been made. In a renewed effort to find out what the EU's capabilities were and where the gaps lay, member states pledged in 2004 what they would contribute to the EU's autonomous action capability, and the result was a force catalog of more than 100,000 troops, 100 vessels, and 400 aircraft.[79] This force catalog enabled experts to see exactly where the capability gaps were and to suggest how they could be resolved. Since 2001, a series of plans—the 2001 European Capabilities Action Plan, Capabilities Improvement Charts, Progress Catalog, 2005 EU Requirement Catalog, and 2006 EU Force Catalog—have sought to identify progress and remaining shortcomings.[80] The advent of the European Defence Agency (EDA) in 2004 was a step toward the permanent collection of military-defense statistics and a push for member states to achieve what is necessary to make CSDP as strong as possible.

In September 2006, more than 8,500 troops were engaged in operations under the EU flag. NATO operations undeniably have involved more troops, but EU operations have grown at a remarkable pace. The EU has a rapid-reaction capability with its creation of 13 battle groups that attained full operational capability in January 2007. These battle groups have around 1,500 troops each and are deployable within 15 days of a crisis; they can remain on location for up to 120 days. Two battle groups are at the ready at any given time. The total personnel involved in a battle group numbers closer to 3,000. Nearly all battle groups slated for the next three years involve forces from multiple countries, one member state serving as the framework nation. Given that the previous Helsinki Headline Goal to create rapid-reaction forces by 2003 has not yet reached fruition, the success of the new Headline Goal 2010 is significant. However, the battle groups have never been used. Enough lead time usually exists to enable EU member states to put together an operation without relying on battle groups. So far, a call for contributions, known as force generation, is the means used to put together troops for CSDP operations. Nevertheless, the advent of battle groups does represent a significant step toward hard integration of military capabilities in Europe.

The military side of CSDP is one of the driving forces behind the need to achieve reform, interoperability, and integration. Moreover, since CSDP operations are currently quite small, even minor hard power contributions add significant value, and bigger member states do not necessarily dominate decision making. The use of a smaller member state's frigate or helicopter can mean the difference between going forward or not. For example, when no other member state could offer a helicopter, Belgium stepped forward, thereby saving CSDP's first military operation in Macedonia.[81] And since the bigger member states may have their resources tied up in NATO, they may prefer to contribute financial support rather than troops or equipment, as the UK did for the recent Chad operation. It is generally recognized that member states that initiate ideas for new missions or are willing to contribute more resources will also have a bigger voice in discussions, regardless of the nation's size. And ideas about CSDP or capabilities management are at times more acceptable if a neutral (non-NATO) country such as Finland, Austria, or Sweden makes the case. Simply put, CSDP is not about least common denominator decision making. It can give a voice and international influence to member states with political will, an attractive incentive for countries to work through CSDP. CSDP's trajectory indicates that if it continues to develop in the coming years, its rewards can create long-term motivations for member states to think more seriously about achieving further integration.

Research and procurement of military technology is one area in which member states are undergoing soft integration. Traditionally, each defense business has only one customer, its national government. Since technology and equipment related to defense are fundamental to a state's national security strategy, EU countries have been resistant to the idea of looking to third countries for these supplies. Beyond the need to influence the choice of defense suppliers, governments must also be careful that they spend taxpayers' money in ways that create jobs, serve the public interest, and protect national capabilities in particular areas of research.[82] Furthermore, Article 296 of the Treaty on European Union exempts the market for defense equipment from the rules of the common market, allowing governments to maintain high levels of protectionism with regard to their defense industries. But shrinking defense budgets across Europe—of the €194 billion per year that member states spend on defense, €41 billion is dedicated to research, development, and procurement[83]—and the changing nature of external threats have led to a gradual rethinking of the traditional system.

Although the process began several decades ago, the rate of industrial consolidation across borders has increased over the past few years. Aerospace and information technology have advanced more quickly than other areas.[84] Aerospace in particular is one of the most integrated sectors of all European industries.[85] It is an extremely expensive area of research and capabilities development, and it is highly politicized. Nonetheless, EU member states have agreed to integrate their endeavors to produce Galileo, the European equivalent of the U.S. global positioning system. They have given the European Commission the authority to run this program, which will require the launching of 32 satellites and quite a bit of research and development. This new technology clearly has both military and civilian applications, and it is beneficial to both internal and external security. Because of the costs, risks, and politics of such an endeavor, the EU is working alongside the European Space Agency (a non-EU institution) and China to get Galileo up and running as soon as possible. While certain challenges remain, and some implementation delays have already occurred, Galileo represents a significant level of will to integrate in the EU's aerospace sector.

More generally, the EDA has encouraged joint contracts, cross-border procurement, and collaboration through its Code of Conduct, under which member states should "open up to suppliers having a technological and/or industrial base in each other's territories, all defence procurement opportunities of €1 m or more."[86] Similarly, the European Commission has encouraged soft integration in this area by proposing the harmonization of licensing arrangements across member states so that cross-border transactions are smoother. The Commission has also emphasized that recourse to Article 296 must be demonstrated by member states each time they wish to invoke it. Individual countries bear the onus of proving that procurement contracts are in their essential interest rather assuming that the contracts are exempt from the rules of the common market.[87] These measures, particularly those put forward by the EDA, are voluntary and nonbinding. Nevertheless, consolidation of top-tier defense industries as well as cross-border collaborative programs have increasingly occurred in the area of research, development, and procurement. For example, various groups of member states have collaborated in producing various fighter aircraft, including the Eurofighter Typhoon, which involved European aerospace companies based in Italy, the UK, Germany, France, and Spain. These developments not only create economies of scale but enable future interoperability in multinational operations and lay the groundwork for common norms about security and the eventual emergence of a common strategic culture.[88] All of these advancements provide evidence for a process of ongoing soft integration among member states in the area of procurement.

Common Security and Defence Policy and Interoperability

With respect to its external influence, the EU has been recognized primarily as a normative power. Indeed, the Union's greatest strength has come from its ability to set normative standards for others around the world, both politically and economically.[89] It has promoted certain behavior by example, especially through its process of enlargement and through the European Neighborhood Policy. Until recently, however, it has not been able to do so through the use of force. Although normative power remains a major EU strength, the operational launching of CSDP in 2003 marked a new era in European influence with a greater number and variety of tools for external influence available.[90] In terms of external security, cooperation is now institutionalized, but there are also signs of an emerging supranationalism.

There are numerous ways in which cooperation has taken off under the rubric of CSDP. At minimum, the EU qualifies as a classic security alliance.[91] But it is important to recognize that its areas and levels of cooperation extend much further, with some even achieving a degree of supranationalism. First, in the area of civilian and military crisis management, committees and working groups in the Council determine the appropriate blend of the two instruments and integrate them to the extent possible in the planning phase. For example, one area of focus for CSDP is security sector reform in third countries—reconstructing state structures so that they conform to good governance and international standards of human rights. Such reform often requires military intervention at the outset, followed by civilian involvement and expertise. The committees and working groups involved in balancing and integrating the civilian and military dimensions are formally intergovernmental, but they sometimes comprise strong epistemic communities that exercise agency independently from states.

Second, the EU formally cooperates in armaments production, capacity building, and research to fortify its defensive capabilities. In practice, soft integration exists in this area. Over time, all parties have accepted the goal of interoperability through a persuasive process pushed forward by member states' military representatives. The advent of the EDA and its subsequent ability to encourage multistate research and procurement is evidence of the growing norm in favor of interoperability.

Third, external security's linkages with internal security give it an element of supranationalism by default. These linkages enable processes of harmonization and integration. The external dimension of counterterrorism, for example, includes the fight against root causes both at home and abroad. As stipulated in the European Security Strategy, the EU now strives to act as one in both arenas. Externally, these arenas include trade, aid, diplomacy, and capacity building in third countries.[92] While CSDP civilian missions and military operations are based on intergovernmental cooperation, they also tackle root causes through peacekeeping, peacemaking, and stabilization. Thus, there is a mixture of a first pillar integrated approach and a second pillar intergovernmental approach.

However, hard integration is already visible in certain aspects of CSDP missions and operations. The relationship between human rights and CSDP is one example. Member states abide by the same guidelines when it comes to protecting women and children in armed conflict and when dealing with gender issues more generally. To that end, each CSDP mission has human rights and gender advisers who ensure that every operational plan takes these concerns into account. Another example is the EU's response to natural disasters. The Union, as a single actor, may deploy its rapid-reaction military resources in the immediate wake of a disaster. Because external security is often an extension of internal security practices, certain common guidelines fully affect how external action is carried out and at what level decisions are made.

Finally, soft integration is occurring with respect to the EU's relationship to third parties. It is taken for granted as a growing norm that the EU should always strive to speak with one voice. Several scholars have described this as a kind of coordination or consultation reflex, a desire to find out the European consensus in Brussels before speaking out on a national position.[93] Of course, this reflex has not resulted in cooperation every time. The high-profile breakdowns over the 2003 Iraq War and Kosovo's bid for independence in 2007–8 exemplify failed cooperation in foreign policy. Although the media tends to focus on these relatively rare situations, these occurrences are not really cause for concern. There is a general pattern evident in much of the integration process that when a breakdown in consensus occurs, member states often respond with more political will for future cooperation. Thus, what might appear to be episodes of failure can also be viewed as triggers for future success.[94] After the disagreements over the invasion of Iraq, the 2003 European Security Strategy took a significant step forward in establishing a European security identity. In the immediate wake of Kosovo, the EU nonetheless established a CSDP civilian mission there. Even after the French and Dutch rejected the Constitutional Treaty in 2005, the Council began immediate work to agree on the Reform Treaty (now called the Lisbon Treaty), which has entered into force just five years later. Most recently, the financial crisis in Greece, in part a result of the EU's lack of enforcement of the Eurozone's fiscal rules, resulted in almost immediate agreement among member states to achieve deeper economic and political integration.[95]

Conversely, little media attention has been devoted to the cases of successful CFSP cooperation. Member states are working toward strong common partnerships with NATO, the United Nations, the African Union, and strategic partners such as Canada, Russia, and Ukraine. The EU's relationship with the United States is of the utmost importance, and it allows special arrangements—even participation—for Iceland, Norway, and Turkey.[96] This aspect of external security is clearly a work in progress, but it is significant that member states' decision makers believe it is appropriate to speak with one voice, and doing so is necessary to cultivate valuable partnerships abroad. In addition, the EU often presents a common front in its diplomacy with nondemocratic countries or those with which it has had less friendly or even hostile relations. For example, the EU has been active in the area of nuclear nonproliferation talks with Iran, from offering incentives to imposing harsh sanctions. But the most prominent among these accomplishments in CFSP have been the 24 civilian, police, and military CSDP operations since 2003.[97]

Military power is one of the key policy tools that differentiates the current EU from its former, largely normative identity. What are the EU capabilities with regard to military power? Can it project a common military identity? The first CSDP military operation was launched in 2003, with six others following. Sixteen civilian missions and several hybrid actions have also taken place. One of the most recent military missions is NAVFOR Atalanta, which tackles the ongoing threat of piracy off the coast of Somalia. This mission shows not only member states' ability to work together to deal with a threat in another area of the world but also their ability to adapt to new challenges. NAVFOR Atalanta represents the first naval operation conducted under the EU flag. Given the newness of CSDP and its position in the second pillar, it should come as no surprise that some crucial gaps remain in the area of cooperation and integration. Chief among them is the fact that there are no permanent operational headquarters to enhance the EU's planning capabilities.[98] In principle, nearly all member states agree that a permanent headquarters would be useful, since there is no controversy over NATO's permanent operational headquarters. But some nations, including the UK, worry that an EU version of the Supreme Headquarters Allied Powers Europe, for example, would result in damaging competition between the two organizations.[99] Five EU member states—France, Germany, Greece, Italy, and the UK—have volunteered their national headquarters to serve this purpose on an as-needed basis.[100]

Despite this shortcoming on the command and control side, military cooperation on third-country operations has been institutionalized relatively quickly, in large part because of the work of the EU Military Committee and its support structure, which primarily includes the EU Military Staff. While national militaries more generally are certainly not integrated, the EU has various groups of specific integrated forces at its disposal from particular sets of member states. These forces have been deployed in Afghanistan, Kosovo, Bosnia, and elsewhere. Eurocorps has 60,000 integrated troops from France, Germany, Belgium, and Luxembourg. Euro Forces, which has both army and navy divisions, comprises 20,000 soldiers drawn from France, Italy, Spain, and Portugal. The European Gendarmerie Force can provide rapid response capabilities in areas that require police action. This integrated, supranational force, consisting of 800 police (with an additional 2,000 on standby) from France, Italy, the Netherlands, Portugal, Spain, and Romania, may work alone or alongside civil or military operations, or it may facilitate transition phases such as military disengagement in a region. Its priority is to serve the EU, but it may also be authorized to serve international organizations like the UN or NATO.[101] Beyond Eurocorps, Euro Forces, and the European Gendarmerie, the EU also has battle groups at its disposal. All of these elements represent hard integration on the operations side of the military sector.

The decision about whether to engage in a particular military action is officially an intergovernmental, second pillar prerogative. However, a form of soft integration is occurring here, too. The diplomatic and military epistemic communities have a strongly held norm of always reaching consensus with respect to important decisions. Thus, a single veto from one member state could prevent any CSDP operation from taking place, and a dissenting member state could control everyone's fate. The so-called silence procedure—a procedural norm that encourages delegates to remain silent rather than oppose an action that already has some level of support—is taken quite seriously. If a particular military operation is on the table and several member states are willing to pledge troops, those who are unwilling can simply remain silent. This does not mean, however, that they can remain uninvolved. If the operation is military in nature, the Athena Mechanism—the permanent funding mechanism for military operations—requires that all member states pay for military operations in proportion to their GDP.[102] Thus, even if a member state is not enthusiastic about a potential operation, the consensus norm and Athena Mechanism push it toward supporting common actions. Of course, those member states that are less enthusiastic about particular operations can weigh in during the planning phase to keep costs down and thus lower their monetary contributions.

The civilian side of CSDP is determined through a similar process in the Council, but funding is completely supranational, coming from the Commission. The EU police mission in Afghanistan from June 2007 to June 2010 was a prime example of integrated capacity and political will to engage in civilian CSDP. The mission sought to help Afghanistan work toward establishing the rule of law, good governance, sustainable development, peace, and security. A total of around 350 EU personnel and local staff provided assistance to the Ministry of Interior in Kabul, regional police command stations, and provincial reconstruction teams. This mission was coordinated with those of the UN and NATO and had U.S. support.

Although civilian crisis management has surprised many observers with its high visibility within CSDP, it displays fewer signs of integration overall. Since civilian crisis management does not require arms to be effective, there is no concern in terms of research and development or procurement. Consequently, there is no need to find a way to integrate such tools. In addition, the types of personnel required for civilian crisis management—such as police officers and experts in rule of law, administration, and civil protection—cannot wait for deployment in the same way that a standing army can. Police, judges, lawyers, and others must serve the needs of their citizens at home on a daily basis or they will not be properly employed and will not keep up their skill levels. Given that they must be occupied in their regular jobs, they have no real opportunity to become integrated across member states in the same way that EU military forces such as Eurocorps, Euro Forces, and the battle groups are able to do.

Although member states in November 2008 pledged a total of 6,050 police, 939 legal experts, 745 administrative experts, and 2,177 civil protection experts to civilian CSDP, they could not guarantee that all of these personnel would be available in the event of an external crisis.[103] Moreover, in the wake of the global financial crisis, the corps of national personnel employed in the service of member state governments is stretched thin, reducing the civilian capacity that each member state can contribute beyond meeting its own domestic needs. By contrast, member states, with few exceptions, maintain standing armies, even though they are far more expensive than their civilian counterparts, and military cooperation and integration is mainly a matter of their priorities and willingness to devote these

resources to CSDP. To be clear, civilian crisis management should not be ne-
glected as an instrument of CSDP. It is in many ways more prominent and
effective than the military dimension, is increasingly integrated with military operations, and is a strong manifestation of the EU's normative
power.[104] But its prospects for growing as an area of CSDP and becoming
more integrated over time are constrained in a variety of ways that military
CSDP is not.

Summary

The various sectors of EU security policy nearly always involve a mix of intergovernmental and supranational, internal and external approaches. The
dividing lines are largely artificial, although they were drawn under the
Maastricht Treaty's three pillar structure. Virtually from the beginning,
cross-pillarization has occurred, as depicted in figure 6. As Ferruccio Pastore
writes, "The external projection of internal security agencies has generated
an increasing overlap, and occasionally open competition, with the policy
communities and public agencies traditionally invested with the task of ensuring external security."[105] It is perhaps fitting that security policies have
emerged in this way. The EU's ability to act as a unit with respect to external security is necessary for the goals of internal security to be achieved,
and vice versa. Consequently, the Lisbon Treaty has finally dissolved this
structure altogether.

    Some areas have advanced more quickly toward integration than other
areas, but a strong instinct to "check with Brussels" tends to move issues
from coordination to cooperation or cooperation to integration. Those areas that have achieved coordination and are moving toward cooperation
include intelligence sharing, the relationship between various national police and justice authorities as well as magistrates and prosecutors, and the
issuance of common foreign policy statements in reaction to international
developments. Cooperation is evident in the harmonization of national
justice and penal law systems pertaining to security, visa policy, the development of a European legal space for the protection of individual rights,
external security more generally, and the civilian side of CSDP in particular.
Complete harmonization in some of these areas has led to de facto integration as well. For example, as certain rules related to external borders are
harmonized, the EU can speak with one voice with respect to third countries and immigration agreements.

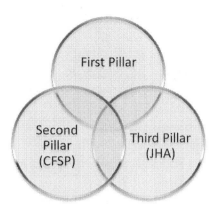

Fig. 6. Cross-pillarization of EU security policy

A number of policy areas are moving from cooperation to soft integration or from soft to hard integration. The European Arrest Warrant and European Evidence Warrant are two prominent examples of soft integration, where there is a common mechanism available to member states. Other areas include rules and norms governing police activity, special investigative techniques, forums for exchanging best practices and forming joint investigation teams, the development and maintenance of common criminal databases, military crisis management, armaments production, capacity building and research, the external dimension of internal security, the EU's relationship with third countries and other international organizations, and decision making about CSDP. Certain policies, including the freezing of terrorist assets and prevention of money laundering, have traditionally been first pillar issues and are heading toward hard integration. Also along these lines are policies covering border security, immigration and asylum, the Health Security Program, air transportation security, strategies to tackle the root causes of terrorism, human rights and CSDP, plans to deal with natural disasters, certain military and police instruments (Eurocorps, Euro Force, European Gendarmerie, battle groups), and the funding of civilian crisis management.

For several reasons, observers tend to clump all of these policies into the two categories of cooperation or noncooperation and to emphasize the latter. First, implementation of these types of security provisions usually depends on individual member states.[106] Second, there are no formal mechanisms to punish a state for not complying, and it is entirely up to each member state to ensure that its national legislation is in line with EU security agreements. Member states can only name and shame those who lag behind.[107] At the same time, many practical obstacles stand in the way of the advancement of security policy. For one, budgetary constraints have been an issue from the beginning. In fact, one of the main reasons why defense budgets across EU member states have declined is that they have to abide by the convergence criteria underpinning the Euro.[108] These criteria mean that member states can neither run a fiscal deficit of more than 3 percent GDP per year nor have a national debt greater than 60 percent of GDP, which heavily constrains the ability to increase defense spending. To make matters more difficult, around the time when member states had to first meet these criteria, the global economy went into a slump, forcing many EU countries to limit their national budgets, especially defense spending.[109] The current financial crisis adds an additional level of complexity as ministries of defense try to restructure, streamline, and modernize their armies. Investment in security research and development suffers most as a result of these financial constraints. Twenty-six EU member states—Denmark has opted-out of defense cooperation—together spend only €41 billion,[110] compared to the €141 billion spent by the United States.[111] Finally, a declining and aging population looms on the horizon as another obstacle. By 2025, estimates show that the average age of European citizens will be 45, pensions will take up a growing portion of the national budget, and there will be fewer people to recruit into the armed forces.

Despite these increasing financial and demographic challenges and the lack of strict implementation enforcement, cooperation and integration are nevertheless occurring. The evolution of security policy consequently rests to a great extent on persuasion, norms, and shifting worldviews among member states, not merely on some kind of self-interested calculation. So the key questions are, Who is doing the persuading? How do they devise these norms? And why are they so convincing?

SECURITY AND THE ROLE OF EXPERTISE

Any Brussels insider knows that the EU is heavily populated with experts. As the following chapters will show, security policy is no exception. EU ambassadors (chapters 3 and 4) reach compromise on issues with political

importance, navigate through controversial passages and technical wording to find workable agreements, and understand how to steer through the
complex apparatus of EU regulation. EU military experts (chapter 5) determine the ideal composition of personnel and equipment to tackle a given
scenario, choose among strategic options, initiate operations, and evaluate
their progress. Technology experts (chapter 6) in the field of security determine new directions for research—among them new surveillance equipment and 3D crisis simulation—that will protect citizens. However, these
groups of experts serve as real agents of policy change—as epistemic communities—when they accomplish more than is expected of them, when
they develop norms of their own, and when they persuade member states
to change their behavior.

EU member states have had widely diverging preferences regarding security integration. The case studies that follow show that initially hard-line
positions can become significantly diluted in the hands of strong epistemic
communities, and the results—further integration—are already evident.
These knowledge-based networks are breaking down member state resistance because of their unique ability to use their expertise to persuade decision makers of the norms group members share.[112] As a result, these epistemic communities have gained acceptance for the beginnings of an
integrated European security space.

The influence of epistemic communities takes place within a larger context. Economic globalization and the growth of transnational crime mean
that nations have increasing difficulty providing for their internal security
alone. Valsamis Mitsilegas, Jörg Monar, and Wyn Rees write,

> Globalisation, economic interpenetration and increased technical sophisti-
> cation reduce national measures more and more often to powerless ges-
> tures. The concept of sovereignty itself seems less and less meaningful at a
> time when global financial transactions, multinational company structures
> and ungovernable communication networks like the Internet do not any
> longer pay any attention to that territorial dimension of sovereignty which
> finds its expression in physical frontiers.[113]

There is a widespread recognition that perhaps the only way effectively to
deal with transnational threats is to employ transnational or even supranational strategies, working together with neighboring countries and even
those further afield. The lack of internal borders makes the EU an attractive

place not only for commerce and trade but also for criminals. As David Spence argues, in the past "the EU was a half domestic polity, providing rights but not providing for obligations and not creating automatic control by civil authorities of the misuse of these rights."[114] This situation is rapidly changing. Moreover, leaders in Europe have wanted an autonomous and coherent identity with the ability to influence for some time. The signing of the St. Malo Agreement and the subsequent launching of CSDP set the stage for the possibility of a security policy that went beyond coordination or cooperation. Plus, participants wanted this experiment into uncharted territory to succeed.

Over time, member states provide a window in which security integration is possible. Presidents and prime ministers sign treaties that put structures into place, express publicly the need to tackle security challenges together, and endorse major documents such as the European Security Strategy. But differences exist between talk and action, intentions and follow-through. When the glare of the media lights fades away, the realities of election cycles, domestic public opinion, and strained budgets set in. There are ultimately many reasons why the EU could stop short of becoming a real security actor. But to focus on these reasons misses important processes occurring behind the scenes. It may not be the usual focus of front-page news, but the confluence of expert-driven influence has pushed member states to start seriously to reconceptualize the idea of sovereignty itself.

CHAPTER 3

Diplomats and Internal Security

"John F. Kennedy thought about what his role would be when he went to Washington. He could either be a senator from a small state, only representing the interests of Massachusetts, and not have any influence, or he could be someone who represented the interests of Massachusetts and the United States as a whole. This would mean that he had much more influence. And that's what he did. This is what we are trying to do in the EU and in Coreper."

—FINNISH AMBASSADOR JAN STORE, COREPER II[1]

PROFESSIONAL DIPLOMATS ARE an essential feature of the Brussels land-scape. A casual look at the daily news in Brussels reveals that behind nearly every major EU action are EU diplomats. Ambassadorial-level diplomats in particular are increasingly recognized as the main drivers behind the EU's daily functioning, from foreign affairs to internal arrest warrants to divorce legislation. Even behind the media glare and political fanfare of a ministe-rial meeting or European Council summit, EU ambassadors are pulling the strings. With the December 1, 2010, launch of the European External Ac-tion Service (EEAS), often referred to as the EU foreign service, attention to the role of diplomats has increased, and it is likely to continue to do so. Af-ter all, once the EEAS is fully established, it will be one of the largest foreign service agencies in the world, with some 8,000 diplomats in its service and a budget of up to €3 billion.

Although diplomats have not typically been included in standard definitions of epistemic communities, the qualities behind this group's composition and cohesiveness make this an appropriate categorization. Diplomats in the Committee of Permanent Representatives (Coreper) con-stitute a relatively strong transnational network that is expertise-driven and held together by strong professional norms. Together, these diplomats are a major force in shaping internal security integration. The concept of epistemic communities is a valuable framework with which to understand

77

security integration because it focuses on how knowledge translates into power. The internal dimension of security integration in particular rests on Coreper's unique knowledge, which enables members to craft complex norms and regulations that EU member states would not have adopted on their own. Examining EU diplomats through the prism of the epistemic community framework enables a better understanding of their processes and accomplishments.[2] An investigation of just the political and contextual circumstances does not explain why certain outcomes are chosen over others. Ambassadors share certain causal beliefs about the role of security integration in the EU by virtue of their expertise. Of the vast number of policy areas that fall under the purview of EU authority, Justice and Home Affairs (JHA) has arguably experienced the most dramatic progress toward integration since the Maastricht Treaty, and this progress is reflected in the Lisbon Treaty, which takes concrete steps toward further EU integration in the area of internal security.

Not all diplomats constitute epistemic communities, and some are less able to affect policy outcomes. The identity of each diplomat is critical to understanding his or her influence in practice, beyond the formal requirements of their positions. Many have met each other at prior diplomatic assignments. They benefit from similar experiences of negotiation and multilateralism and have undergone similar training. They find that they have much in common from the start, and evidence suggests that they share similar worldviews, professional protocol, and causal beliefs. The following section briefly maps out the historical background of professional diplomacy in Europe, arguing that an epistemic community of diplomats has existed for some time, although it has not always been strong. Next, I lay out the diplomatic apparatus in today's EU. I then turn to Coreper itself as a strong example of an EU epistemic community and examine its impact on a particular policy example, the Strategy on Radicalization and Recruitment.[3]

HISTORICAL BACKGROUND

As many great works of European diplomatic history attest, professional diplomacy has been a significant part of statecraft since at least the Renaissance.[4] In the sixteenth century, European statesmen sent formal plenipotentiaries to congregate in major capitals throughout the continent and beyond, with the authority to represent their interests abroad. These diplomats constituted an epistemic community even as state formation was still under way. Diplomats in Europe have for many centuries comprised an epistemic community of varying strengths, though its evolution has not simply been an upward path-dependent trajectory over time.[5] Rather, the strength of the epistemic community has relied on certain key causal variables—mainly similar training and social background, high status, high meeting frequency, and shared professional norms. These qualities have contributed to cohesiveness within the corps and to the development of a common culture.

During the mid–seventeenth century, for example, the epistemic community of diplomats could be characterized as strong in some ways and weak in others. European ambassadors comprised a distinct professional group residing in the major capitals of Europe, but the profession was not yet fully standardized, with training still coming entirely on the job and selection based on political appointment. Even before the advent of the telegraph and postal service, these ambassadors corresponded regularly with each other, cultivating a kind of nascent international society and European transnational network. They met informally at royal courts across Western Europe and gained a high level of status as influential representatives of their sovereigns. These diplomatic relationships meant that when major negotiations occurred—beyond the day-to-day sharing of information to which they were accustomed—these actors already had a basis of understanding and certain norms of interaction. But alongside these growing transnational ties was the absence of bureaucratization and standardization of the diplomatic profession. Diplomats from the same state were often rivals, sometimes with competing aims. At the time, the Treaty of Westphalia was one of the first major multilateral conferences among states—bilateral meetings were much more common—and diplomats influenced some aspects of it.

By the late nineteenth century, often described as the golden age of diplomacy, the bureaucratization and early democratization of states paved the way for a more professionalized corps of diplomats in Europe. Diplomats benefitted from high status and shared strong professional norms, although selection was not yet meritocratic. They came from a similar social background, which helped contribute to a kind of automatic cohesion within the corps. They met more frequently than their predecessors but less often than EU diplomats do today. The advent of the telegraph meant that diplomats of the period could correspond regularly with their capitals, al-

though instructions tended to be short. Diplomats found themselves sup-
plementing their own instructions, sometimes taking license with them,
and exercising a degree of agency. The inventions of the steam engine and
railroad enabled statesmen to attend conferences more often, but diplomats usually carried leaders through the negotiations. One of the major
conferences of the time, the 1878 Congress of Berlin, was a strong example
of diplomatic professionalism and influence.

In the twentieth-century interwar period, professional diplomacy was
again transformed, but this time there was a significant drop in status as
the diplomatic corps received the brunt of the blame for the breakdown in
the prewar alliance system. Before the First World War, the field of diplomacy was making great strides in terms of becoming a more meritocratic,
professional, and career-oriented practice. Not only were these reform efforts pushed aside during the war, but statesmen were also meeting more
often to participate in international negotiations rather than sending their
professional diplomats. The Supreme War Council, formed to coordinate
the strategies of the Allied powers in the autumn of 1917, was the epitome
of this growing practice of summitry. Diplomats maintained many of the
shared professional norms that had characterized their interaction for centuries, but they had little influence, especially during the critical negotiations leading to the 1919 Treaty of Versailles. They were invited to be present at the Paris Peace Conference but were not even allowed in the same
room as the statesmen, who were engaged in the real negotiations. David
Lloyd George, Woodrow Wilson, Georges Clemenceau, and Vittorio Orlando—the Gang of Four—attempted to design a treaty on their own, in
the absence of professional diplomatic expertise. In the end, the statesmen's radical personalities, stubbornness, and lack of diplomatic experience made a workable peace out of reach.

The advent of international governmental organizations later in the
twentieth century brought another distinctive phase of diplomacy: permanent negotiations. Professional diplomats posted to multilateral organizations such as the United Nations and EU in many cases have a more important role than their colleagues in bilateral embassies. For example, the
negotiations leading to the 1992 Treaty on European Union (the Maastricht
Treaty) demonstrated the high level of influence achievable by a strong epistemic community of diplomats. EU ambassadors hold a very high status,
meet frequently, are selected and promoted based on merit, and receive
specialized training followed by decades of on-the-job experience. Diplo-

mats are still drawn largely from a similar social background and tend to be male at the highest echelons, but the situation is slowly changing. In the years leading to the Maastricht Intergovernmental Conference, ambassadors serving as personal representatives of ministers played a significant role, persuading their capitals to change their instructions based on the climate in Brussels and on the diplomats' knowledge of how far the other diplomats could go to reach a compromise. Without a strong epistemic community of diplomats and their ability to convince statesmen, an agreement in Maastricht would have been impossible. The Maastricht Treaty was a critical development, as it set the stage for further political and security integration.

Thus, European professional diplomacy did not simply emerge as a fully formed profession. Instead, initial socialization of the diplomatic epistemic community occurred alongside a gradual process of professionalization that began as early as the seventeenth century. Diplomats effectively professionalized themselves. At first, each diplomat's influence was closely tied to the relative power of his home state. Later, diplomats gained reputations in their own right. They developed norms of protocol, precedence, and procedure based on what worked best to preserve order and to reach an efficient outcome. They gained expertise on the job. Some of these earlier choices were institutionalized into the profession, enabling the more structured selection and training of diplomats beginning in the nineteenth century. Each new generation was socialized into the existing body of norms based on this ever-evolving collective enterprise. While many things have changed since the early modern period, such as increasing bureaucratization, professionalization, and meritocratization within foreign services, many qualities have persisted, including the respect for protocol, cultivation of relationships, and general esprit de corps in European capitals.

Expertise has been a major part of this evolution. Historically, diplomatic expertise involved a combination of at least three factors. First, diplomats had to be experts in the substance of the specific negotiations taking place. Second, throughout their careers, they cultivated nuanced understandings of different countries' positions, gradually developed reputations independent of the statesmen they represented, and gained expertise in reading the personalities of their foreign colleagues. Third, and perhaps most enduring, they acquired an overarching knowledge of the process of diplomacy itself. As in all epistemic communities, the process of deliberation is so important among diplomats that it plays a major role in determining whether a successful outcome is reached. The nature of diplomatic expertise is quite similar today, although in the context of the EU it is far more specialized. Chiefs of state and ministers have increasing difficulty understanding the complexities of EU negotiations. In many if not most cases, issues have become so technical that EU ambassadors must rely on legions of experts to work out smaller parts of agreements before even beginning to discuss their political flavor.

THE EU DIPLOMATIC APPARATUS: EPISTEMIC COMMUNITIES OF DIPLOMATS

There are currently two major groups of ambassadors involved in EU security policy, the Committee of Permanent Representatives II (Coreper II) and the Political and Security Committee (PSC). Coreper II was formed approximately a decade before PSC, but the origins of the two bodies are somewhat similar in that both were formally created as a result of EU institutional developments. Epistemic communities can arise either in or outside of an institutional environment. While nongovernmental epistemic communities tend to be more visible, it is important to look broadly to find epistemic communities, whether or not they are embedded within formal structures. How individuals come together to form a network is not as critical as what they do once they meet and how their relationships evolve from there. While the epistemic communities of diplomats do comprise formal Council committees, they can also act together as more than the sum of their parts.

Coreper, both at the ambassadorial and deputy ambassadorial levels, sits at the pinnacle of a complex apparatus of professional EU diplomacy. Given the size and scope of its authority, particularly in policy areas that are usually reserved only for sovereign states, it is perhaps appropriate that Coreper ambassadors most closely approximate the idea of a traditional diplomatic corps. They manage relations among states and negotiate agreements that require consensus. They do so on an ongoing basis, spending large amounts of time together.

Coreper was first created through a Council decision on January 25, 1958. It is formally defined as "a committee consisting of the Permanent Representatives of the Member States [that] shall be responsible for preparing the work of the Council and for carrying out the tasks assigned to it by the Council."[6] Thus, it has not officially been granted the power to make substantive decisions. In practice, however, when Coreper agrees on an issue (labeled as an A item), it is accepted without debate at the level of the Council of Ministers. The dynamic within Coreper and the qualities of the individuals in this group have meant that it has evolved into a very powerful entity. Since its inception, Coreper has also had the authority to establish working groups to aid in more specialized negotiation or preparatory research.[7] At this point, Coreper has roughly 250 such working groups, and each ambassador has a team of advisers seconded from his or her home ministry.

Coreper is unique for its institutional position within the Council of the European Union; it is officially a high-level intergovernmental committee within the Council, appointed by political leaders, but it comprises ambassadors from each of the member states.[8] Each member state has a permanent representation in Brussels—effectively an embassy to the EU— with the Coreper ambassador as the delegation's head. Candidate member states also set up permanent representations to facilitate accession negotiations. Within each permanent representation is the typical hierarchy of diplomats, experts, and support staff. But what makes these embassies different from others is the fact that many of the diplomats are also members of specific Council committees.

Soon after Coreper was established, it became bogged down in work until it no longer had the time to discuss everything. The sheer volume of policy areas transferred either in whole or in part to the EU level meant that the work had to be divided, which was done on two separate occasions. The first occurred in 1962 when Coreper was split into I and II. Coreper I, the original Coreper, dealt more with technical and internal matters such as agriculture, the internal market, and energy, while Coreper II was responsible for more horizontal and political issues. Despite being newer, Coreper II became the more powerful of the two. With the passing of the 1992 Maastricht Treaty, which included provisions for a monetary union, political union, JHA, and Common Foreign and Security Policy, among other things, the roles of Coreper I and II became even more differentiated. Now, Coreper I prepares Council meetings on issues related to employment, competitiveness, transport, agriculture, environment, and education, while Coreper II does the advance work for the Councils on General Affairs and External Relations, Economic and Financial Affairs, and JHA.[9] In December 1999, the Helsinki European Council augmented Coreper's jurisdiction in light of increasing numbers of Council committees. Officially, Coreper now has the responsibility to bring together the work of other bodies and ensure that they consistently reflect the main principles of the EU, such as subsidiarity, transparency, and proportionality. This responsibility has transformed Coreper into a body that informally makes decisions on its own issue areas as well as a gatekeeper for other agreements. Scholars who have studied Coreper in detail often conclude that it has become "a *de facto* decision-making body."[10]

Although Coreper II commands a great deal of influence, Coreper I remains a key part of the EU's diplomatic apparatus. The Council's deputy ambassadors possess an important dynamic of their own. Coreper I deals with a greater variety of issues than Coreper II, and its members tend to debate entirely new areas of policy more regularly than in Coreper II, where similar, more difficult debates are often repeated.[11] The ambassadors in Coreper I also tend to be slightly less experienced than those in Coreper II, but they are well respected in their capitals and are sometimes being groomed for the higher-ranked position. It is an advantage if a Coreper II ambassador has served in Coreper I.[12] In the first half of 2009, five Coreper II ambassadors had previously held the Coreper I post.[13]

Coreper I deals with issues that are usually unrelated to those of Coreper II, yet they operate similarly in terms of their internal dynamic and the relationship with their capitals.[14] On very rare occasions, the two Corepers collaborate to some extent if overlap exists on an issue. Energy policy is an example of a policy area that can have crossover between Coreper I and II, as in the case of the 2009 gas crisis involving the Ukraine and Russia. The Swedish Coreper deputy ambassador described the incident as "the first time Coreper I dealt with issues in parallel with Coreper II."[15] Climate change is another example. But typically, each ambassador has only a broad awareness of what the other is doing.[16] Many observers also have a sense that Coreper I is becoming overloaded.[17]

In addition to having distinct issue areas, Coreper I is distinguished from Coreper II in that the former works largely under the codecision procedure, which means that only a qualified majority (QMV) is necessary for agreement; in contrast, Coreper II usually requires unanimity. Coreper I operates based on QMV about 95 percent of the time.[18] Members of Coreper I thus face more pressure than do Coreper II members to change positions rather than to be outvoted.[19]

As the original permanent representatives, members of Coreper I still have a sense that their work is in many ways more critical to the function of the EU than that of the Coreper II ambassadors despite their higher rank. First, it is an unprecedented diplomatic group in terms of the kinds of issues it discusses. As Luxembourg's Coreper II ambassador, Christian Braun, said,

> Coreper II is dealing with defense, money, justice, foreign affairs, all basic powers of the state, eighteenth–nineteenth century competencies of the state. These powers have been transferred much later, not entirely, and in a completely different way. Coreper I is a Coreper which is new—transport, agriculture, environment, social policy, telecommunication, all these are twentieth-century competencies.[20]

Second, there is a sense that Coreper I produces policies that are more tangible to average citizens. According to Danish Coreper II ambassador Claus Grube, formerly the Coreper I deputy ambassador,

> [Coreper I] is more technical and in the vast policy areas of society—agriculture, health, and environment—it means that Coreper I has to be able to negotiate on a highly technical level. At the same time, the kinds of dossiers in Coreper I are the bread and butter of any daily life in any government. In that respect, Coreper I is much more connected to government and the overall intentions of society. Therefore, it is very important to perform the work well, to the satisfaction of the administration at home and to have a clear sense of what will work within these interests. . . . On a professional level, I felt more rewarded working in Coreper I compared to II. Sometimes you have more of an impact on society as a whole in Coreper I.[21]

Coreper I is typically not yet involved in security policy, although certain issues at times touch on that area indirectly. One example is migration. The JHA pillar includes third-country migration rules, and Coreper I affects migration policy when it negotiates rules regarding worker rights and obligations. As JHA evolves, the work of Coreper I may become more relevant to security, but it may also result in increasing areas of conflict. Swedish Coreper I ambassador Ulrika Larsson said, "Frontex's rationale is to keep people out. But we need people to come to the EU. We need more skilled labor."[22] Coreper I strives to make sure that internal policy keeps the EU running well. As a group, Coreper I clearly deserves more scholarly attention than it has received.

In 2001, yet another ambassadorial layer was created in the Council to focus on the Common Security and Defence Policy (CSDP). The Political and Security Committee (PSC) represented the second division of Coreper, which had previously been charged with anything falling under the rubric of the Common Foreign and Security Policy (CFSP). As the Treaty on European Union stipulates, the Council is charged with "taking decisions necessary for defining and implementing the common foreign and security policy on the basis of the general guidelines defined by the European Council."[23] Coreper is the main body that prepares and implements the work of the Council. PSC's predecessor, the Political Committee, was based in the capitals instead of Brussels and did not meet nearly as frequently. Like Coreper, PSC is housed in the permanent representations, and its members hold the title of ambassador. Coreper technically outranks PSC. According to a January 22, 2001, Council decision, the PSC's main duties are to

> keep track of the international situation in the areas falling within the common foreign and security policy, help define policies by drawing up "opinions" for the Council, either at the request of the Council or on its own initiative, and monitor implementation of agreed policies. . . . Furthermore, in the event of a crisis the PSC is the Council body which deals with crisis situations and examines all the options that might be considered as the Union's response within the single institutional framework and without prejudice to the decision-making and implementation procedures of each pillar.[24]

With PSC's creation, a support structure of deputy ambassadors and working groups also arose to aid these new ambassadors in their work. PSC ambassadors consistently consult the EU Military Committee (EUMC) and the Civilian Committee on Crisis Management (Civcom). EUMC is populated with high-ranking military officials whose job it is to inform PSC of what types of actions are possible militarily. EUMC members can indicate the EU's hard-power capabilities for a given operation and how much political will backs certain types of actions. Civcom comprises a more diverse mixture of officials who with a focus on civilian tools such as judges, lawyers, police, and regulators. If PSC is negotiating a specific CSDP operation, it also relies on the relevant regional working group. If all three are consulted, PSC ambassadors tend to give equal weight to each group's advice.

In addition to these key diplomats within the Council, many others influence policy in Europe but are somewhat less involved in issues of EU integration. In Brussels as well as in capitals throughout Europe, there are bilateral embassies with ambassadors representing each country individually to other countries or institutions. This structure has been in place for centuries, but newer diplomatic structures increasingly overshadow it, especially with regard to economic, political, and security issues. When obstacles to agreement in Brussels are particularly difficult, national decision makers might occasionally try to persuade other countries' bilateral ambassadors, but it is more common in these situations for capitals to talk directly to each other.[25] Newer member states, however, sometimes find this bilateral option beneficial, especially if they have a smaller diplomatic corps and have not yet cultivated the necessary relationships in Brussels. As Latvian Coreper II ambassador Normunds Popens said,

> Our ambassador in Rome knows the Italian minister well. . . . We can get things done by going beyond Brussels to the capitals of the member states, and then the ministers in the capitals can change what happens here in Brussels. This is only possible if the bilateral ambassador has a strong network and can call the right person.[26]

In effect, diplomats in Brussels can use bilateral embassies to create a boomerang effect, triggering processes in other capitals that come back to affect efforts in Brussels.

The Commission also forms a part of the EU's diplomatic apparatus through its missions of civil servants who represent the EU to outside countries or institutions. The Commission has more than 130 delegations overseas, and much of their work involves public diplomacy initiatives.[27] Their work is typically restricted to policy areas of supranational authority that fall within the Community pillar. Rather than striving to find common ground through deliberation on new policy as diplomats within the council do, Commission missions seek to project abroad decisions that have already been made. In a sense, Commission diplomats are public relations experts, whereas Council diplomats carry out more of the traditional diplomatic role of actually determining policy outcomes among states through negotiation.[28]

Finally, a new component of the European diplomatic apparatus that will likely cause fundamental changes in the future of EU diplomacy is the

EEAS, which was envisioned as part of the Constitutional Treaty and was then carried over to the Lisbon Treaty. According to former high representative Javier Solana, "The foreign service is contemplated in the treaty as an effort of the member states to create a global common diplomacy. I like to think that in time we will be one of the most important diplomacies in the world, along with U.S., China and other big players in the world."[29] Once the EEAS is fully functional, it will comprise one of the largest foreign services in the world.

While many professional diplomats are involved in various aspects of EU policy, the role of Coreper II (referred to as Coreper for the rest of the chapter) is significant. The processes within Coreper lead to critical policy outcomes in the realm of internal security.

COREPER

An epistemic community's strength can be measured by the selection and training of its members, the frequency and quality of its meetings, its shared professional norms, and its common culture. Selection and training indicate the competitiveness, level of expertise, and status of a group. The nature of meetings points toward whether members of an epistemic community have the opportunity to cultivate relationships, engage in real deliberation, and develop a common culture. Shared professional norms are a sign of intuitive and sometimes inarticulate practices that smooth the interaction between network members, enabling them to reach consensus more easily. And finally, common culture encapsulates the esprit de corps and identity that holds the group together. A strong common culture carries with it a shared worldview and substantive norms (or shared causal beliefs) about the best way to achieve their goals and what these goals should be. Altogether, Coreper is a strong epistemic community.

Selection and Training

Diplomats in Europe are typically selected through a standardized exam system administered by the foreign ministries of their respective countries. Candidates for entrance usually come from Europe's top universities, meaning that they share similar social and educational backgrounds even before they take up their first postings. Until recently, most members of the

European diplomatic corps were white men from upper-middle-class families. Until 1993, all permanent representatives in Brussels were male. Diversity has gradually been increasing but will take some time to reach the highest levels. Diplomats usually receive their initial training at their national foreign ministries and then alternate between postings overseas as foreign service officers and at home as foreign ministry officers, working their way up through the diplomatic hierarchy. Coreper ambassadors go through this process and after decades of service have shown themselves to be the best at what they do.

Ongoing professional training generally occurs at the foreign ministries as well as on the job. Each member state has a different means of preparing its diplomats for new assignments, but time in the field—performing the daily duties of a diplomat, navigating through difficult multilateral negotiations, and learning the nitty-gritty of foreign policy—is the best training. The ambassadors at the top have an authoritative claim on diplomatic knowledge after years and years real experience. As Cypriot Coreper ambassador Andreas Mavroyiannis said, "Expertise comes from experience, long exposure, and whether you know the people, issues, and procedures."[30]

One might be tempted to dismiss the notion that diplomats constitute an epistemic community, in large part because of the perception that diplomats are generalists rather than experts. The current scholarship on epistemic communities usually focuses on groups of scientists, particularly environmentalists and economists.[31] However, although diplomats, especially those at the highest levels, must have general knowledge of a wide range of policy issues, they may also be experts in specific issue areas. The process of promotion and assignment to different postings means that the most successful diplomats eventually become recognized experts in trade, development, humanitarian aid, security, or the like. In particular, being a generalist on EU issues constitutes a unique kind of expertise. Many Coreper ambassadors have dealt with European issues throughout their careers.[32]

If they did not already have these skills, EU ambassadors quickly become experts in how the EU apparatus works (both formally and informally) as well as in the diverse range of member state preferences and the ongoing challenges to EU integration. A Coreper appointment is considered one of the most prestigious as well as most challenging ambassadorships. It is also taken very seriously. In Denmark, for example, the selection of the ambassador to the EU requires governmental approval twice, with two weeks separating the votes.[33] In most countries, however, the Ministry of Foreign Affairs is in charge of selecting ambassadors for appointments abroad. The EU ambassadorial post is at least as important as the London, Washington, D.C., Berlin, and Paris posts. For many countries, the EU position is the most important ambassadorship, since decisions in Brussels affect such a high percentage of domestic legislation.[34] By the time a chief of state is looking at the roster of potential diplomats to appoint to Coreper, only a handful of qualified candidates remain. A process of elimination based on personal circumstances or other such factors typically narrows the pool down to the single ambassador qualified for the position. One ambassador explained that it is easy to predict who the people in the pool will be for the next three or four generations of ambassadors.[35] Years of experience in EU matters, strong relationships with those in the capital, and demonstrated skill are prerequisites.[36]

The top ambassadors remain keenly aware that the EU post requires long hours and is far less glamorous than other positions. According to Braun, "You don't get to have a house in Rome with a view, live an exotic lifestyle in Beijing, or experience the social life of Vienna. [Coreper II ambassadors] are all people who love power."[37] Those who take on this job are extremely ambitious.

Few in the member states or in Brussels have attained the level of expertise on specific EU issue areas that these ambassadors hold. Those in the capitals spend much of their time focused on a variety of policies or are not as informed as those in Brussels. For newer member states, there is the additional challenge that not enough time has passed for diplomats to circulate in and out of Brussels to add to the expertise and understanding of EU issues at home.[38] In Brussels, the only diplomats who approximate Coreper's level of expertise are those in the Mertens and Antici working groups, whose job it is to prepare Coreper I and II meetings, respectively. In many ways, Mertens and Antici diplomats—relatively young members of member states' foreign services—are EU ambassadors in the making. Those in Mertens or Antici frequently become future Coreper I and II ambassadors, just as there is a natural progression from Coreper I to Coreper II. Many Coreper II ambassadors are better off for their prior experience as deputy ambassadors and are recognized as being among the most influential ambassadors in Coreper II.

Second, Coreper's expertise is also evident in that European countries tend to emphasize career diplomacy rather than political appointments—as opposed to the United States, where around 30 percent of ambassadors are appointed from outside the foreign service.[39] In Europe, an ambassador is not appointed to the EU primarily as a way of fulfilling political patronage. Rather, each ambassador has been working on the EU in one form or another even in the case of new member states. Even the ambassadors from member states added in the 2004 and 2007 enlargements have received quite a bit of exposure to their future posts by working full time on the accession negotiations. Indeed, Edward Best, Thomas Christiansen, and Pierpaolo Settembri find that the impact of enlargement on EU institutions is often exaggerated.[40] In the period preceding membership, each of the 10 + 2 member states set up permanent representations in Brussels. When they joined the EU, the prior existence of these permanent representations meant that most member states had diplomats with well over a decade of EU experience. These ambassadors may on occasion find themselves to be a bit newer to the issues than other ambassadors, but they are nonetheless highly knowledgeable and experienced in the area of EU competences.

Third, EU ambassadors are also experts in the technical skill of negotiation and consensus building. The art of compromise cannot be easily acquired, and it embodies a number of shared professional norms. This kind of expertise is unique to the profession. In contrast to the more traditional notion of an epistemic community, diplomats are more directly involved in the policy-making process than are independent groups of scientists or economists who are trying to influence policy. But Coreper ambassadors are not simply transmission belts for states. They are constantly coming to agreement among themselves, then seeking to persuade their politician counterparts of their decisions. Although they work with instructions, in the EU context they often play a role in writing those instructions and frequently persuade their capitals to be flexible.

The EU ambassadors have more expertise on EU issues than do the politicians at home. Examples abound of statesmen trying to conduct negotiations themselves but being unable to find a solution because they do not fully understand the issues, are stubborn, or lack a common language with which to facilitate compromise.[41] In fact, several diplomats noted in interviews that one reason why ministerial-level meetings are sometimes useful is that the ministers' lack of knowledge enables them to gloss over differences and thereby overcome previous gridlock. An issue that might have occupied Coreper for weeks with a focus on slight nuances in wording could be dismissed as unproblematic in a Council meeting. This situation is more the exception than the rule, however, as ambassadors generally can push for compromise at their level.

Diplomats' ability to persuade those in their capitals is indicative of their claim to authoritative knowledge about the issues at stake. They are usually in a unique position to understand all sides of the debate and to take into account the preferences of other negotiators. Moreover, they are true members of international society. Their high professional status, meeting frequency, training, and similar social background can allow them to reach compromise even in situations previously thought to be insurmountable. Knowledge of diplomatic protocol as well as common identity, norms, and worldviews are in place before negotiations begin.

Meetings and Shared Professional Norms

Face-to-face meetings are necessary for an epistemic community to flourish. Meetings are where dialogue occurs, information is shared, and policy norms are agreed upon or reinforced. Both the quantity and quality of meetings are important, and the biggest distinction for Coreper ambassadors is that between formal and informal meetings.

Coreper meets formally each Wednesday and follows an agenda circulated in advance. The meetings do not last long enough for every delegate to speak on every issue, so all participants must choose how to strike the right balance. They do not want to be either too quiet or too domineering, both of which are signs of weak diplomatic ability.[42] The only ambassador who speaks on every issue is the chair, the individual from the member state that holds the six-month rotating presidency of the Council. But generally, since formal meetings are far less frequent than informal ones, most decisions occur during the latter.

Since the 2004 enlargement, informal meetings often occur in smaller formats of between six and eight ambassadors with a shared interest in a particular policy. These meetings typically take the form of working coffees, lunches, or dinners. Ambassadors also attend various social activities. For example, at the beginning of each presidency, all of the Coreper ambassadors, their spouses, and their Antici delegates spend three or four days on an informal visit to the major institutions and companies in the member state that holds the presidency. This trip offers an opportunity for the diplomats to get away from their regular schedules and bond in an informal setting. Attendance is mandatory. During regular informal meetings, ambassadors discuss what will happen at the formal meetings and prepare for ministerial meetings.[43] These informal meetings enable participants to speak much more frankly and to discuss issues more efficiently. As a result, informal meetings also build relationships within the group. Said Slovakian ambassador Maroš Šefčovič, "We are not only ambassadors, but friends on the other side of the table. We spend more time together than with our wives. We are permanently together. Our wives know each other. . . .We are a quite close-knit unit."[44]

The ambassadors strive to be as interconnected as possible with the rest of the EU structure. They meet most frequently with representatives of the Commission and have occasional but less intensive meetings with representatives of Parliament. Coreper members do not meet very much with other committee groupings such as the PSC, Civcom, or EUMC, since they are too busy to deal with policy issues that do not overlap with their responsibilities.[45] Outside of the EU structure, Coreper ambassadors could meet with a variety of groups and actors and regularly receive such requests.[46] Ambassadors are selective about how to use their time most productively and about which meeting invitations to accept. In particular, there is a shared norm that ambassadors should not meet with members of the media before a negotiation. They will also avoid meetings with lobbyists at any point. But they are occasionally open to meetings with nongovernmental organizations (NGOs), think tanks, off-record media, and groups from their states.[47] In general, however, actors outside of the EU such as lobbyists and NGOs usually target capitals or the European Parliament rather than Coreper.[48]

In addition to the quantity, type, and style of meetings, the quality of the interaction is crucial to Coreper's ability to exert influence and reach consensus. Members of an epistemic community who have strong shared professional norms are more likely to find agreement on policy that is within their domain of expertise. Coreper has recognized and shared practices that enable the process to work better. For most epistemic communities, the process of reaching consensus on policy goals is virtually unrelated to their area of expertise; however, for epistemic communities of diplomats, consensus and expertise are closely related. Diplomats are not merely experts in the process of compromise, but it is a large part of what they do. Diplomats become experts in substantive policy areas such as EU integration, but their expertise also lies in their ability to root out common areas of understanding among the member states. Thus, the line between shared professional norms and expertise is, in this case, somewhat blurred.

Many textbooks lay out the way in which decision making is supposed to work from the Council's perspective. The Commission sends a proposal to the Council (and to the Parliament, if it is a codecision area). The dossier goes to the relevant working group and works its way up the hierarchy to Coreper I or II, depending on whether it is of a more technical or political nature. Extensive negotiations occur, and the issue eventually reaches the appropriate configuration of the Council of Ministers, at which point (1) it will be rubber-stamped with no further negotiation (labeled A); (2) it will go back to Coreper for further negotiations; or (3) if will be labeled B and can be put to a qualified majority or unanimity vote, depending on the issue. After the dossier clears the Council of Ministers, it becomes legislation. If it is subject to codecision, it must also clear the European Parliament, which carries out its own processes of ratification.

Beyond textbook accounts, however, the story looks quite a bit different. Coreper diplomats are recognized in Brussels as being powerful decision makers whose job it is to represent their member states to the EU. To varying degrees, such representation entails making decisions on behalf of ministers, sometimes pushing for consensus beyond their instructions. All ambassadors, regardless of how closely they are bound to red lines, maintain constant interaction with their capitals throughout their negotiations. In fact, ambassadorial culture seeks to avoid having the ministers come to Brussels to deal with an issue that could not be resolved by Coreper. Ambassadors have developed a sense of when they must ultimately delegate the work or pass it up to the level above them. For some, this sense is a gut feeling gained through decades of experience; for others it is more practical. Thus, shared professional norms—a sense of how the practice of diplomacy should be carried out—is a critical part of how governance works in the EU.

One major professional norm is that Coreper seeks involvement in the policy process much earlier than formal accounts might indicate. Ambassadors want to ensure that their preferences are incorporated into any new document before it is circulated. Much of the serious, behind-the-scenes maneuvering takes place before the Commission has initiated a new dossier. Diplomats believe that after the Commission has committed a particular proposal to paper, the proposal cannot be changed substantially.

A second major professional norm governing Coreper's operations involves the management of relationships with the working groups below them. How do Coreper ambassadors use of their working groups? Mainly, they determine when and to whom to delegate. Once the Commission sends a dossier to the Council, either it goes directly to the working group with the appropriate expertise, or the Coreper ambassador whose member state holds the rotating presidency decides which working group will received the dossier. Coreper can decide to provide some political guidance before the working group discusses the dossier, but typically it goes straight to the bottom of the hierarchy without such guidance.[49]

The type of working group tasked with an issue plays a large role in the outcome. The particular expertise of the working group will naturally affect the ultimate result. As Estonian Antici delegate Klen Jäärats said, "The division of the dossiers should follow the logic of the Commission distribution, but the lead committee influences the outcome. It's inescapable."[50] For example, working groups specializing in security and on human rights may work on similar dossiers, but their outcomes are likely to be very different because of the nature of their goals. A working group focused on security issues is more likely to stress efficiency and effectiveness of the policy, while one focused on human rights would stress the importance of protecting civil liberties even at the cost of expediency.

Whether the working group is based in the capitals or in Brussels will also affect the outcome. Capital-based groups meet less frequently than Brussels-based groups. Brussels-based working groups would seem to be inherently more effective since they are constantly in close proximity to each other, but capital-based working groups also have benefits. When individuals come directly from the capitals on a regular basis, they can more easily ensure that the capital remains aware of the issue and invested in the outcome.

Although working groups exist to serve Coreper's needs, the independent role of working groups has grown over time. They play a strong role in deciding what can be settled and what cannot. In some cases, they label the whole dossier A, and no further discussion takes place in Coreper or in the Council. Everything is more or less rubber-stamped. In others, they label parts of dossiers A and escalate other parts, labeled B, to be negotiated in Coreper. However, ministers or Coreper members can always reopen something that is closed if they feel the need. One motivation for reopening a dossier might be that the Council—or more often Coreper—feels that the

Council's negotiated stance could go further or achieve more. Even if an issue is marked B, Coreper can send it back to the working group for further discussion, just as the ministers can send something back down the hierarchy to Coreper. This shuttling of dossiers up and down the hierarchy is known as the *navette*.

In addition to reopening files that have been settled at lower levels, Coreper frequently sends items that remain unsettled back down the hierarchy for further discussion. Since working groups are far more technical than Coreper (which is in the technical-political gray area), the items that Coreper sends back for renegotiation are usually quite narrow, often involving the phrasing of a few sentences. Thus, Coreper ambassadors decide the extent to which they handle issues at their level or decide to delegate decision making, and they determine when a working group's job is complete.

When a dossier is at Coreper's level, and the ambassadors have determined that it is the right time for their input, they strive to be as efficient and results oriented as possible, resulting in a third kind of professional norm. One of the requirements for a dossier to be finalized by the Council is its approval based on either a unanimous or qualified majority vote. The nature of the issue determines which type of vote is necessary, with first- or third-pillar issues usually requiring QMV and second-pillar issues requiring unanimity. Coreper, however, does not vote. Rather, the presidency determines whether sufficient support exists for a policy to be accepted. In a purely rationalist framework, the expectation is that actors bargain for their best individual self-interest, usually finding Pareto optimality as a group. Under this reasoning, some winners and some losers would exist for each issue passed under QMV, but the whole package of issues would reflect a Pareto frontier. That is, all negotiators would have made some trade-offs, but they would also have achieved their preferred conditions and feel that no change could make them better off.

In reality, however, Coreper strives to ensure that everyone is on board with each individual policy regardless of the voting requirements. As Šefčovič explained, "If it is a very vital, superimportant interest, even though it is QMV, there is a gentleman's agreement to search for unanimity."[51] Coreper ambassadors want to prevent anyone from losing, even though the system of voting could easily enable several actors to be voted out of consideration. This practice goes against the more rationalist expectation that diplomacy is about bargaining and maximizing personal gain. Rather, the ambassadors deliberate and feel it is proper and professional for them to discuss issues on their own merits. For them, the best way to reach compromise is to negotiate one issue at a time rather than to try to strike bargains through trading various positions across issues.[52] As Finnish ambassador Jan Store described, "We are not always sailing at a cruising speed, but we are really dealing with the subject."[53] He said that Coreper typically deals with four or five different sectors in a day but rarely tries for a package deal. Even though finding unanimity is the modus operandi regardless of whether an issue requires it, issues designated as subject to QMV are ultimately more creative and constructive. When ambassadors know that they could be outvoted, they have to be more flexible. This process also has the added value of making the negotiations run more quickly and smoothly. Now that the Lisbon Treaty has entered into force, QMV for Coreper's policy areas will increase significantly.

A fourth professional norm governs when it is desirable to escalate an issue to the ministerial level. Coreper ambassadors regard escalation of an issue quite negatively, seeing the entire group has having failed if it cannot resolve something at the Coreper level. For their part, ministers from the member states are content when they do not have to deal with an issue. And Coreper ambassadors recognize that having ministers grapple with an issue instead of dealing with it themselves has important ramifications. Ministers can devote much less time than ambassadors can to discussing EU issues, while ambassadors sometimes stay up all night in meetings to reach a successful outcome. In Grube's words,

> We often ask ourselves, "Is it worth putting it to the ministers, or should we deal with it ourselves?" . . . But a Council meeting of ministers is a limited span of time to deal with a certain number of dossiers. Ordinary Council meetings consist of a three-hour meeting, a two-hour lunch, and a three-hour meeting. They won't stay past six or seven at night. We have to be careful about what goes to the level of the ministers. A normal Council meeting can only handle one dossier with several questions or two dossiers with one question on each. If there are so many issues, then nothing will get done.[54]

When ministers are involved in controversial negotiations, heavy media attention results. If the media misconstrues the issue, a minister could get bad press at home even if the policy clearly benefits his or her country. According to Šefčovič,

The media coverage is important if a minister comes to Brussels. We don't want to give the impression that the EU is harming us [when] 99.9 percent of the policy is good for our country. [We don't want to have a situation where] the media focuses on one negative part and steamrolls us.[55]

Similarly, Portuguese Antici delegate Francisco Duarte Lopes said, "The Council is more open to the public, more bound to be checked by the press, more bound to be used for media games."[56] Ambassadors could be taking a risk, exposing a policy to potentially negative public scrutiny, when their intention is to see it resolved at the ministerial level. Moreover, issues presumably are escalated only when member states cannot see eye to eye, and ministers may thus fight something only to lose publicly.[57] Romanian Antici delegate Alina Padeanu stated, "A small political problem can become a big political problem at the ministerial level."[58] Because of these potential downsides, ambassadors may on occasion use escalation as a threat, a last-ditch effort to push colleagues to move on a particularly controversial topic.[59] This approach is not the standard modus operandi for ambassadors, who typically reach consensus willingly and through positive dialogue, but they sometimes find it helpful to remind each other that if no one gives way, the matter will be entirely out of their hands, a situation that involves certain risks.

Of course, ambassadors realize that the process at times benefits when the ministers come to Brussels and participate. The ministers might want the media attention associated with the policy—as long as it is fair—so that those at home can see that they are actively involved in EU issues.[60] Such publicity helps convince citizens at home that EU policy is good for them and provides more transparency on potentially sensitive issues. Coreper might also escalate a dossier when the presidency has a timetable and political importance will help to push through a policy.[61] This strategy depends on the strength of the presidency's feeling about the matter. In the end, certain ambassadors may only have the authority to make certain moves, and even if the ambassadors would like to move forward, they must escalate the issue to do so.[62] According to Ambassador Mavroyiannis,

There's a fundamental idea in the EU, at the end of the day, that you need a purely political body. The ministers get together and the idea is for them to shed another light beyond the technocratic light, to bring to light a broader political context. Not because they are more clever and intelligent, but because they bring another perspective. . . . You need the right combination of the political and technical.[63]

A gathering of ministers in Brussels is accompanied by a lot of fanfare. Police set up barbed-wire barricades in Rond Point Schuman, roads are closed off, and the media are poised to get statements. Even when an issue is escalated to the Council of Ministers, Coreper works very hard to prepare everything. Statesmen do not typically have the same EU expertise as their ambassadorial counterparts and thus usually need to rely heavily on them even when the ministers are in Brussels. On arriving in Brussels, ministers are often immediately briefed by their permanent representatives and told what to say during the Council meeting. Bringing the minister to Brussels can be symbolic, with the Coreper ambassador retaining the reins, or ministers may not be able to get to Brussels, so Coreper ambassadors stand in. Ambassador Grube related, "I sit in on the meeting and tell him what to do. . . . In many Council meetings, we are the ministers because they can't come."[64] When ministers are present, ambassadors sits next to them, providing an indispensable resource. Everyone knows an ambassador is really powerful when his minister says exactly the same things as he or she does.

A dossier might also be escalated above even the Council of Ministers to the European Council itself, a summit of prime ministers or foreign ministers. At this level, Ambassador Popens said, "Sometimes they get things through because they don't understand it. They are preoccupied with other things so they just do not care about it."[65] Discussions are highly political, and statesmen may not even be concerned with the highly detailed and technical debates that have occurred in the layers below them. In contrast to Council of Ministers meetings, Coreper ambassadors are not allowed in the room during a European Council meeting. They go to the building with their president and minister but wait in a nearby lounge. They receive updates about events in the negotiation room but also use their time productively. Said Mavroyiannis, "We share information and it's very valuable because we can't go anywhere else. . . . Very often we come to agreement in the lounge and tell the officers in the European Council to get them to prepare papers and give them to the presidents and ministers in the room." In the end, it is estimated that 90–95 percent of the results of a European Council summit are determined by Coreper or the General Affairs Council.[66] Thus, even when an issue becomes highly politicized and the ambassadors are not even present, they still play an overwhelmingly important role as quiet directors behind the scenes.

After a ministerial or European Council meeting, Coreper's work may have only just begun. Just as Coreper may send issues back to working groups for further discussion, ministers may send matters back to Coreper. The logic, however, is different. Ministers may send a dossier back to Coreper because they do not understand the issue or they simply do not have the time to deal with it. Coreper sends a dossier back to working groups so that they can hash out further technical detail. More than technical experts, the permanent representatives are skilled at navigating a path to political compromise based on their expert knowledge of diplomacy and EU integration.

Common Culture

Common culture is similar to but distinct from shared professional norms. While shared professional norms provide an epistemic community with a roadmap of best practices, common culture is more a state of being. It encompasses not only the esprit de corps of a group but also its identity, heritage, symbolism, and sense of purpose. Individuals who share a common culture align their interests with those of the group and thus have similar substantive norms. For epistemic communities, the policy goals they share reflect their common expertise.

Coreper's esprit de corps is manifested as a feeling of being part of a club and empathizing with each other. As Romanian ambassador Mihnea Motoc said,

> A very special kind of solidarity bonds us. For most of us, we have had previous assignments as ambassadors, so we have a duty and natural inclination to respect each other for past achievements and accomplishments. We have a natural courtesy towards one another even if it's a situation where one of us has an uncomfortable issue to discuss.[67]

New member states are no exception to this feeling of solidarity. They have been socialized into the system. In many cases, ambassadors from the newer member states have more autonomy to act because their capitals do not yet have the administrative wherewithal to cope directly with EU affairs.[68] Enlargement has affected the way Coreper works, but not because new member states' representatives are somehow fundamentally dissimilar. Rather, ambassadors argue that the main difference is that there are a greater number of voices and interests at the table.[69] More important than the newness of the member state is the newness of the Coreper ambassador. Slovenian ambassador Igor Senčar said, "Even if you are from an old member state, if *you* are new, then you have to take time to be an observer. . . . Some have a real talent for some issues or a real talent for other issues."[70] Those ambassadors with a greater depth of experience and talent as negotiators have greater pull in meetings. Thus, there is no correlation between the more experienced ambassadors and the bigger member states.

But the distinction between bigger and smaller member states could still mean divisions in the overall esprit de corps in other ways. Popens expressed the feeling that bigger member states are more immediately aware of their positions in negotiations because they have more at stake in more issue areas. Smaller member states may not be involved in a number of policies and thus may not have dedicated resources to even determine their stances in these areas.[71] The issues may also be unprecedented from their point of view. In general, however, the group dynamic within Coreper emphasizes ambassadors' equality regardless of the size of their member states. Given the wide diversity of policy areas within the security realm, smaller member states often can take the lead on initiatives that are not priorities for bigger member states. Outcomes of negotiations are more than simply a matter of relative power and bargaining.

At the level of Coreper, cohesiveness exists across big and small as well as new and old member states. This cohesion is significant because if an issue is escalated to the ministers or the European Council, power differentials among member states are much more evident. Bigger states wield more influence at purely political levels. In this sense, smaller member states benefit from resolving issues in Coreper or other legally binding intermediate bodies, especially in the issue areas where smaller member states have already taken the lead.[72]

Members of Coreper also share substantive norms with respect to the EU that are an important part of their common culture. The members of Coreper believe that continued integration is the best path forward. They consistently describe themselves as pro-Europe and in most cases as more pro-Europe than those in their capitals. They see their role as reconciling national and EU interests, but to a great extent, they believe integration is inevitable and desirable. Given that they could just as easily approach negotiations as a game of bargaining and strive to gain as much as possible for their national interests, it is significant that these diplomats are serious about the EU's common good. In Mavroyiannis's words,

> We are conscious of the need for us to reconcile pursuit of national and pursuit of general interest. This has to do with the idea that one should never— except in extreme cases—put one above the other. This is not an ordinary intergovernmental institution. This is about integration, building something. . . . The EU is not outside. It's part of what you're doing.[73]

One manifestation of this approach is that the ambassadors take one issue at a time, and no fixed alliances exists among certain groups of member states.

A second substantive norm is that ambassadors believe the best way to improve the lives of European citizens is to focus on the common benefit rather than the interests of each member state individually. They view the Council as a kind of common EU government and feel that their role is to operate within it to serve a common constituency of European citizens. For example, according to Motoc,

> In the end we have one constituency. We have to mold together what we are doing. We all read the European media. We know reports from various countries. . . . It's a fantastic experience because you get to look beyond the surface of things into areas of politics that you only otherwise have in government.[74]

Similarly, Store contended, "What is good for Europe is good for Finland, even if we didn't get all that we wanted."[75]

A third substantive norm Coreper ambassadors share is the belief that their diplomatic expertise should bridge both technocratic and political decision making. They often regard themselves as maneuvering in a gray area between the two. Jäärats said, "Something that used to be seen as technical is becoming political. There's no clear definition on what is political and what is not. Ideologically, Coreper is one, so they are members of the same government."[76] In Duarte Lopes's view, Coreper "has technical tasks and takes political decisions."[77] Some member states rely heavily on their high-ranking civil servants and lack extensive hierarchies in their prime ministers' cabinets. While diplomats are fundamentally civil servants, they may have to do politicians' work.[78] But because they do not have politicians' identities or motivations, policy preferences rely on diplomatic expertise.

Coreper ambassadors favor of more internal security integration, which they believe will greatly benefit European citizens and will result in more efficient EU operations, especially since cross-border interaction is constantly increasing. The ambassadors broadly define security as encompassing all aspects of everyday life in Europe, and they believe that a strong interdependence exists between internal and external security.[79] This view contrasts sharply with that of their PSC counterparts, who do not share a consensus that there is overlap between the two.

Ambassadors spend quite a bit of time deliberating over nuances, some of which are highly technical. Nevertheless, Coreper members agree on the fundamentals of security and see integration as involving the "convergence of minds and values."[80] Leaving aside resistance and differences in how much integration each of the 27 capitals sees as desirable, much of the ambassadors' discussion involves balancing the interests of security with the need for civil liberties. They do not debate the fact that they need a legal space, nor do they debate the general principle that integration provides more and better security for all. They take these ideas for granted. But their expertise is needed to find the right balances to push integration forward and to convince their capitals to go along. The path toward more integration is by no means an easy one, and at times Coreper can introduce only a few new regulations.

Overall, how cohesive is this epistemic community of Coreper diplomats? Diplomatic selection and training, meetings and shared professional norms, and common culture all indicate that Coreper diplomats can be characterized as highly cohesive. Their selection and training give them recognized expertise in EU issues and the art of compromise. They meet frequently in informal settings and share a multitude of professional norms that smooth their interaction and enable them to settle on shared policy goals based on their expert knowledge. They identify with one another despite being charged with representing diverse member state interests, and they share substantive norms and worldviews about EU integration and security policy. In short, they are a strong epistemic community. Assessing their impact requires looking outward, beyond the group's internal dynamics. The primary means through which they exert influence on policy outcomes in the EU is by persuading their capitals of their policy goals.

Persuading the Capitals

These processes, conventions, and procedural norms play no small role in substantive policy outcomes. Diplomatic interaction with the capitals is the final and critical piece of the puzzle in determining whether Coreper achieves its aims. Given that these ambassadors share substantive causal beliefs, even regarding the contentious issues of security, do they succeed in convincing their capitals?

A major part of the permanent representatives' work consists of persuading their capitals of the need for further internal security integration. However, they face a lot of resistance from the capitals, where the tendency is to try directly to control the direction of JHA and to guard national regulations, some of which have been in place for centuries. As Austrian ambassador Hans-Dietmar Schweisgut put it, it is a "situation where the ministers of home affairs are obsessed with secrecy and obsessed with keeping information as close to their chests as possible. They are reluctant to give things early to Coreper. They precook things to the extent possible."[81] The ministers also feel pressure from domestic actors, especially judges and lawyers, who are accustomed to national rules and do not want to see them changed.[82]

From their standpoint in Brussels, the members of Coreper are fully aware of the common benefits internal security integration would have for European citizens, and one of the ambassadors' challenges is to try to persuade their capitals of this. Popens explained, "Everybody is guarding his own legislation, [but] I'm always saying there's a good objective in the EU, and [resistance makes Latvia] look ridiculous."[83] This level of resistance is much higher for internal security than for other issue areas, so Coreper ambassadors must exercise agency, sometimes in opposition to their capitals, to see their policy goals reach fruition. They do not always succeed, given the controversial nature of JHA and how it affects national rules and practices. On some occasions, Coreper has no choice but to escalate the issue to the next European Council meeting and hope that top politicians have been persuaded and can simply cut through domestic resistance. On other occasions, ministers in the capitals drag their feet, drastically slowing the process in Brussels. Nonetheless, over time, the dynamic of push and pull between Coreper and capitals favors Coreper.

Ambassadors are more European in their orientation than are their capitals and tend to shape policy in this direction. In turn, those in the capitals recognize that Coreper ambassadors are always seeking compromise and understand that pressure, whether or not they ultimately give in. Rogier Kok, a policy officer in the European and International Affairs Department of the Dutch Ministry of Justice, said, "In the end, if [the ambassador] doesn't want to say something, he doesn't. In the end, he's in charge. He's in control. It's his interpretation of what's important or not, and what's achievable."[84] For their part, permanent representatives report that they usually get their way in dealing with their capitals. Of course, certain lines cannot be crossed. In such cases, ambassadors face obstacles, but they are not entirely insurmountable.

Those in the capitals do recognize that the representatives in Coreper are more aware of EU developments and have greater expertise. According to Emma Gibbons, the head of EU section of the International Directorate in London's Home Office, "It's about being on the front line, exposed to the day-to-day dynamic. Here you get Westminster and ministers."[85] The distance from Brussels is even further for some of the newer member states that have not yet had a large number of diplomats circulating through the European capital. Diplomats who have spent time in Brussels know better how to write instructions from the capital, have more knowledge of EU issues, and understand the necessary margins for maneuvering. Said Padeanu,

> If you see the issues debated in Brussels, when you go back you understand how to write instructions for Brussels, how to allow a margin for negotiations. The longer-term member states have empathy towards Brussels-based decision making in their capitals. Of the countries from the 2004 enlargement, a few of them have Euroskeptic governments. They have difficult instructions. They always have to check with their capitals. We [from Romania] have flexibility. We have the possibility of negotiating our instructions. In most cases, our opinions are taken into account.[86]

Gibbons, who served two postings in Brussels, concurs: "Having exposure to both, you can get the big picture."[87]

Internal security integration is progressing quickly and is becoming more important, but a contentious process of persuasion still occurs in advance of the adoption of each new policy. On the one hand, those in the capitals tend to focus on mainly national interests rather than on the big picture of what might work well for Europe.[88] In the Netherlands, for example, the general approach is to handle internal security on the national level, but if a broader focus has added value, policymakers are willing to put national policy into a European context.[89] Some member states more strongly favor integration than others, and even some sectors of government within a single member state are more pro-Europe than others. According to Kok, his department is more Europe-minded than the experts who write Dutch law. In his experience, national traditions involving Dutch law are the main obstacles to further integration in the field of JHA. Pieter Jan Kleiweg, head of the EU external department in the Dutch Ministry of Foreign Affairs, believes that all member states are effectively acting in accordance with their own national interests.[90] Thus, disparities occur even between ministries in the Hague. Rita Faden, director general of internal affairs in the Portuguese Ministry of Internal Affairs, said that it is important to have a mix of national and EU preferences but that it is counterproductive to consider internal security only from a national perspective since the EU is nearly internally borderless.[91] On the other side of the spectrum, Peter Storr, director of the International Directorate in the UK Home Office, described his country's involvement in EU common security policy as mainly altruistic: "We give more than we get out."[92]

On the other hand, the ambassadors fundamentally believe that everyone is better off if member states collectively strive to accomplish what is in the common good. In Faden's view, the members of Coreper

> have more of an urge to compromise. . . . Trust in the ambassador is really important. . . . In the capitals, we may not have the complete pictures. [Coreper ambassadors] have asked to change the instructions, and we have been flexible. They are pushing for compromise, and we understand the pressure to compromise.[93]

Thus, for the most part, ambassadors find themselves negotiating with their capitals just as much as they deliberate among themselves.[94] Because they have a large support system of working groups below them, most of the straightforward parts of JHA agreements are resolved and only the one or two most difficult issues are left for Coreper. The controversy is boiled down to its essence by the time it reaches the ambassadors, and they focus their persuasive efforts in this area.

In addition trying to persuade capitals on specific issues, diplomats also push capitals to change more fundamentally the way they approach Brussels. For example, Estonia's Jäärats reports that he is trying to get "Tallinn to treat Brussels issues like internal government issues."[95] Given the types of areas in which the EU is involved, if governments were to regard EU decision making as an extension of their actions, he argued, understanding and approaching integration in a constructive manner would be much easier.

Instructions and Flexibility

The primary way in which the capital has leverage over its ambassadors is through formal instructions, and the primary way in which ambassadors exercise agency is through flexibility with those instructions. Nongovernmental epistemic communities do not typically have to deal with instructions from their national governments but still must coordinate with government officials and persuade them, working within the system, to see policy goals implemented. While receiving instructions from the capitals is a big part of how the epistemic community of diplomats operates and is constrained, in practice instructions serve as a more formalized means of coordination and persuasion between relevant governments and an epistemic community. Instructions are rarely set in stone for high-ranking ambassadors, and they serve as a basis for deliberation. A set of instructions denotes what the capital wants, and an ambassador's efforts to gain room for maneuver or to change the instructions denote what the epistemic community wants. If ambassadors play a role in writing their own instructions, then what the epistemic community collectively wants may already be wrapped into the first set of written instructions. Coreper ambassadors are not simply transmission belts for states but are experts in their own right with the ability and desire to influence outcomes both individually and collectively.[96]

Each member state's government has a different system of compiling instructions for Coreper ambassadors. In Estonia, for example, the foreign ministry streamlines the instructions from all the other ministries before sending them to the attaché, who then provides them to the ambassador.[97] In Finland, the instructions from various ministries are funneled through the EU secretariat in the prime minister's office, where they are screened and coordinated.[98] For the British, instructions are coordinated in London with input from Brussels, and the briefing of the ambassador is the responsibility of the desk officers.[99] In other words, the ambassadors are briefed in Brussels on the basis of the instructions to which they had previously contributed. The Netherlands has a strong culture of coordination in the Hague, where face-to-face interministerial meetings take place every Tuesday morning in advance of each formal Wednesday Coreper meeting.[100] It is rather unusual for high-level civil servants from separate ministries to know each other personally, as the Dutch do, but that is a key feature of their governance style. More generally, all member states seek to streamline instructions and make sure that both the capital and the experts in Brussels have had input into the final product.

The ambassadors report having a high degree of flexibility with their instructions, but varying degrees and types of flexibility exist. Depending on circumstances in their home states, certain Coreper members may be more constrained. States with less domestic flexibility fall into three categories. First, coalition governments present more of a challenge for Coreper ambassadors hoping to persuade their governments to move on an issue simply because coalition governments always have more difficulty agreeing on anything. Thus, countries Germany and Estonia are likely to be less flexible, and Portugal is likely to be more flexible. A second challenging situation is when a government lacks a strong parliamentary majority.[101] In this situation, the government must tread a fine line to ensure that it keeps its advantage. And third, in member states where ambassadorial selection is more political and the majority party has just changed, Coreper ambassadors may suddenly find themselves facing increased resistance at home as the new government prepares to appoint a new ambassador. Greece, Italy, Austria, and Spain tend to be more political in their nominations of ambassadors and may on occasion fit this situation. In early 2009, for example, the Italian Coreper ambassador who was appointed by former prime minister Romano Prodi was still in his position when the government came under Silvio Berlusconi's leadership.

More generally, ambassadors gain flexibility and autonomy through their own initiative. All Coreper ambassadors frequently talk to their capitals via video conferencing, telephone, or e-mail. Ambassadors who judge that instructions are unworkable given the climate in Coreper will communicate with their capitals to get the instructions changed. This process can occur in varying ways. Some ambassadors are involved in writing their own instructions from the beginning. Others receive instructions but are permitted some license during negotiations without checking with the capital. In Denmark, for example, the ambassador has the same powers as the minister and can make binding decisions on behalf of the Danish government. Still others receive broad but not very detailed instructions, giving the ambassadors room to maneuver. In the words of Slovakia's Šefčovič, "The minister is quite pleased if he doesn't have to give too many instructions."[102]

Even though flexibility is ultimately part of the working relationship between ambassadors and their capitals, ambassadors must earn this margin of autonomy, first through a career built on trust and second through a desire to exercise agency as a member of Coreper. Since ambassadors have a unique viewpoint from their permanent base in Brussels (for the duration of their appointment), they report back to their capitals what will or will not work, reports in which they have quite a bit of discretion. Also, officials in the capitals do not know what happens in informal discussions among diplomats unless ambassadors share that information. As Schweisgut put it, "If we feel strongly about an issue, in most instances, our position [will be] approved."[103]

In sum, Coreper has transcended its formal role of preparing the work of the Council and in many ways substitutes for the Council.[104] These ambassadors generally hold a common set of professional norms involving diplomatic protocol, procedure, and practice. These norms govern the process of conducting negotiations and are enduring. There is a long-lived diplomatic norm of reaching compromise—the idea that it is better to give up some of what you want to secure a workable solution than to insist on particular priorities at the expense of the common goal of cooperation. In essence, diplomatic success is defined as a compromise solution. Coreper has developed certain substantive norms on EU policy outlooks, such as the causal belief that further security integration will benefit all member states.[105] Thus, the existence and evolution of the EU has in many ways resulted from diplomatic initiative over time.[106] And internal security integration is the hard test for Coreper's influence.

COUNTERTERRORISM: THE STRATEGY ON RADICALIZATION AND RECRUITMENT

The 2005 Strategy on Radicalization and Recruitment (SRR) defines the terrorist threat to the EU, highlights the challenges the EU faces in overcoming extremist ideologies and threat vulnerabilities, and outlines the proactive measures the EU will take to undermine al-Qaeda's radicalization and recruitment in Europe.[107] The SRR exemplifies what Coreper typically engages in with regard to internal security, although it is one of the more conceptual rather than technical policy areas. Coreper broadly monitors the progress of the EU Counterterrorism Strategy, provides updates, and follows up on implementation. It also receives support from a number of working groups, most importantly the CFSP Working Group on terrorism of the second pillar and the Terrorism Working Group of the third pillar.

The SRR's section on responses to radicalization and recruitment is perhaps the most significant part of the strategy, as it requires new policy initiatives undertaken at both the member state and supranational EU levels. The three main parts of the response strategy involve

1. disrupting the activities of the networks and individuals that draw people into terrorism;
2. ensuring that voices of mainstream opinion prevail over those of extremism;
3. vigorously promoting security, justice, democracy and opportunity for all.[108]

The strategy is now part of the broader EU Action Plan on Combating Terrorism, which the Council revises every six months.[109] The specific records of Coreper discussions involving SRR are still classified, but a picture of Coreper's influence can be gained by comparing the draft strategy submitted to Coreper and the final version, which reflects Coreper's revisions. Interviews are also valuable, although regular turnover in Coreper makes it somewhat challenging to put together a complete picture through interviews alone.

Since Coreper was involved in a special session to initiate the strategy in September 2005, even the original draft reflects the ambassadors' input on policy goals. On September 12, 2005, the UK presidency specifically requested that Coreper reexamine its draft of the strategy. This process took about two months, and on November 11, the presidency circulated the new draft, with Coreper's revisions. The final version of this document was made public on November 24, and it was nearly identical to the November 11 draft. Coreper's revisions were accepted in toto. These final drafts reflect the input of Coreper and its working groups (Article 36 Committee, Political Security Committee, Terrorism Working Party, and CFSP Working Group on Terrorism) and shed light on the ambassadors' substantive norms.

To isolate Coreper's specific input in crafting the final version of the Strategy, table 2 summarizes the key differences between the old and new drafts. These data show that Coreper shared norms about the need to (1) enact a comprehensive response, (2) elevate perception of threat, and most important, (3) legitimate the action taken by the EU. All three encouraged a further degree of Europeanization of the strategy. Despite the fact that member states had initially regarded the problem of radicalization and re-cruitment to terrorism as country specific, over the course of several years they had accepted a highly integrated approach to tackling these problems. They began to see these challenges as European and did so as a result of Coreper's initiatives.

In terms of enacting a comprehensive response, Coreper emphasized the existence of a dangerous, distorted version of Islam that must be com-bated with efforts to integrate Muslims into society so that they are less sus-ceptible to radicalization. To accomplish this goal, Coreper argued that member states should not only ensure that discrimination is minimized but also seek the help of NGOs engaged in helping immigrant and religious communities. This approach gave credence to the importance of nonstate, transnational actors and decreased the responsibility of member states alone in tackling the problem. Coreper believed that empowering moder-ate voices and involving elements of civil society would weaken the influence of extremist Islam.

The second major norm reflected in Coreper's vision for the strategy was that the perception of threat was greater than had been recognized. Therefore, the ambassadors believed, more people are at risk and more cit-izens could be affected by terrorist activity than had been anticipated. Coreper argued that radicalization and recruitment take place not only in prisons but also in educational institutions, religious training centers, and places of worship. Moreover, the pattern of radicalization and recruitment is more prominent than had been assumed. Individuals have similar rea-sons for adhering to distorted versions of Islam: they use propaganda, in-cite anger, and are always growing their target base. Coreper's effort to ele-vate the perception of threat again contributes to the Europeanization of the strategy. Even if certain regions and member states have seen no evi-dence of the rise of extremist ideologies, Coreper emphasized that they might be the next targets. Therefore, the ambassadors argued, participation in a collective effort would be necessary, even for those who felt they had nothing to worry about. This idea represented a big shift given that only six

TABLE 2. Coreper's Influence on the Strategy: Three Norms

Norm	Old Emphasis	Coreper's Emphasis	Significance
Enact a comprehensive response	Protection against a version of Islam Member states must do "much of the work"	Protection against a *distorted* version of Islam. Must empower moderate voices. The "key to our success will be on non-governmental groups"[a]	Longer-term strategy highlights radical nature of extremist Islam and need for nonstate actor support
	Target inequalities and discrimination	Need long-term integration	
	As a broad range of people are susceptible to recruitment, need adequate and appropriate education	Also need *cultural* opportunities in immigrant communities	
Elevate perception of threat	Prioritize vulnerability to attack ahead of reducing the threat No mention of Europe's history of terrorism	Prioritize reducing the threat ahead of vulnerability to attack "Europe has experienced different types of terrorism in its history." But Al Qaeda is the biggest threat.	More distinctive and pattern-based threat. Things will get worse before better.
	Monitor prisons	Monitor prisons *and* places of education, religious training, and worship	
	Radicalization of Muslims in Europe is not new, but it is relatively recent	Areas where radicalization is not yet a problem and Muslim populations are small *may still become targets* for extremism	
	Combat "argumentation" that convinces people of a clash between Islam and the West, especially by "eloquent leaders" who convince people to express their grievances	Combat "*propaganda*" that convinces people to express their anger (no mention of eloquent leaders)	
	An individual becomes involved in terrorism for unique reasons; there is *no profile of a terrorist*	Motives to become a terrorist are *similar*, even though it is an individual decision	

TABLE 2.—*Continued*

Norm	Old Emphasis	Coreper's Emphasis	Significance
Legitimate action	No mention of legitimacy or fundamental rights	Counterterror policy will be considered a "legitimate course of action"; must respect fundamental rights "put in place the right legal framework to prevent individuals from inciting and legitimizing violence"; pursue *political dialogue* and technical assistance	Significant new interest in legitimacy of action within a legal framework; desire to make process more political and participatory
	No mention of legal framework; pursue technical assistance		
	Consult Muslim communities	Consult academic experts, other governments, and Muslim communities	
	Promote justice, democracy, and opportunity for all	Promote *security,* justice, democracy, and opportunity for all	

Note: Italics added for emphasis.
[a]NGOs include "communities, religious authorities and other organizations."

countries—Germany, Italy, Spain, Portugal, France, and the UK—had ever suffered from domestic terrorist threats prior to 9/11.[110]

The final norm reflected in Coreper's revisions to the strategy is the idea that actions taken by the EU must be legally and normatively legitimated. In keeping with this norm, the ambassadors added to the final draft specific mention of protecting fundamental rights, putting in place a legal framework, encouraging a political dialogue, and involving experts such as academics in shaping policies. The idea of fundamental rights, common to all citizens of the EU, once again shows a belief that through asserting Europeanness, radicalization and recruitment to extremism can be counteracted. Policies can be legitimated by showing respect for rights as well as for the legal system on which much of EU legislation rests. Coreper argued that a political dialogue had to be pursued and the process made more participatory, involving academics, other governments, and Muslim communities. This approach reflects the diplomatic culture of reasoned, democratic processes and respect for plurality.

Since the SRR's public release, Coreper has revised its policy goals as a

result of ongoing value shaping and in response to real events. Such updates have occurred regularly since the strategy is now part of the more
general EU Action Plan on Combating Terrorism, a policy for which
Coreper also performed the preparatory work.[111] The most significant evolution in policy since November 2005 involves increased information sharing among the member states. In this regard, the influence of the technology epistemic community described in chapter 6 overlaps with Coreper as
projects that were part of the Preparatory Action on Security Research provide the technology to enable effective and rapid information sharing.
Table 3 illustrates the key policy evolutions since 2005. Starting with the
December 2005 EU Action Plan, the categories of policy areas were divided
into Prevent, Protect, Pursue, and Respond. The SRR was entirely subsumed
within the Prevent category. The table reflects the policy changes that were
not explicitly included in the original SRR but were added as Coreper revised the EU Action Plan.[112]

Council documents indicate that the strategy remained organized
around the three areas of response, but specific tasks within each category
evolved over time as a result of Coreper's deliberations. In the first category,
the policies became more specific but continued to seek various methods of
curtailing extremist propaganda. Over time, the SRR also added funding
programs for citizens interested in conducting research on transnational
terrorism or in finding ways to strengthen the relationship between civil
society and European authorities.

In the second category, the revised policy initiative stated that all religions have moderate voices and that they should be encouraged. Moreover,
in place of extremism, Coreper suggested that "religious communities
should embrace the fundamental norms and values of European society."[113]
Thus, the ambassadors diluted the emphasis on local imams and Muslim
communities, and by treating the issue of extremism as a problem within all
religions, Coreper communicated that all of society must grapple with these
problems. A program of public diplomacy was also mentioned as an important policy goal in terms of explaining and legitimizing EU actions to the international community. Such a campaign to improve Europe's image also
works to solidify the idea that Europe has a common image.

Finally, in the third category, the emphasis again was on offering
funding programs to support citizens in designing initiatives. Coreper's
idea of involving citizens directly in policy research is also evident in
chapter 6 with respect to technology development. These projects, which

TABLE 3. Coreper's Influence on the EU Action Plan

SRR Category	Revision Date	Policy Evolution—Strategy on Radicalization and Recruitment (Nov. 2005)[a]
Disrupt the activities of the networks and individuals who draw people into terrorism	2/13/2006	Act in common against extremist web sites; promote Community policing; exchange information on incitement of violence; police training inside and outside of the EU; implement measures against illegal extremist literature and media; set up network of European experts; have conference on ways media can counter radicalization; journalist training programs
	5/24/2006	Add: Research program on transnational terrorism
	3/9/2007	Add: On January 10, 2007, the Commission published a call for tenders (deadline March 5, 2007) for a study on the best practices in cooperation between authorities and civil society with a view to the prevention of and response to violent radicalization; on January 30, the Commission published a call for proposals for projects in field of prevention of violent radicalization.
Ensure that voices of mainstream opinion prevail over those of extremism	2/13/2006	Empower moderate voices in Muslim community; support availability of moderate religious literatures; *encourage Muslim communities* to rely on *local Imams* and develop enhanced training; develop non-emotive lexicon for discussing radicalization; comprehensive communication strategy to explain EU policies to media and terrorist experts, train journalists in Europe, Middle East, and North Africa
	5/24/2006	Change: Empower moderate voices of *all religions* in the EU; encourage religious communities to embrace the fundamental *norms and values of European society* Take out: reference to local Imams
	3/9/2007	Add: Media Communication Strategy was approved by the Council in July 2006
Promote yet more vigorously security, justice, democracy, and opportunity for all	2/13/2006	Promote intercultural dialogue
	5/24/2006	Add: Research projects funded under the Sixth Framework Programme for RTD (research and technological development) that address intercultural dialogue
	3/9/2007	Add: "Facilitating cross-cultural dialogue between media professionals" is one of the themes of the Commission's call for proposals on projects for countering radicalization, issued in January 2007

Note: Italics added for emphasis.

[a]The EU Action Plan on Combating Terrorism did not contain any reference to the Strategy on Radicalization and Recruitment until February 2006, although there were four prior versions. Revisions continued after March 9, 2007 as well.

are multinational in scope, encourage policy plans that require a European approach.

Coreper's Motivations

What motivated this particular evolution in policy? Ambassadors described an overarching norm: Radicalization must be regarded as a European problem with a European response. Estonia, Finland, and Slovakia, for example, do not have problems with radicalization, yet all three ambassadors agreed that they must take a European approach and engage in the debate about what should be done. As Estonian ambassador Raul Mälk said, "The EU provides a collectively prepared understanding. We're not specialists on Islam, so we can use the whole EU's approach. This is very important. Immigrants know that when they go to Estonia, we have a European attitude and approach to legislation."[114] He emphasized that EU funding to provide training for lawyers and language courses for immigrants has been important. Store, the Finnish ambassador, argued that the debate in his country resulted in solutions that are "local and immediate." For example, "we decided that new people should be dispersed all over the country, not just one area in the suburbs, and we try to integrate them as well as possible through education, involvement in life, making them into normal citizens."[115] One ambassador indicated that even though his country does not have a single mosque, he believed the problem to be a European one. He stressed that the fact that the Dutch were surprised when they started to hear radical ideas coming from their mosques should be a lesson for everyone.[116]

The SRR distinctly emphasized European rather than national initiatives, thereby triggering an integrative approach. The draft of the SRR presented to Coreper for deliberation mentioned European approaches:

> Addressing this challenge is beyond the power of governments alone. . . . We will continuously develop our collective understanding of the problem. . . . We need to spot such behaviour by community policing and effective monitoring of the internet and travel to conflict zones. We should build our expertise by exchanging national assessments and analyses.[117]

But the subsequent revisions and specific policy initiatives took this idea further, emphasizing the establishment of a "European picture." Coreper's decisions reflected a desire for a comprehensive, pan-European response to radicalization and recruitment. New factors such as protections for fundamental rights, legal frameworks, public diplomacy, media relations, funding opportunities, and NGO involvement pushed the strategy to a more European level, enhancing the idea that a contiguous homeland exists and must be protected. And the policy would be legitimated for the EU and by the EU.[118] These were big steps along the path toward internal security integration, particularly in light of the fact that member states had previously regarded radicalization and recruitment as only national problems with national solutions.

Outcomes and Implementation

The outcomes and implementation of the SRR have been carefully documented through progress reports. The high level of response to Coreper's policies is quite significant, as evidenced by the large number of new initiatives. First, by November 2006, Germany launched a program, Check the Web, to "ensure synergies in the efforts of Member States and the EU to counter terrorist use of the Internet."[119] Second, member states held several meetings to promote interfaith and intercultural dialogue, including a conference led by the Finnish presidency in Jakarta "aimed at challenging stereotypes in Europe and the Islamic World."[120] Third, many member states began to support Community policing training. To encourage this effort, the European Police College sponsored multicountry police training to bring together officers from different states to learn from each other. Many other initiatives have also been launched.

A November 2006 progress report states,

> Radicalization has moved from a somewhat specialist issue to a central theme with profound implications for the future of our society. The first success of the EU Radicalization and Recruitment Strategy is that it has brought this issue to centre stage and focused minds on how we tackle the problem collectively.[121]

To disrupt networks, the intelligence services of the member states have begun to share important information with Europol and the Situation Centre, creating a supranational strategy. The Austrian presidency organized a conference in Trier to enable policy practitioners to meet and exchange information about how best to handle the problem of radicalization in prisons and educational institutions. By November 2006, 21 member states as well as Romania and Bulgaria signed the Convention on the Prevention of Terrorism, agreeing to abide by EU laws criminalizing both direct and indirect incitement to engage in terrorist activities.

In terms of ensuring that voices of mainstream opinion prevail over those of extremism, member states followed through with Coreper's suggestions through the implementation of a media communication strategy. This strategy focused on developing a "common lexicon of terms"[122] to enable the actors involved in implementing the SRR to understand one another better and to use suitable language in describing their observations. Among other things, member states began deliberately to support moderate Muslim groups in their efforts to combat extremism, and numerous conferences were held to promote intercultural and interfaith dialogue. The Anna Lindh Foundation, an international organization of European and Mediterranean countries, supported programs aimed at media, education, and youth through the arts, music, school magazines, summer exchange programs, books, libraries, translation, and civil society organizations for intercultural exchange. In particular, these efforts targeted Coreper's call for public diplomacy initiatives.

In terms of promoting security, justice, democracy, and freedom for all, the EU launched military and police operations in third countries to try to restore stability to conflict-ridden areas. Such operations enable the EU to diffuse hotbeds of radicalization and recruitment before the problem reaches the EU's borders. Member states work together as a common force to construct judicial, police, and governance structures in many regions of the world. Through programs like Erasmus and Tempus, the Commission supports higher education in countries where radicalization sometimes occurs and brings students from these countries to the EU. Thus, in just one year, a combination of efforts from the Council, Commission, member states, and nonstate actors in response to Coreper's detailed strategy resulted in very concrete steps toward security integration.

Six months later, a new progress report noted several new initiatives alongside the continuation of the previous ones.[123] In addition to the Check the Web program, Europol launched a portal enabling member states to monitor potential terrorist web sites. Experts from the member states met to deliberate on these two resources and determine the best ways of dealing with identified problems. And a number of EU institutions as well as member states organized seminars and conferences on all aspects of the SRR. The European Police College set up new programs on regional police training involving forces from non-EU member states including the Balkans and the Mediterranean countries. Coreper members agreed that their countries would exchange information about the expulsion of all third-country nationals involved in terrorist activity or radicalization.

A November 2007 progress report described progress in these earlier areas as well as a fresh set of initiatives, again fulfilling Coreper's call to action. Member states' efforts to combat radicalization in schools and places of worship include training programs for local authorities and outreach to civil society groups. Austria, Germany, and France began working together on a project that teaches prison staff how to recognize and combat radicalization. Germany also put forward a proposal to the Commission to bring together visible members of the Muslim community from all over the world—media personalities, academics, pop culture icons, and religious leaders—to encourage a more moderate version of Islam. The UK applied for funding from the Commission to set up an overarching network of European civil society groups to spread messages countering extremism and radicalization. This network would subsequently expand outside of the continent, ultimately becoming global. The Commission launched a formal dialogue between EU and religious institutions, and the EU named 2008 the European Year of Intercultural Dialogue, with a budget of 10 million.

The EU enhanced its dialogue on radicalization and recruitment with the Mediterranean through EuroMed, with Asia through ASEM, with Southeast Asia through the ASEAN Regional Forum, and with the Islamic world in general through the Organization of the Islamic Conference. The Union also enhanced its cooperation, especially in the legal sphere, with the United Nations.

In November 2008, several member states took the lead on a number of new initiatives.[124] Germany continued its lead on Check the Web, the UK took over a communication strategy to improve further the common lexicon and combat the narrative often used by extremist groups, Spain took leadership on training of religious leaders, the Netherlands oversaw training of local authorities, Sweden took on Community policing, and Denmark focused on helping young people avoid radicalization. A closed-circuit television initiative launched in 2007 identified areas where member states could use a common legal framework and merge best practices in the use of CCTV. Finally, EU member states agreed to cooperate with the Alliance of Civilizations, an international organization under the auspices of the UN, in five areas: promoting human rights, improving media access, enhancing an intercultural dialogue, working together on immigration and integration, and involving civil society in the prevention of radicalization.

Coreper's SRR has of course received some criticism, and it is clearly an ongoing project for the ambassadors.[125] In some areas, progress has been uneven, and cooperation has been limited to sharing best practices. In other areas, such as third-country missions, numerous educational programs, and the communication strategy, real strides toward integration have occurred. The SRR is just one example of Coreper's ability to influence the direction of security integration. Coreper has affected internal security integration involving terrorism in a variety of policy areas. The European Arrest Warrant, Joint Investigation Teams, framework decisions on freezing property or evidence and attacks against information systems, and the Protect, Respond, and Pursue areas of the EU Action Plan on Combating Terrorism are just a few of the areas that have come under Coreper's purview.[126]

EU security outcomes thus are shaped by the internal processes of an EU epistemic community. Diplomatic selection and training, meetings, shared professional norms, and common culture all indicate that Coreper diplomats constitute a transnational network of experts that is highly cohesive and effective. Coreper ambassadors are the crème de la crème of the diplomatic services in Europe, and only a handful of individuals qualify for Coreper appointments. Once they arrive in Brussels, the ambassadors meet frequently on an informal basis and benefit from centuries of evolution of the profession. Consequently, a rich body of shared professional norms exists: These norms include getting involved in policy initiatives very early on in the process, understanding when and how best to delegate, searching for unanimity even if an issue only requires a qualified majority vote, and knowing when to escalate to the ministerial level. Coreper members also share substantive norms about the desired direction of EU integration. The ambassadors firmly believe that integration benefits the common good of European citizens, especially in the sphere of internal security protections, and consistently follow through with these aims as they engage in day-to-day decision making.

The case of the SRR shows that the influence of the epistemic community of diplomats can lead to significant steps forward in security integration. The ambassadors exert influence on policy outcomes in the EU primarily by persuading their capitals and others of their policy goals as well as continually refreshing and updating their strategies. They have clearly kept the problem of radicalization and recruitment on the radar for member states, NGOs, and other actors. The outcomes of the SRR provide clear evidence that Coreper can set into motion a variety of policies. Coreper thus has transcended its formal duty of preparing the work of the Council, in many ways taking over the Council's role as a key knowledge-based network.

CHAPTER 4

Diplomats and External Security

THE POLITICAL AND SECURITY COMMITTEE

The Political and Security Committee (PSC, also known by its French acronym, COPS) is an appropriate comparison to Coreper, as it is another key grouping of ambassadors influencing security outcomes.[1] It is also a valuable comparison because while Coreper is a strong example of an epistemic community of diplomats, PSC is weaker in comparison, demonstrating the added value of the epistemic community framework. Relative weakness in an epistemic community is clearly reflected in network cohesion and the ability to exercise independent agency. Without the epistemic community framework, it would be easy to assume that PSC is for all intents and purposes the same as Coreper but with a different policy focus. PSC, too, is involved in an important part of EU security policy, and its jurisdiction has grown over time. But just because PSC as a committee does more and more work does not mean that PSC as an epistemic community is getting more and more influential. The ambassadors who comprise PSC clearly qualify as an epistemic community: They constitute a professional network with a shared body of expert knowledge and seeking to affect policy outcomes. But not all groups of experienced ambassadors achieve their policy aims. Moreover, the prospects for strengthening PSC, beyond its current level of cohesion, may be quite minimal.

Coreper and PSC share the historical background discussed in chapter 3. Both are the product of processes and professional norms that have evolved for centuries, and both are now organized under the umbrella of the Council of the European Union. Like Coreper, PSC comprises an ambassador from each member state, and all have undergone the same training and selection procedures that bring them to their current high-status positions. They have typically met each other in other settings, as is the nature of diplomatic corps across Europe, and their work involves constantly persuading each other and their capitals to agree to new levels of compromise.

At the same time, some visible differences separate PSC from Coreper. PSC focuses on external rather than internal security, and especially Common Security and Defence Policy. Coreper formally outranks PSC; Coreper's members thus tend to be somewhat more senior than PSC ambassadors. And Coreper has existed for more than forty years longer than PSC. Some distinctions are less visible but just as crucial. PSC deals primarily with crisis situations, meaning that the amount of time its ambassadors have to deliberate on a particular issue is typically shorter than Coreper's. In fact, crises are often unique, so that when they strike, ambassadors must spend a great deal of time reading various texts to prepare for their discussions on how to craft an EU response. In addition, since external security is the most difficult area for governments to hold at arm's length, member states on occasion prevent PSC from deliberating on certain issues that should fall under PSC's jurisdiction. One example is the 2002–3 Iraq crisis, when ambassadors were forbidden to put Iraq on their agenda.[2] This may not be surprising given the major differences in Paris and London at the time. In other instances, PSC ambassadors may be permitted to discuss a sensitive issue, but member states may also require additional representatives to attend the meeting to ensure that their preferences are effectively conveyed. In these cases, meetings become quite large, often topping 100 individuals, making consensus building and real deliberation nearly impossible. This may sometimes be the case in certain formal meetings of Coreper, but there is more occasion for this in PSC.

As an epistemic community, PSC is weaker than Coreper not because of any quality inherent in the ambassadors but because of the circumstances that bring them together and the dynamic into which they fall after arriving in Brussels to assume their posts. The four main qualities that determine an epistemic community's cohesiveness and ability to influence are selection and training, meeting frequency and quality, shared professional norms, and common culture. In terms of selection and training, although PSC ambassadors are slightly more junior than those in Coreper, they are otherwise subject to the same rigorous selection procedures. The other three qualities, however, are quite weak compared to Coreper. For PSC ambassadors, informal meetings are less frequent, and many other actors are in the room during formal meetings. PSC ambassadors have difficulty consolidating professional norms specific to their environment and have less opportunity to develop strong substantive norms or a common culture. Ultimately, PSC ambassadors have less autonomy from their capitals than Coreper representatives and do not seem to influence outcomes in a way that pushes integration forward.

This chapter is based on my interviews of PSC ambassadors and deputy PSC ambassadors as well as supporting interviews of Coreper, EUMC, and Civcom members. Evidence is also drawn from Jolyon Howorth's 2007 interviews and survey of 27 PSC ambassadors. Very little research has been conducted on this committee and thus there are limited secondary sources on which to draw data. Only two policy articles,[3] one academic article,[4] and one book chapter[5] give detailed attention to the committee. Moreover, no documents are available to trace processes of deliberation within PSC, since it often deals with crises of a highly sensitive nature. In some cases, PSC ambassadors may engage in a flurry of telephone discussions over of a day or two to try to find a common EU response without committing anything to paper except their final conclusions. Indeed, the results of the PSC's "crash deliberations" are reported in the news practically on a daily basis.

Despite these two limitations, it is important to start to build a basis for understanding this key emerging actor in external security matters in Brussels. This chapter focuses on the distinctions between PSC and Coreper and underlines PSC's impact on external security integration.

Because PSC ambassadors are drawn from the same pool as Coreper ambassadors, I do not repeat the background discussion that appears in chapter 3. Rather I begin by highlighting PSC's formal role and then analyze the four main qualities that shed light on the strength of this group as an epistemic community. I subsequently discuss the relationship between PSC ambassadors and their capitals, an interaction that resembles more a transmission belt for state preferences than a two-way process of mutual persuasion. Finally, I conclude by addressing the question of whether Coreper and PSC compete with or complement each other, laying out the implications of increasingly fragmented decision making on EU security policy.

A NEW AMBASSADORIAL LAYER

In March 2000, member states put into place the PSC as an interim replacement for the Political Committee (PoCo), which was established in the Maastricht Treaty. PoCo, comprised of the political directors from each member state's ministry of foreign affairs, did not represent as firm a commitment to a common approach to foreign policy as could be achieved. It met formally once or twice per month, primarily in the capital of the member state holding the rotating presidency. The idea was to keep PoCo separated from the supranational atmosphere that pervaded Brussels institutions and to keep those Brussels institutions safe from the intergovernmentalism that pervaded PoCo.[6]

British foreign secretary Robin Cook is believed to have suggested the creation of a permanent committee to replace PoCo. When other EU leaders agreed, discussion began on the details. Thus was born the idea of a body to be dedicated to the Common Foreign and Security Policy (CFSP) and to be based in Brussels, to meet frequently, and to provide greater continuity and expertise.[7] While the British suggested the creation of PSC to stress the Council's role in CFSP (as opposed to the supranational Commission) and to ensure national oversight of the new CFSP High Representative, others saw the new group as a step toward emphasizing the growing need for the EU to develop a more viable and successful common security and defense policy and to make the Common Security and Defence Policy (CSDP) operational.

In January 2001, PSC became a permanent committee. Article 25 of the Treaty of Nice gives PSC its official mandate:

> A Political and Security Committee shall monitor the international situation in the areas covered by the common foreign and security policy. . . . It shall also monitor the implementation of agreed policies. . . . [T]his Committee shall exercise, under the responsibility of the Council, political control and strategic direction of crisis management operations.[8]

While PSC does not technically have a broader mandate than its predecessor, its duties are described in more concrete terms than were PoCo's rather vague responsibilities under the Maastricht Treaty. Moreover, CFSP High Representative Javier Solana made a special contribution to the Nice Treaty, describing PSC as the "linchpin" of CFSP/CSDP.[9] Over time, PSC has gained a greater role, and some scholars contend that it has done so through its own initiative and collective agency.[10] Howorth argues, for example, that the intergovernmental processes within PSC include normative socialization, which has resulted in the development of a supranational strategic culture that transcends national strategic cultures—what he describes as supranational-intergovernmentalism.[11]

PSC spends most of its time deliberating the nitty-gritty of CSDP, from providing the initial response to a crisis and developing a strategy for dealing with it to following through with implementation and monitoring. New initiatives are usually put forward by the chair of PSC or by one of the other member states. The Commission also has the right to put proposals forward, but so far it has refrained from doing so. The Commission's presence is critical, however, as it controls the CFSP budget for nonmilitary operations, possesses the administrative apparatus to collect information, and runs numerous secondary missions in the same crisis areas.[12] After members agree to an operation, all information from member states and EU instruments must be given to PSC so that it can draft a crisis management concept. PSC then manages the drafting of the joint action, the concept of operations, and finally the operational plan. Every six months, all relevant information must be sent to PSC for review. PSC provides recommendations on whether an operation should be ended, changed, or continued.[13]

Shortly after the establishment of the permanent committee, some rivalry arose between PSC and Coreper. The latter had previously been responsible for producing the EU's common responses to crises. According to treaty, all the work of the Council is supposed to flow through Coreper before going to the ministers, and as both Coreper and PSC were populated with senior ambassadors, the new division of labor led to much ambiguity and competition.[14] Should PSC serve as a kind of preliminary negotiating body for Coreper? Or should PSC have its own area of authority? If Coreper is "responsible for preparing the work of the Council," where is the dividing line between Coreper and PSC?[15] Coreper ambassadors apparently were so concerned about PSC's new duties that they began scheduling emergency Friday meetings before every Monday meeting of ministers to formally "approve" the work of their PSC counterparts.[16]

In June 2002, the Seville European Council helped to resolve this rivalry by establishing Coreper's internal focus and PSC's external focus.[17] In terms of security policy, this change meant that PSC would deal with all aspects of CFSP, while Coreper would focus on Justice and Home Affairs. A degree of competition remains between the two groups in terms of where final decision-making authority lies. PSC ambassadors sometimes come to decisions that leapfrog Coreper's jurisdiction. As Estonian PSC ambassador Sander Soone described,

We are an independent body, not subordinated to anyone except the Council. The issues that we decide ourselves, without going through Coreper, are the ones that the Council has entrusted us with. As a principle, all matters concerning operations are only for PSC to discuss.[18]

But Austrian Coreper ambassador Hans-Dietmar Schweisgut said,

My COPS ambassador—and I say "my COPS ambassador" for a reason—in our system, I am his superior internally. . . . COPS cannot finalize documents to go to the Council. In strict terms, everything has to be approved by Coreper.[19]

Similarly, according to Rochus Pronk of the Political Affairs Department of the Dutch Ministry of Foreign Affairs,

If the PSC is not in a state or position to come to agreement, Coreper can do it. They have to admit that Coreper is the highest body, and for Council conclusions, very often PSC is not in a position to agree, but Coreper is. In the composition of the PSC and Coreper, Coreper is quite a bit more senior.[20]

Formally, everything should go through Coreper, but in practice such is not always the case. If PSC is unable to resolve an issue, it is escalated to Coreper. But for CSDP crisis management, PSC acts more or less autonomously, and the ambassadors receive dedicated instructions directly from their capitals.[21] According to Schweisgut,

COPS has an oversight role. In this area, COPS is more or less completely independent. But talking about the overall framework, and relationships with third countries, this isn't for COPS, this is for Coreper.[22]

PSC is managing a process that is shaping new and important external action. Thus, to the extent that it has taken the initiative to gain new levels of influence, it has done so mainly in the area of CSDP.

PSC is certainly fulfilling its mandate well, enabling CSDP to run smoothly and creating the overall image that CSDP is of great significance. But is this influence fostering a significant emerging European strategic culture? Integration requires longer-term processes to reach fruition. PSC must often grapple with issues about which member states care deeply, with little time to decide. PSC ambassadors are regularly instructed to protect strongly held national interests and to avoid crossing national red lines. While PSC regularly fosters cooperation under CSDP despite these national restrictions, in comparison to other security epistemic communities, it does less to consciously affect the longer-term trajectory of security integration. While it is possible that PSC's overall work may ultimately result in more integration over time, as Howorth argues, a strong epistemic community would purposefully and consciously pursue its policy aims. To systematically compare PSC to the other epistemic communities, I now turn to the key variables that determine cohesiveness.

Selection and Training

Some discussion initially took place about the seniority of the ambassadors appointed to PSC. The French government saw the launch of PSC as an opportunity to enhance the EU's security profile and wanted to appoint senior ambassadors to the post, while British leaders worried that doing so would somehow interfere with the goals of the North Atlantic Treaty Organization (NATO) and wanted second-tier appointees. The British suggested at one point that PSC ambassadors be double-hatted to both NATO and the EU, much in the same way as the EU Military Committee. In the end, the December 1999 European Council in Helsinki agreed that these ambassadors would formally be at the senior level. However, all of the larger member states refrained from appointing very top ambassadors because they wanted to be able to exercise close control in this very sensitive policy area.[23] This decision provides implicit evidence that member states are aware of the agency often exercised by the most senior diplomats, like those in Coreper, and wanted to minimize the possibility that such actions could occur in PSC.

The overall impression, however, is that PSC seniority has gone up slightly with each generation. Most PSC ambassadors have previously served as European correspondents; when they arrive in Brussels, therefore, they already have expertise in coordinating European policy.[24] Finnish PSC ambassador Anne Sipiläinen described several categories of expertise among PSC ambassadors: general EU expertise, specific CFSP expertise, a Coreper background, or regional expertise. But she noted that all PSC ambassadors are of very high caliber, more capable than appointees to bilateral embassies.[25] A PSC appointment brings much prestige, differentiating group members from participants in other diplomatic committees working on CSDP, such as the far more junior diplomats of the Civilian Crisis Management Committee. Despite the bit of controversy at its founding, all PSC appointees are career diplomats and come from the same background as Coreper members.

PSC ambassadors gain a great deal of new knowledge after they take up their posts in Brussels. Sipiläinen, who was deputy director general of the Political Department prior to her PSC appointment, compared Helsinki and Brussels: "We here in Brussels know much more than the capitals can ever know, so it's a different type of knowledge. The instructions are quite broad, and that is very good because it is difficult for the capital to adapt to what's going to happen in the PSC meeting."[26] Overall, however, PSC ambassadors are distinguished from other types of ambassadors only in that they are very near the top of their profession.

Meetings and Professional Norms

Despite PSC's high level of professionalism and expertise, its potential to exercise collective agency has not been entirely realized, in part because of the nature of their meetings. PSC meets formally on Tuesdays and Fridays but also schedules meetings on an as-needed basis. The emergency meetings follow the same rules of procedure as the regularly scheduled gatherings but deal with only one issue.[27] As CSDP has grown more robust, PSC's schedule has become increasingly overloaded. Formal meetings usually last the whole day and often go into the night.[28] The ambassadors now rely on the Nicolaidis Group, established in 2003, to sort through all of the issues in advance and highlight areas where achieving consensus might be difficult. The Nicolaidis Group is essentially the PSC's version of Coreper II's Antici Group or Coreper I's Mertens Group.

A key characteristic of these formal meetings is that more than 100 people regularly attend,[29] even though on paper only about 30 individuals—the ambassadors and a few other institutional delegates—should be present. A representative from the Commission and four from the Council Secretariat are required to attend at every meeting. Next to each ambassador sits the national expert on the topic being discussed (who waits in an adjacent room until that issue is raised). Candidate countries—currently Turkey, Macedonia, Croatia, and Iceland—have representatives present as well, and various note takers always sit in. Member states can also send other national officials, who sit behind the ambassadors and their experts. While only 28 of these individuals actually get to speak in the discussion, the result is that the room lacks an intimate atmosphere.[30] Simon Duke writes, "The national 'representatives' can often comprise more than the COPS members, which means that on issues that are particularly emotive or complex the meetings can easily consist of over one hundred people—so much for collegiality."[31]

PSC also meets informally, a practice that to some degree offsets the impersonal nature of the formal meetings. However, the growing workload means that members have less and less time to socialize in these informal settings. Tight schedules and impersonal formal meetings have become such a problem that the ambassadors have specifically set aside Tuesday lunches as a formally scheduled informal meeting with just the core group in attendance. The ambassadors admit to frequently being quite overwhelmed with information, which takes a toll on their ability to foster close ties.[32] According to Ana E. Juncos and Christopher Reynolds,

> A glance at the PSC's working procedures illustrates that although meetings take place in Brussels, the Committee's workload has reduced opportunities for socializing and has rendered the diplomatic work closer to a government in the shadow (and therefore also blurring the distinction between diplomacy and civil service). Even though something of a club atmosphere appears to remain [after the change from PoCo], not least because of the highly frequent contacts between ambassadors and officials which are far more intense than had ever been possible previously, the PSC increasingly appears as being "outside the charmed circle of diplomacy."[33]

Hense, these ambassadors are close to the pinnacle of professional diplomacy in Europe, but the declining quality of their informal meetings and staid nature of their formal meetings is transforming the group into something that resembles less a diplomatic community than a bureaucratic organization. This phenomenon is particularly visible when contrasted with the informal meetings of Coreper ambassadors or even those of EU military generals (see chapter 5).

In terms of meetings with individuals or groups outside of PSC, those with their NATO counterparts are particularly important.[34] Since September 2000, joint meetings between PSC and the North Atlantic Council (NAC) have become a regular feature of coordination between the EU and

NATO. On occasion, the presidency may also decide that PSC should meet with key members of nongovernmental organizations, such as Gareth Evans of the International Crisis Group.[35] PSC members also take part in special seminars that enable them to gain information about relevant topics—for example, small and light weapons.[36] The PSC never meets with the EU Military Committee or the Civilian Crisis Management Committee, receiving written recommendations from those groups, a practice that hints at the growing fragmentation of decision making in Brussels.[37]

Meetings can be an opportunity for diplomats to develop and consolidate a body of shared professional norms. The quantity and quality of meetings provide a strong indication of the strength of these norms in binding a network together and making it professionally cohesive. Beyond standard diplomatic norms and protocol, this group seems to be held together by specific shared substantive norms about CSDP's direction, but the basis of this network overall is not as strong as that of Coreper or EUMC.

Certain professional norms govern formal meetings, but they tend to be based on expediency rather than on any desire to drive the process forward permanently to advance overarching objectives. For example, ambassadors address each other on a first-name basis and speak directly to one another at formal meetings. There is no translation for these meetings. Between 70 and 80 percent of the time, English is spoken; the rest of the time, delegates use French.[38] To accommodate the large number of individuals in the room, one norm holds that no delegation should speak more than once on a particular topic. Ambassadors who speak a second time must apologize to the presidency and explain why they need another turn. Since the 2004 enlargement, another norm holds that each ambassador should speak no longer than two minutes. Thus, PSC operates in a very efficient fashion.[39] While these procedural norms help the committee accomplish its tasks in a reasonable amount of time, they do not encourage real deliberation. An increase in informal meetings with smaller groupings of ambassadors would likely be necessary to permit such discussions.

Interviews reveal that a major professional norm is the ambassadors' strong desire to reach consensus at their level, as is the case for Coreper and many other groups within the Council. Reaching consensus is PSC members' highest priority outside of representing their national interests and is a built-in quality of the diplomatic profession. They will examine an issue on two to three separate occasions, seeking common ground, before determining that it is time to escalate the issue to Coreper or the ministers. PSC ambassadors try to avoid sending an issue to Coreper. Greek deputy Coreper II ambassador Joannis Vrailas said,

> We have been less and less involved with external relations because of the PSC ambassadors. There's a gentleman's agreement that PSC will not come to Coreper. PSC will not want to be seen as not being relevant. The PSC ambassadors are proud; they have an esprit de corps. They believe that once they have agreed on something, they agree not to open it up again in Coreper.[40]

PSC members are less hesitant to escalate an issue to the ministers, who meet once per month. In many cases, the ministers will debate CFSP issues regardless of whether PSC finds compromise, since political components and strong national interests are often involved. Pronk reported, "A lot of details are being discussed in Brussels, but they won't be able to participate in anything without clear guidance from the Hague."[41] Thus, the root of the motivation to reach consensus at the PSC level comes more from the need to be relevant than an anxiety about failing to find a solution to a given issue.

With regard to CSDP operations, however, the ambassadors take the lead more than the ministers, and PSC's growing influence is discernable in this area.[42] PSC largely plays an oversight role. Much of the details of operations planning are hashed out in other bodies—the military committee, military staff, Civcom, Civilian Planning and Conduct Capability, and the Policy Unit—before these matters reach PSC's table. While the Council's CSDP apparatus helps to relieve PSC's workload, this division of labor has a key disadvantage. In the words of Christophe O. Meyer, "The proliferation of working groups and alternate formations on various issues also pose a problem to the overall coherence of the PSC machinery and its capacity to facilitate persuasion and attitude change."[43] Despite PSC's tangible presence in the area of CSDP, decision making involving civilian or military operations requires different types of expertise, and the delegation of certain aspects of planning to experts takes away from the ambassadors' ability to exercise independent agency, leaving them with a largely coordinating role.

How do the ambassadors make decisions in the area of CFSP/CSDP? The process tends to balance bargaining and persuasion. Larger member states sometimes have a disproportionate pull, as they can contribute most to an

CSDP operation.[44] Thus, meetings have a strong element of bargaining based on relative power. Lithuanian PSC ambassador Darius Jonas Semaška said, "Everyone has exactly the same chances to talk. We are all equal in the discussion around the table, but of course the opinion of the country participating most has bigger weight."[45] At the same time, there is room for persuasion. The quality of the argument itself is important. Each ambassador spends time crafting an argument to pitch to the others,[46] and all participants have a sense that they must be willing to listen to other points of view. Estonia's Soone reported that "persuasion and willingness to consider seriously the problems that the countries are bringing to others and the willingness to find the solution are all important."[47] When persuasion is the modus operandi, ambassadors may meet in advance of formal meetings to settle certain key issues.[48] But again, with growing pressure to spend a lot of time reading documents on short notice and with emergency meetings that last all day, holding advance meetings informally is challenging. Juncos and Reynolds argue that persuasion occurs more often than bargaining but that the process is better described as problem solving: PSC ambassadors "are there to sound out other national positions, gain information, and find out what is and is not possible."[49]

While PSC's role has grown alongside the expansion of CSDP, the ambassadors are not pushing for higher levels of cooperation or integration beyond the day-to-day management of these operations. The job of coordination is already a feat in itself, given the numerous and distinctive types of operations simultaneously being carried out. Meeting frequency may be high, but the meetings offer limited opportunities for socialization. A body of shared professional norms has not flourished beyond what typically exists in a diplomatic setting, and the norms that have evolved over time tend to emphasize expediency rather than a deliberative, persuasive process. This state of affairs is ultimately reflected in policy outcomes. Again, it is possible that the entire corpus of PSC's work may ultimately support more integration in the long run, but a strong epistemic community must behave as an agent for change that consciously shapes outcomes.

Common Culture

PSC ambassadors share a natural esprit de corps as a consequence of the amount of time they spend together and their common backgrounds. This esprit de corps gets stronger the longer each ambassador serves in Brussels. The average term is three to four years, which is somewhat longer than typical diplomatic postings. Such tenures give the ambassadors more fluency with the issues on which they work and enable them to obtain a wider body of knowledge pertaining to CFSP. After a while, they usually start to think from a Brussels-oriented perspective. For example, according to Estonian Antici delegate Klen Jäärats, "Our PSC ambassador has changed a lot in terms of CSDP. It is a learning process, and one in which he is going native."[50] The ambassadors feel that they understand each other well and that they can build relationships during informal meetings. The ambassadors from the newer member states are somewhat younger but are nonetheless very skillful at quickly internalizing the PSC's norms.[51] The growing importance of CFSP and CSDP also brings ambassadors together as they pursue common goals that are increasingly influencing the greater trajectory of EU integration.

Is this esprit de corps strong enough to support a common culture? Do ambassadors equate their interests with those of the group? Do they share substantive norms? Do their policy goals reflect their common expertise? To some extent, PSC ambassadors share a common sense of purpose and certain substantive norms, but these qualities tend to lack complexity. First, ambassadors speak a common language when it comes to security. As Dutch PSC ambassador Robert Milders said, "We have a common understanding of what security means. We are familiar with the ins and outs of our discussions. We don't need to explain to each other the basics. The negotiations are more about the detail, the practical side."[52] Similarly, the main controversy is not whether something constitutes a threat to security but how to prioritize various threats and what actions to take.[53]

Second, Howorth's interviews and surveys of PSC ambassadors show that they strongly support the development of CSDP and a security identity for the EU.[54] They, as well as decision makers in the member states, ultimately want CFSP/CSDP to succeed.[55] Thus, PSC's existence is predicated on a desire to find consensus, and capitals realize that compromising their positions may be necessary. This desire for consensus also manifests as a desire to speak with one voice whenever possible, a so-called consultation reflex.[56] Member states tend to look to Brussels before publicly stating their national positions. In addition, ambassadors indicate that the best strategy for conveying national preferences is to couch them in terms of what is good for the EU.[57] As Sipiläinen said,

> We are willing to have an EU common policy. This aspect is very strong, but we all realize that there are certain limits. We are trying to combine EU and national interests. We have to find a single voice somehow. Sometimes that voice is not always that loud, but it is improving. Some say that we are so intergovernmental nowadays, but we're doing much more than five years ago.[58]

Thus, the main aim is to speak with one voice, but instances often arise when ambassadors can only settle on a lowest common denominator. The specific circumstances of an issue determine whether it goes one way or the other.

Beyond this broad support for security cooperation and the basic ability to start negotiations on the same page, few substantive norms extend below the surface of these PSC relationships. Ambassadors do not see military capacity as a major part of their work and do not discuss it. Either the capacity exists or it does not, but they do not feel they can encourage member states to develop greater military capabilities. Furthermore, they see the goal of military interoperability as the purview of the ministers of defense and the EU Military Committee and as marginal to the PSC's work. They discuss interoperability only on a case-by-case basis. The ambassadors have different views on the connection between internal and external security and have no consensus in this arena. In Milders's view, "External security has nothing to do with internal policy. . . . There is no overlap."[59] French PSC representatives, in contrast, see multiple areas of overlap between the community pillar and external security but not with internal security.[60] Soone, the Estonian ambassador, recognized the relationship between internal and external security but emphasized that PSC does not discuss it in this way. Rather, "Coreper II takes the step to discuss the internal security issues that might be related to our negotiations."[61] Finally, each member state has different geographic goals. Estonia, for example, is more active in the Balkans and Eastern Europe. Portugal spearheaded the security sector reform operation in Guinea-Bissau, while France took the lead in Congo. Afghanistan is a rare example in that all member states see it as a priority.

Persuasion instead of bargaining is one of the main indications that individuals within an epistemic community align their interests with those of the group. PSC decision making is not simply about bargaining. If this were true, the UK, Germany, and France would frequently determine outcomes.[62] Rather, expertise and the personal qualities of ambassadors play a role. Sipiläinen said, "There are some who have more experience and have more weight in persuading. In all these kinds of groupings, it's really the person and his expertise and not as much the formal position of the member state."[63] Thus, expertise can translate into successful policy goals. But when does relative power and bargaining matter, and when do persuasion and expertise take over? Given the vast differences in the nature of instructions ambassadors receive from their capitals, whether an issue is resolved through bargaining or persuasion is determined on a case-by-case basis.

The Capitals-Brussels Transmission Belt

The dynamic between the capitals and their PSC ambassadors resembles a transmission belt more than any other relationship between the capitals and their representatives handling security policy in Brussels. PSC ambassadors are more concerned than other security actors about conveying national interests and consciously define themselves this way. They are not on such a short tether that they are obliged to read instructions out loud in meetings, but they believe that the process of finding consensus involves only some compromise and mostly consists of finding areas of natural overlap within the restrictions they are given. Meyer finds that PSC reflects a high level of cohesion with shared norms and high levels of trust. As long as ambassadors are working within this shared normative framework, he argues, they can often persuade each other by building a good case for something.[64] Similarly, Howorth argues that one strategy PSC ambassadors employ is to present their country's preferences as close as possible to where they believe the consensus lies. To do so, he argues, ambassadors must constantly be aware of the "collective mind-set," a process that is closer to consensus seeking than bargaining.[65] However, PSC falls short in achieving a persuasive, deliberative process in which ambassadors seek to persuade their capitals of compromise solutions that they have crafted on their own by virtue of their collective expertise.

PSC ambassadors are highly effective at overseeing coordination and cooperation after member states agree to engage in particular military operations or civilian missions. Howorth argues that PSC ambassadors can cite numerous examples of negotiations in which certain individuals started off with very different positions and were able to narrow the gap through deliberations and phone calls to the capitals, sometimes achieving unanimity.[66] In its role as crisis manager, PSC agrees to various documents that form critical steps in the CSDP process. Furthermore, the dossiers concluded at PSC's level are rarely reopened for further discussion at the ministerial level. Again, PSC ambassadors have remarkable success at managing cooperation, but little evidence indicates that they are consciously shaping the long-term trajectory of CSDP. And they are not pushing for new levels of security integration, as Coreper does. For example, they are potentially in a good position to encourage the use of battle groups (not yet ever deployed). They could also push member states to follow through with the original Headline Goal of having 60,000 rapid-reaction forces at the ready. They might also try to persuade capitals of the need for further capacity building and interoperability. These as well as other goals fall within the purview of PSC influence and would clearly smooth the path for all future CSDP initiatives. It may be that the ambassadors are too busy to take on these additional goals, but the fact remains that they have taken no concrete steps toward achieving them. In the end, despite being senior ambassadors with a high level of expertise, they fall short of achieving any significant level of collective agency.

One reason for this failure is that ambassadors have vastly differing degrees of maneuverability within their instructions. As Juncos and Reynolds argue, the degree of latitude depends on the member state, the ambassador's seniority, and the issue at stake.[67] Big member states may provide 50 pages of detailed instructions, whereas small member states may allow decisions to be made quickly and in Brussels. Slovenian deputy PSC ambassador Mirko Cigler said, "I've got four lines, and my French colleagues have four pages of instructions."[68] The length of the instructions typically reflects the importance of the issue, but it is understood that if instructions contain little room for maneuvering, the process will be difficult for the ambassador as well as the committee as a whole. Again, instructions serve as a formalized means of coordination and persuasion between governments and an epistemic community. A capital has leverage over its ambassadors through the formal instructions it issues, and ambassadors exercise agency by achieving flexibility with those instructions. But if the level of flexibility across member states differs substantially, collective agency becomes difficult, and a network is always stronger if it wields the strength of all its members.

PSC ambassadors report that they usually have flexibility and can get their states to change instructions within reason. According to Cigler, "It's not just what you got, but also how you use it." In some cases, flexibility may exist but ambassadors are still very closely watched. Whatever they say in meetings is closely scrutinized back in the capital.[69] In other cases, ambassadors must decide how much of personal risk they are willing to take by stretching the boundaries of their instructions. As French deputy PSC ambassador Didier Chabert said,

> We try first to negotiate with third delegations. We look for a compromise within the red lines of Paris. Before giving final word, we do have to check with Paris. We have to make sure it is within the red lines of Paris. Sometimes it is very obvious, and we don't have to check. When we have doubts, we have to cross-check with Paris.[70]

At the end of the day, ambassadors must be able to tell their capitals that they arrived at a consensus agreement without violating any national red lines. PSC ambassadors often call their capitals in the middle of meetings to convey the consensus and find out whether they have the go-ahead. This practice may allow PSC ambassadors' to acquire a bit more flexibility.

Adam Sambrook, who instructs PSC ambassadors from London, expressed the idea that these diplomats are essentially negotiating within the spaces between their red lines: "There are sharp red lines, but not insofar as they are restrictive. We give people in Brussels flexibility."[71] The Portuguese director for security and defense affairs, João Pedro Antunes, who previously served in Brussels during his country's presidency, said that he is particularly sensitive about ensuring that his ambassador has flexibility with instructions: "Unless it's a key issue and we want to be strict about the output, all 27 have to agree. I let the ambassador manage with a free hand. The meeting can go in a different direction."[72] He is often asked to change the instructions because of a compromise reached in Brussels.

> Every member state is persuaded by negotiations in Brussels. In the end, we have to compromise, and sometimes we are convinced by others' arguments. On many issues, we don't have a strict position from the start. . . .We are Europe-oriented.[73]

However, ambassadors rarely do the persuading because that type of two-way, interactive teamwork usually happens at lower levels, especially with Civcom or the Political Military Group. When asked whether decisions are made primarily in Lisbon or in Brussels, Antunes explained,

> In our area, by far most [decisions are] determined in Brussels, $1/3$ in Lisbon at most. Many issues are very technical, and probably we're fine either way. We have a very small structure in Lisbon, and it is very difficult to follow very technical issues. We are not always motivated to look into technical details here. There's a head of division and one desk officer. It's much easier to follow if you are in the meetings. It's much easier if you are sitting there.[74]

Thus, the British and Portuguese perspectives show variation in the degree of flexibility, with the latter having more.

The story is also different in the Hague, where the Ministry of Foreign Affairs has a complex and formal process for compiling and synthesizing instructions from many different government departments. The instructions are eventually uploaded to a secure computer database that is accessible to ambassadors all over the world and visible to everyone with security clearance. Pronk said, "Sometimes PSC ambassadors may say that they don't need instructions, but we say you need clear guidance. You need framework instructions. We need to be able to react, and ministers must be informed."[75] According to Pronk, Dutch PSC ambassadors have often called the capital and asked for more flexibility with instructions, but "usually the answer is no. He has to stick to it, and fight for it, and tough luck that you're alone. The minister will stick to it also at the Council. We try to find a compromise, but on some issues there's a principled stance."[76] As in the Portuguese example, any changes to instructions are far more likely to happen at the Civcom level, where the two-way interaction between the capital and Brussels remains relatively informal. Henrick van Asch of the Dutch Ministry of Foreign Affairs's Security Policy Department said, "The PSC is like an oil tanker. It can't change course very quickly. Once things are agreed to in Civcom, they can't really be changed. Otherwise, it takes quite drastic measures."[77]

The Lithuanian ambassador barely receives instructions at all. According to Semaška, "We didn't have thorough discussions on whether it is in Lithuania's interest to have a stronger military pillar in the EU because it's not a matter of our participation. We have limited resources, and we concentrate all of them on NATO."[78] Ambassadors who have less to contribute in terms of security have less in the way of instructions, but they also lose influence.

Given PSC ambassadors' high levels of skill and experience, it is not surprising to find, as some scholars do, that on some occasions certain ambassadors persuade their capitals to compromise their positions. Juncos and Reynolds argue that "interaction in Brussels-based committees can and frequently does impact upon the definition of preferences."[79] While this is certainly true, it is important to take into account that member states differ in the way they instruct these particular ambassadors and the extent to which they are willing to grant flexibility. They tend to engage in two-way diplomacy with those in lower-ranked groups such as Civcom rather than PSC, although Coreper still benefits from a high degree of flexibility. In sum, the PSC-capital dynamic as well as the processes within PSC itself mean that this particular knowledge-based network has a moderate basis—in comparison to Coreper—for influencing outcomes beyond what instructions allow.

THE INSTITUTIONALIZATION OF EXTERNAL
SECURITY COOPERATION

At the broadest level, PSC negotiates three major types of issues. First, it strives to craft a common EU voice in response to international crises or incidences, like the 2008–9 Georgia-Russia crisis, the 2007–8 Kosovo bid for independence, and various human rights violations around the world. Second, it discusses and manages ongoing relationships with third parties such as the African Union, Iran, and Russia. Third, it oversees CSDP operations and missions from inception to withdrawal. The bulk of PSC's work is in the third category. However, outcomes might have been improved in several ways if PSC had taken a more active role and used its collective expertise to improve the process. CSDP missions may evolve quickly, but PSC need only focus on short-term exigencies. Decision making can be improved with each new mission, and lessons can be learned.

PSC has not streamlined the overly complex process of CSDP operational decision making in Brussels, making it very difficult for implementation to be coherent on the ground. A recent report from the European Council on Foreign Relations (ECFR), which is admittedly harsh in tone, argues that the PSC is guilty of bureaucratic mismanagement. The report criticizes PSC for falling victim to naive transference (applying a previous model to a new situation even though the conditions are very different), ignoring the advice of officers on the ground, micromanaging missions, and neglecting to build connections between internal and external security bodies in Brussels.[80] Essentially, PSC makes it difficult for those on the operational side—the crisis management experts on location—to carry out their work effectively. The ambassadors send out a constant flow of e-mails and instructions to those carrying out CSDP operations, but these documents are often not very practical. Micromanagement from afar cannot take into account day-to-day risks, the nuances of the local situation, and the need to act decisively in response to new developments. The ECFR report concludes that PSC ambassadors are misusing their time "to focus on trivialities as a proxy for substantive discussion" and that the ambassadors' interactions with operatives provide "little strategic guidance but instead a stream of instructions about operational matters they are in a better position to decide upon themselves."[81]

PSC clearly has a strong coordination reflex that has played a role in institutionalizing external security cooperation, but it does not often push beyond immediate exigency to find longer-term solutions. For example, the EU's Chad mission, which took place from January 2008 to March 2009, resulted in a flurry of PSC discussions about the shortage of helicopters. Chabert recalled, "We needed six transport helicopters and three combat helicopters. We had no ability to find these helicopters because everywhere there was a lack of them. They were all off in different locations."[82] The PSC had to ask external partners to provide the helicopters, and Russia ultimately made up the shortfall. In the first half of 2009, the Czech presidency scheduled a Helicopter Initiative Seminar to address this problem, but it was attended by military experts from NATO and the EU. Although PSC has firsthand knowledge about what capability shortfalls mean for the success of CSDP, it is "usually a marginal issue" in PSC deliberations.[83] Thus, PSC effectively slaps a Band-Aid on the problem of capabilities instead of trying to make some headway in addressing the disease.

While the record shows a veritable flood of new CSDP operations and missions in a relatively short period of time, PSC has been bogged down with minutiae instead of grappling with the greater trajectory of security policy in Europe. As such, it has done little to establish a workable template for the future. Such an effort would likely require the ambassadors to exert a stronger persuasive force on behalf of soft integration. It would certainly require at least the recognition that internal and external security and civilian and military instruments need to be brought together. A significant reason why institutionalized cooperation in the external security area has occurred—apart from PSC consensus building—is that the decision to launch a new CSDP mission does not require that all member states participate. The silence procedure enables those member states that do not wish to contribute simply to refrain from objection. Enough participation is required only that the mission forward, but the end result is that most of the missions are not quite as strong as they should be. This phenomenon is particularly acute on the civilian crisis management side. The 2003 police mission in Macedonia lacked 30 percent of the required personnel, and the current police mission in Afghanistan lacks 50 percent.[84] If PSC ambassadors used their persuasive expertise to influence member states' choices, CSDP missions could have greater participation, lessening the burden on each country and enabling a quicker resolution of crises.

COMPLEMENTARY OR COMPETING DIPLOMATIC COMMUNITIES?

PSC has the potential to be enormously powerful, especially as CSDP grows in scope and range.[85] Much of its potential influence lies in its broad-ranging responsibilities under the Nice Treaty. It would be natural to expect PSC to constitute a strong epistemic community. After all, little differentiates these ambassadors from those in Coreper: They clearly share diplomatic and EU expertise, and the CSDP area has broadened rapidly over the past ten years. When these ambassadors arrive in Brussels, however, they find relatively limited opportunity to meet informally, develop strong professional norms that go beyond those typically found in the diplomatic profession, and they ultimately share a broad-based culture that lacks deeper and more specific substantive norms. Consequently, PSC's shaping of its identity and role reflects a rather narrow focus on CSDP crisis management. While this was their intended formal role, stronger epistemic communities would have pushed beyond their boundaries. Instead, PSC ambassadors tend to operate on a case-by-case basis, and the range of flexibility across member states varies sharply according to national circumstances and what is at stake.

Qualities fundamental to this community of ambassadors will likely preclude it from exercising high levels of agency in the future but go some considerable distance toward fostering cooperation among member states. PSC's contribution to cooperative outcomes under the Common Foreign and Security Policy is no small matter, but in comparison to other groups, it has done relatively little to take CSDP beyond cooperation. One may question whether cooperation itself is PSC's shared goal and thus claim that the measure of success lies somewhere short of integration. However, this idea would be somewhat counterintuitive and not entirely accurate. Ambassadors stress that their overarching goal is for the EU to speak with one voice in the external security realm. In the words of Quentin Weiler, the French chargé de mission for the PSC,

> The whole idea is that the EU is stronger united than divided. We are not playing name and shame. Unanimity is required so we have to take on board everyone. That plays a key role. Unanimity obliges you to find a compromise.

As diplomats generally do, PSC members define success as a compromise solution. Integration by definition institutionalizes compromise and enables a group to make a permanent mark. While it is understandable that decision makers in the capitals would be content simply to achieve consensus based on each circumstance as it arises, high-level diplomats typically strive for more, for a variety of reasons. Consensus is achieved simply by finding areas of overlap or identifying the lowest common denominator.

Another important lesson from this case study is that the EU's diplomat decision makers are highly compartmentalized with regard to security policy. While Coreper ambassadors see an intimate connection between internal and external security, they focus on the former and look for ways to create synergies with the latter. PSC ambassadors tend to see less connection between the two and to work exclusively on external security. Compartmentalization or fragmentation of policy areas may provide one explanation for the EU's rapid progress in internal security integration but less progress in the external arena.

This strong division of labor may afford ambassadors more time to focus on their own specialties, progressing further than would otherwise be possible if all tasks fell into a single ambassador's portfolio. At the same time, segmentation means that related policy areas are not discussed together as much as they could be or as much as might be expected given their inherent interconnectedness. To the extent that coordination between internal and external security occurs, it happens in the capitals, in Coreper, or informally among ambassadors from the same permanent representation. Given this procedural pattern, integration would seem to be quite hampered. Indeed, Howorth writes, "With so many cooks in the kitchen, it is, in some ways, amazing that any broth is produced at all. And yet, decisions *are* taken, policy *is* made and CSDP *has,* over the last few years, gone rapidly from strength to strength."[86] The puzzle is why integration has actually progressed relatively quickly despite this compartmentalization.

The strength of Coreper has been the main source of diplomatic influence, with PSC playing a relatively weaker role as a moderate-strength epistemic community. Romanian Antici delegate Alina Padeanu explained that overlap exists between internal and external security but that "Coreper puts the pieces together. . . . PSC is a preliminary discussion. Everything except discussion of the [C]SDP missions goes to Coreper."[87] Coreper looks at the whole picture: PSC's contributions are complimentary to Coreper's work but do little to help achieve Coreper's aims. Rather, the EU Military Committee and to some extent the Civilian Crisis Management Committee are doing more to advance integrative processes on the external side and to enhance synergies with internal security.

As security integration accelerates, so does fragmentation of key groups. Austria's Schweisgut noted that "over time, it's been difficult to maintain the central role of Coreper as coordinating and directing everything. Once the EU is deeply integrated in an area, specialized bodies emerge."[88] While it seemed necessary to offload key aspects of CFSP/CSDP to the PSC given Coreper's growing workload, too much fragmentation can certainly slow the process of integration and make it difficult to see the big picture.

CHAPTER 5

The Military Community

"Around the world, militaries are identical, not just very similar. If you have a group like the [EU] military committee and have a question of organization or efficiency of organization or a particular military operation, there will be consensus around the table."

—GENERAL JO COELMONT, FORMER BELGIAN EUMC REPRESENTATIVE[1]

IN THE CONTEXT OF EU security integration, the military representatives (milreps) of the European Union Military Committee (EUMC) lie at the core of a wider epistemic community that extends below them in the military hierarchy, above them in the capitals, around them in their national and EU-level defense staff offices, and horizontally to their counterparts in other international organizations and third-country operations. Each representative in the EUMC rarely acts as an individual.[2] Together they form a hub of influence, but feeding into their decisions are a variety of actors.

The dynamic between the chiefs of defense and their milreps in Brussels is not unlike that between member states' ministers and the Brussels-based Coreper ambassadors on the political-diplomatic side. A relatively strong transnational network of high-level military officials exists in Europe, although they have only recently coalesced into an epistemic community. With the combined newness of both external security policy and an emerging EU military capability, the EUMC has so far had a minimal impact on hard integration in terms of concrete outcomes. However, the cohesiveness and persuasiveness of this network are high, and they have triggered processes of Europeanization or soft integration. Of the EU's various transnational security actors, the EUMC is a good indicator of the future trajectory of security integration on the external side and is therefore an important group to which to pay attention.

Milreps meet frequently in informal settings, share tangible professional norms, benefit from similar training, and have a strong common culture. In particular, the EUMC's internal processes of cooperation result in very quick consensus, even on nuances, and evidence suggests that its long-term impact on capabilities planning may be significant.[3] Yet the military representatives are not simply fulfilling national instructions but are also exercising collective agency. One of the central qualities underlying the strength of this epistemic community is that although it is relatively new and has yet to have a wide-ranging impact, it benefits from centuries of military culture and tradition in Europe. Karen Dunivin defines military culture as "learned (via socialization training such as boot camp); broadly shared by its members (e.g., saluting); adaptive to changing conditions . . . ; and symbolic in nature (e.g., rank insignia and language jargon make sense only within a military context)."[4]

Military culture is distinctive from strategic culture, which Paul Cornish and Geoffrey Edwards define as "the institutional confidence and processes to manage and deploy military force as part of the accepted range of legitimate and effective policy instruments."[5] Strategic culture, for example, might indicate the extent to which a particular society is militaristic. In this sense, it is more closely related to a country's overarching military doctrine. Military culture, by contrast, shapes the practice of daily life in the military and the context in which officers carry out tactical decisions. The historical backdrop for military culture in Europe—and to a lesser extent strategic culture, among other things—firmly differentiates the military epistemic community from other relatively new epistemic communities, such as that of technology experts (chapter 6). The rich historical background underpinning military culture today does not necessarily lead to a strong epistemic community, just as the shared background of Coreper and the Political and Security Committee (PSC) has not led both of those groups to form strong epistemic communities.

Given that countries in Europe have fought many long and violent wars, it might be hard to imagine that any element of transnational military culture could lend support to some level of normative convergence. While this chapter focuses on the current military epistemic community, European military transnationalism has a basis in the seventeenth century. Prior to early state building, evidence also shows a kind of transgeographic diffusion of military culture and expertise. The spread of ideas and level of interaction among military officials might not have been strong enough to constitute an epistemic community per se, but shifting alliance formations and professional learning at times brought various key individuals together, resulting in some degree of ideational diffusion and normative convergence. Just as in the case of the diplomatic epistemic community, it is not possible to point to any path dependence or inevitability in the existence of a military epistemic community, but historic developments shed some light on the conditions that enable such a community to exist today.

At the same time, the story of military epistemic communities in Europe is not as clear-cut as that of the diplomatic side, not least because soldiers and diplomats have essentially opposite aims: the former to vanquish an opponent, and the latter to prevent conflict. Thus, while an epistemic community of diplomats has existed in varying strengths since at least the seventeenth century,[6] the same cannot be said of a community of high-ranking military officials. Although military experts were studying each other's strategies, developing the same kind of expertise, and interacting with each other to the point that it is possible to speak to some degree of a coherent Western military organization,[7] the military epistemic community that exists today was never inevitable, and its existence is to a significant degree predicated on the formation of the EU.

The following section highlights some historical patterns behind the development of European military culture. Each civilization or nation has very specific and distinctive elements to its military norms and practices, but some important similarities exist and provide a foundation for current developments. The bulk of the chapter analyzes the EUMC's internal dynamics and agency and how its members have collectively influenced the Long-Term Vision for European Defence Capability and Capacity Needs, setting in motion an important component of external security integration.

HISTORICAL CONTEXT

The work of military officials has as old a vintage as that of diplomats. The groundwork for the EU military epistemic community was laid gradually over centuries. Despite much evidence for varying degrees of transnationalism over time, whether these relationships and interactions before the second half of the twentieth century could be characterized as an epistemic community is open to question. However, a brief look at the historical development of military, knowledge, expertise, and transnational (or trans-

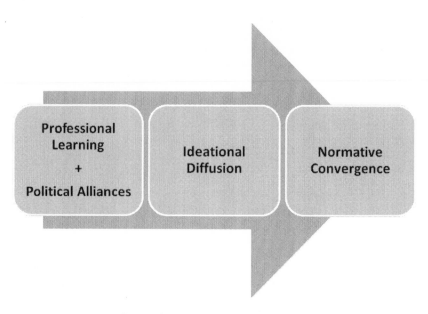

Fig. 7. The diffusion of military ideas

geographic) interactions sheds some light on the foundations of today's military epistemic community. Over the course of European history, ideas have been shared across geographic space primarily through (1) professional learning or emulation and (2) political-military alliances (figure 7).

Before the gradual consolidation of the modern nation-state and at least as far back as ancient Greece and Rome, military conflict and the accompanying military culture, norms, and philosophy have been a part of human existence. Critical distinctions existed, even within supposedly similar cultural communities such as Sparta and Athens.[8] But military cultures were often tangible and enduring, with new generations of warriors and commanders socialized into existing cultures with the passage of time. Following ancient Greece, the military culture of the Roman Empire was based on strict discipline, training, and esprit de corps. Professional training and hierarchy were sharply delineated. The Roman military machinery was so central to daily life that an enormous proportion of state activity was wrapped up in running it. Since at least several centuries B.C., high-level military officers in both Greek and Roman civilizations studied each other's conquests and learned how best to strategize based on their successes and failures.

The experiences of these ancient civilizations served as a common history for the militaries that arose centuries later. In other words, professional learning occurred across both space and time. Ancient Greek philosophers such as Thucydides, Herodotus, and Xenophon wrote rich accounts of the details of battle and military life during their lifetimes. Similarly, Polybius, Onasander, and Julius Caesar preserved the memory of military strategy and daily life during the Roman Empire, creating a common legacy for the future. Many of these writings survived, and the advent of the printing press in the fifteenth century facilitated their spread. By the sixteenth century, works such as Onasander's *The General (Strategicus)* were translated and circulated throughout France, Spain, England, the Low Countries, and the various German and Italian territories.[9] These accounts have often served as a basis for the training of soldiers and officers and have influenced military strategy in countless areas and times. It is therefore no surprise to find eighteenth-century commander Marshal Maurice de Saxe citing Onasander's writings as critical to battle planning or the early-twentieth-century Count Alfred von Schlieffen studying Polybius's description of Roman tactics through historian Hans Delbrück's account. Military leaders simply used these texts to learn their craft.

The premodern era generally saw adaptation rather than growth of military knowledge. Although circumstances of warfare changed, sometimes dramatically, with advances in military technology, the process of professional learning remained more or less the same for some time, with generals and commanders learning from allies and enemies alike as well as reading and emulating the same military philosophers.

Long before nation-states began to emerge, from the ancient period through the medieval and early modern eras, military alliances were common. In ancient Greece, critical alliances included the Hellenic League, the League of Delos, and the Peloponnesian League. The conflicts between and within the Christian and Islamic worlds in the Middle Ages led to numerous military alliances spanning Europe, the Middle East, and North Africa. The later dynastic struggles between Habsburg and Valois, Ottoman and Safavid blurred significant lines between supposedly fundamentally disparate worldviews. And the Thirty Years' War (1618–48) saw states divided not only into the Catholic League and Protestant Union but also and simultaneously allied with their confessional opposites. Virtually no major conflict in European history failed to involve some kind of coalition or alliance of powers. These conflicts also provided high-level commanders, generals, and admirals with opportunities to strategize more broadly, learn from each other, and create plans together based on potential scenarios. Sharing, adapting, and emulating tactical knowledge of battle planning was generally uncontroversial in comparison to the grand strategies of political leaders, which often caused wars. Some of these plans were ultimately enshrined into treaties.

Once the modern nation-state began to coalesce in the seventeenth century, the two processes of military learning and alliance formation came to entail a degree of transnationalism. But at the same time as the ability to communicate and share information was facilitated with advances such as the telegraph and railroad, the rise of territorial boundaries and political identity made it more difficult for military officials at the top to learn from each other. In some ways, the rise of the nation-state created barriers and meant that military strategies and tactics had to be guarded in the interest of sovereignty. Nations were much more concerned with maintaining any possible military advantage, leading to secrecy.

The outcome of nation-building remained uncertain for a long period, and political organization remained very fluid. Different forms of governance emerged—city-states, city leagues, and empires—before Europe at last settled on the modern nation-state. The continent is arguably now going through a transformation of a different sort in the form of EU integration, and it is starting to resemble the premodern era in a number of ways. In the early modern period, however, the rise of military organization was heavily tied to the rise of centralized nation-states.[10] A rich historical literature describes how technological innovation in military weaponry necessitated the creation of certain political structures to pay the cost and manage the administration of war, favoring larger political units that had the resources to create these structures and pay these costs. For example, the advent of gunpowder weapons and subsequent building of defenses against these weapons could only be handled by the central state. Technological advances and knowledge about strategies for countering new weaponry similarly spread across Europe. A variety of factors converged—military technology, the rise of the nation-state, the concentration of military power, and state sovereignty—to increase the scale of war in Europe during this period.[11] Nevertheless, technological advances also meant that borders were no longer as porous, and militaries could keep their borders more or less secure.

Although the concept of transnationalism entered the political science debate in the 1970s, it is not simply an invention of the late twentieth century. Specifically, military culture, know-how, and professionalism have crossed borders—either inadvertently or through purposeful contact and political alliances—for quite some time. Even before the rise of nation-states as the primary form of political organization, various types of military coalitions or alliances sought more efficient warfare or shared goals. With the advent of nation-states, this type of interaction became literally transnational, but in practice, it differed only slightly from earlier interactions. In the modern era, the nature of military alliances is quite broad. They are sometimes backed by treaties but at other times are informal; they can be bilateral but are also often multilateral; some include security guarantees, while others do not.[12] Perhaps the most well known more recent alliances were those in the lead-up to the First World War (when the Russian Empire, the United Kingdom, and France were the main countries allied against Germany, Austria-Hungary, and Italy, among others) and in the lead-up to the Second World War (when the British Empire, United States, and Soviet Union were the biggest powers allied against Germany, Italy, and Japan). In both cases, alliances shifted over the course of these wars, and many small and medium-sized countries also became involved. Standard accounts of military history should thus be considered in a different light, one that shows not simply nations jostling for power and survival but also shifts in the balance of power that enabled the spread of military ideas, doctrines, tactics, and expertise. In the early to mid–twentieth century, alliances brought together different powers, providing the context for convergence, especially in Western Europe.

With the founding of the North Atlantic Treaty Organization (NATO) in 1949, multilateralism became permanent among certain Western European countries and the United States. The fall of the Berlin Wall forty years later, advances in communications technology, and subsequent enlargements of NATO have further increased transnational interactions within this multilateral framework. A few studies have examined the question of whether and to what extent transnational networks exist within NATO—security communities, epistemic communities, and communities of practice.[13] While the study of specific transnational networks within NATO is beyond the scope of this volume, it is not difficult to imagine that a nascent epistemic community might have been percolating among early NATO officials. Today, at least one cohesive epistemic community of military generals exists. But the extent to which transnational networks of security officials and experts within NATO have been able to convince their capitals of their goals is open to debate.

From ancient Greece to the founding of NATO, military culture and expertise spread across space and time through learning and alliance formation. It was not inevitable that this diffusion of ideas would result in more convergence, and fluctuations certainly occurred in the level of cohesiveness of shared military culture over time. But after the two world wars all but destroyed Europe, a more linear trajectory toward convergence began to emerge in military practices and norms. In contrast to events on the diplomatic side during the same period, these processes could never have resulted in anything far beyond a nascent or short-lived epistemic community because of the circumstances of war and the shifting compositions of allies and enemies. The business of war is simply not the same as the business of diplomacy.

The founding of NATO certainly constituted a critical juncture in terms of the contextual and structural factors conducive to the flourishing of epistemic communities. Moreover, the military side of Common Security and Defence Policy (CSDP) is not entirely separable from NATO. Perhaps NATO paved the way for the security component of EU integration, but that is an entirely different debate. While NATO boasts a high degree of cooperation and coordination, with more than 60 years of solid, institutional memory under its belt, the nature of NATO's functions and structures still to some extent restrains the potential impact of epistemic communities, while CSDP's functions and structures are more conducive to the influence of such communities.

THE EMERGING MILITARY EPISTEMIC COMMUNITY

The EU Military Committee is central to the process of security integration in Europe. It was established by a January 22, 2001, Council decision. The committee is formally composed of chiefs of defense (CHODs) of the member states, but in practice it comprises their permanent military representatives.[14] The CHODs come to Brussels only twice each year to participate in the committee. The chief of the EUMC must be a four-star officer, while the other committee members who represent the CHODs should hold the rank of a three-star general or admiral. The Council's decision stipulates that "the EUMC is responsible for providing the PSC with military advice and recommendations on all military matters within the EU. It exercises military direction of all military activities within the EU framework."[15] The EUMC is charged with carrying out the Petersberg Tasks,[16] the European Security Strategy,[17] and EU operations in third countries.

On June 11, 2001, the EU Military Staff, consisting today of around 200 civilian and military personnel, was established to assist the EUMC by preparing draft papers and proposals. The EUMC Working Group, populated by lieutenant colonels, is also a critical lower-level support structure for the committee's work. The members of the working group are an important part of the military epistemic community as well, although they are not as central to outcomes as the EUMC.[18] Representatives from the Council Secretariat and Commission always participate in formal meetings, and the heads of the EU Military Staff and the European Defence Agency are frequently present as well.

The EUMC is the highest-level military body of the European Union, but it is only a midlevel committee in the Council, technically ranked below the PSC. This status indicates the newness of EU military power. While several other actors in both the Council and the member states are heavily involved in the preparation of military advice, the EUMC is where the final stage of consensus is achieved among member states regarding military CSDP. Each country's security agendas are developed according to its domestic governance structures and traditions. But in the realm of EU security policy, capitals' preferences are also significantly shaped by two-way dialogue with their representatives in the EUMC.

With a few exceptions, military representatives are double-hatted—that is, represent their countries simultaneously in both the EU and NATO.[19] For NATO, the milreps are just one step below the North Atlantic Council (NAC). For the EU, they generally handle three types of tasks. First, they perform the typical role of high-level military officers, discussing what is happening on the ground in EU operations, receiving briefings from operational commanders, and determining long-term needs. Second, they deliberate on issues that need an immediate decision, such as planning CSDP operations. They determine the requirements and contributions from the member states and try to reach consensus before passing their advice to the PSC ambassadors. Finally, they have ongoing discussions on informal issues, checking each other's points of view and figuring out what is possible before any formal proposals are put forward on such matters as future operations, ongoing security challenges, and prospective projects (for example, the installation of an air traffic management system).[20]

How can a midlevel Council committee comprise an epistemic community? An epistemic community may or may not be embedded in a formal structure. It is often more difficult to recognize such a community that is part of an official bureaucracy, since its members are simply assumed to be doing their jobs. Thus, it is important to look beyond a transgovernmental group's formal role to see if it is acting as more than the sum of its parts. Does the committee accomplish more than its official purpose? Do its members share expertise, possess a common culture, and meet informally outside of the committee structure? Did they perhaps know each other before their appointments?

The EUMC is a relatively cohesive Brussels-based committee with a wealth of shared expertise; a rich culture of shared professional norms and common values; a high frequency of informal meetings, enabling persuasion to occur and compromises to be found; and a significant level of trust among members and from their individual capitals. The internal qualities of the committee—selection and training, shared professional norms, common culture, and meeting frequency—have smoothed the path to compromise on a variety of issues, including in the context of EUNAVFOR Atalanta and EUFOR Chad and long-term capabilities development.

Selection and Training

High-ranking military officials have a specific, authoritative claim on technical knowledge that comes from career experience, education, and training. EUMC military representatives have spent an average of 35 years in their countries' militaries, working their way up through the ranks.[21] They have previously served as commanders and chiefs of staff, attended military academies, and served as faculty at defense colleges, among other experiences.[22] In 2009, at least eleven EUMC members had received advanced midcareer training in the United States, and all but two had received training outside of their own country. At least one held a doctorate, and two held master's degrees. Seven attended the NATO Defense College in Rome, five went to Washington, D.C., to further their education at the National Defense University, and a handful attended the U.S. Army War College in Carlisle, Pennsylvania. Most were posted to either NATO or the UN earlier in their careers. The remarkable similarities in training and education contribute to a culture of shared values within the broader epistemic community. Many of these representatives have decades of experience with the defense industry, providing advice on security policy research, leading military operations, and working on multilateral issues.[23]

What type of expertise results from this wealth of experience? The most technical type of knowledge that high-level military officers possess is tactical expertise, defined as the best way to execute military strategy on the ground, especially on the battlefield. This specialized knowledge has increasingly come to encompass a range of other military activities in which states are occupied, such as crisis management, civil-military relations, and humanitarian intervention. EUMC generals find reaching compromise on military advice involving tactical knowledge unproblematic. Training and career experiences, alongside the historical learning underpinning the military profession, has resulted in a body of shared knowledge that is virtually taken for granted at their level of expertise. It is firmly a part of the practice of military thinking and deliberation at these upper echelons of the profession. If EUMC members disagree about tactics, it is usually because there is a lack of information about certain conditions on the ground. As Belgian general Jo Coelmont put it, "If we have different opinions, then we look for better intelligence."[24] When they acquire the intelligence to clarify the situation, they can agree very quickly on tactics. In short, if a political mandate is in place, they will likely reach consensus on what to do in the field.

Tactical expertise is clearly a major component of what makes this military epistemic community uniquely valuable to the EU's external security goals.[25] This particular type of expertise must be distinguished from military doctrine and grand strategy, both of which are more political in nature.[26] While military doctrine is an important part of the EUMC's work, grand strategy typically occupies policymakers. Grand strategy is the act of keeping a given territory secure and determining the overarching security goals of a state or political entity. High-level military officers are often asked to provide advice on grand strategy, but they do not determine such strategy in a democracy. If a state is about to engage in or is the middle of war, grand strategy also includes the overarching plan about how to conduct the campaign and win.

Military doctrine, conversely, is in some ways just as central to the work of these military officials as tactical expertise. It is defined as "how one wages war, including ideas about how best to fight the enemy and assumptions about what part of the enemy is most important."[27] Thus, it is one level removed from tactical expertise, but not so political that it constitutes grand strategy. Deborah Avant argues that "most agree that doctrine falls between the technical details of tactics and the broad outline of grand strategy."[28] It also encompasses strategic culture, the institutional ability to determine effective use of force and the shared norms that legitimate use of force in a given scenario.

To the extent that EUMC milreps encounter obstacles, they are almost always in the form of political disagreements coming from PSC ambassadors or their capitals. Red lines from the capitals can make consensus impossible at the EUMC level. However, if the political barriers are more related to doctrine than to grand strategy, military representatives can help resolve disagreements by finding technical solutions with political impact. Just because milreps are very skilled when it comes to finding consensus on tactical advice does not mean they are apolitical. At the same time, they will avoid as much as possible providing advice that is politicized. That is, they will strive to ensure that their tactical military advice reflects their objective, professional expertise rather than any kind of national, group, or personal interest. As British general David Bill said, "We are trying to challenge politicized arguments. There is a difference between this and taking into account the political side."[29] In other words, the EUMC consistently seeks to add political value while avoiding politicized military advice.

Much of the literature addressing the role of militaries in international relations tends to focus on military doctrine rather than tactical expertise and often characterizes it within the realist or rationalist framework.[30] In terms of military doctrine, organizational theorists argue that militaries will strive for success in battle, low uncertainty about outcomes, and autonomy from political interference. Realist arguments generally support the idea that military doctrines tend to be offensive.[31] But other scholars argue that military doctrines can conform to a variety of typologies—defensive, innovative, static, and deterrent doctrines. Avant contends, for example, that military doctrines can also adjust based on the strategic needs of a state.[32] In effect, military doctrine is a subset of grand strategy. In the case of the EU, military doctrine tends to conform to organizational theorists' expectations while adjusting as the EU's grand strategy evolves. One aspect of the EUMC's added value is a keen awareness that if the group allows an operation to go forward and it is not successful, CSDP would experience a major setback from which recovery could take 15–20 years.[33]

Because of this awareness, the role of expertise can equally mean that the EUMC may advise against potential EU operations despite political agreement. For example, political actors were interested in sending a battle group to Congo's Kivu province to help protect refugees and provide aid, but the military view was that doing so was impractical. There were not enough troops, the region was in the middle of Africa, and the lack of roads was a problem. Military representatives thus advised against using a battle group, and their expertise affected the political outcome.[34]

In terms of long-term military planning, especially capabilities development, some degree of transnational convergence has occurred with regard to EU military doctrine. This convergence is more visible within the EUMC than in member states' ministries of defense.[35] A long-term perspective is an important part of evolving EU military doctrine because it involves making decisions about how the EU will wage war as a collective in the future, what types of threats member states will face and where to focus capabilities development. Because of their unique, authoritative claim on knowledge, milreps exert influence both on short-term decisions about whether to embark on an operation and on the long-term trajectory of defense planning. The European Defence Agency (EDA) is designed to help member states achieve these goals, but it cannot deliver anything until the EUMC articulates the common will.

In the context of the EU, common or EU-level grand strategy is still extremely narrow, since CSDP itself is still a small policy area. So far, all external security goals are humanitarian or secondary to the immediate security threats to EU territory. Most EU member states are individually quite weak in the area of traditional military capabilities and defense. To the extent that the EU projects hard power, outsiders will often only pay attention to a handful of member states—Italy, France, the UK, and Germany—all of which have vastly different priorities. Smaller member states may not constitute a significant part of the EU's external image, but they are still involved in creating a common grand strategy.

In sum, there are three main types of military expertise. At the most technical level, EU military representatives share identical tactical expertise. Knowledge about shaping successful military doctrines, while more political in nature, also falls within the domain of EUMC influence, both in terms of short-term and long-term planning. The latter will be discussed in more depth in the case-study of the Long-Term Vision.[36] Grand strategy, however, falls fully within the political realm of decision making and is thus the prerogative of democratically elected leaders. Over time, however, the exigencies of military doctrine can affect grand strategy, especially from a longer-term perspective. Overall, expertise in shaping successful military doctrines and determining battlefield tactics are the key tools of the EU Military Committee. Those who play a supportive function in the wider epistemic community—in capitals and the Council—also share in this kind of expertise. As French general Patrick de Rousiers said, "We have trust in each other due to previous backgrounds, trust in that what we say will not be our own operation, but an operation that has been matured by ourselves, team, and capital."[37] The high level of professionalism and objectivity with which milreps determine their military advice provides them with a great advantage in seeking to influence outcomes.

Meetings and Professional Norms

The processes within an epistemic community are a key part of whether it succeeds at shaping policy outcomes. An epistemic community must be internally cohesive to be persuasive as a group, and the amount of time that members of an epistemic community spend together makes cohesiveness possible. Quantity of meetings is one simple measure of cohesiveness, but digging deeper also requires considering the quality of the meetings—that is, if a meeting is too formal or structured for the individuals to speak openly, then it is less productive. An esprit de corps will naturally arise when meetings are frequent, but an epistemic community requires more. When the quality of meetings is high, shared professional norms are robust. Meetings must be an opportunity for real deliberation. The strength of common culture and the quality of meetings are mutually constitutive, as meetings are the primary forums in which professional norms are expressed and culture is consolidated.

Formal EUMC meetings are held every Wednesday, and additional meetings are quickly scheduled if there is a crisis. Representatives really make decisions during the informal meetings, outside the walls of NATO. They have frequent working coffees and dinners at each other's homes—on average, three or four times per week, but with dinner five times in a week not unusual.[38] In addition, there is a reception with each presidency as well as "away-day" visits to EU military operations—for example, in Chad.[39] When their schedules allow, military representatives also meet at conferences, seminars, and think-tank events. In particular, NATO-CSDP generals and ex-generals, as part of the wider military epistemic community, regularly participate in these types of outside seminars. All of these events are all good opportunities for military representatives to get to know each other and, most important, to gain a sense of what the others are thinking before they are on the spot at their official meetings. Informal meetings are also where milreps pick up new subjects that may appear on the agenda in the future.[40]

Milreps spend most of their time in their NATO offices, whether they are working on NATO or EU issues, but Wednesdays are generally spent at the EU's Council building. According to Romanian general Sorin Ioan,

> I spend Wednesdays in the EU, and dedicate all day to EU issues and discussing in detail. We also have working lunches and receptions. There is an equal divide of work between NATO and the EU. We are responding to all, but there is overlap of activities. We choose based on which is more important, and our deputies can participate in others.[41]

Beyond the overlap evident in NATO and CSDP areas, double-hattedness means that the military representatives are doubling up on both formal and informal meetings, and NATO involves its own set of meetings. Hungarian general István Békési said, "NATO has the same type of meetings, but there is much more possibility for special committee meetings, which must be held."[42]

Since the memberships of the two organizations are similar but not the same, meetings must be scheduled carefully. For example, it would be unacceptable for the generals formally to discuss a purely NATO issue at a Wednesday EU meeting, where no American representative is present. Ultimately, more meetings mean more time together and tighter cohesiveness.

What happens in the meetings? Does real deliberation take place? First, even the "formal" meetings are conducted more or less informally. Translation is not a part of these meetings, a practice that aids in direct communication. A strong military norm is to speak in English or French, meaning that the generals share language as part of their culture. Latvian general Raimonds Graube explained,

> Formally, the military committee is different from other committees. If agricultural ministers get together, they can speak in their own language. This costs a lot of money. The only exception is the military. We can't

speak so many languages. If you are on the battlefield and everyone is speaking seventeen different languages, nothing can work. It must be French or English.[43]

In practice, only the French and Belgian generals use French, while the others use English. To add to the informality, milreps are on a first-name basis, and regardless of when they arrived in Brussels, they treat each other as equals.[44] Despite this informal atmosphere, participants attend all meetings in uniform, not to appear formal but as a visual display of their literal esprit de corps.

Second, a central aspect of the military representatives' body of shared professional norms is the distinction between flags up and flags down. In formal meetings, flags are up, and everything is recorded. Generals are obligated to serve as mouthpieces for their chiefs of defense. Reports of their discussions become official papers and are circulated to those with high enough security clearance. Very few are declassified for general public consumption.[45] When flags are down, the generals can discuss frankly with one another whether or not they agree with their instructions. Discussions take on a tone of expediency. Said Graube, "There are subdynamics to the process when flags are down. In an informal meeting we are always honest."[46] Participants are free to express their perspectives as professionals rather than as transmission belts for state preferences. They can distance themselves from their instructions and speak honestly about how to reach consensus based on their expertise. None of these generals have any significant traditional diplomatic experience, yet they find themselves achieving the same level of consensus that usually characterizes Coreper negotiations. But an important distinction exists: While their ambassadorial counterparts rely on finely tuned negotiation skills, the generals rely more on a desire to get things done.

Subdynamics in flags-down meetings include signaling. For example, if a general begins his statement with "I have instructions to say . . . ," listeners are alerted to the likelihood that he has strict red lines from his capital and that even though he does not personally agree with his instructions, he may not be able to move from them. An even clearer signal is when a general sends his deputy to the meeting. The deputy's arrival indicates to other group members that he will read aloud his instructions verbatim. As Dutch general A. G. D. van Osch described,

You know something is really wrong if Cyprus sends a deputy and he starts with reading instructions. I never have to do it that way, but we all know that if this is happening, maneuvering space is zero. The military representative does it that way so that he never has to see the emotional reaction. He's protecting himself from the anger of the others, because it can be very frustrating.[47]

This particular kind of signaling behavior serves as a protection mechanism. All EUMC members understand that any one of them might find himself in a tough position, with strict instructions that he personally does not support. Yet they collectively define success as reaching a compromise, and tempers can flare when this success is threatened by one stubborn position. By sending a deputy, a general protects himself from the anger of his peers and preserves the cohesiveness of the whole. France's de Rousiers said, "Because we believe in what we do, we all want things to move forward."[48]

Another signal of possible obstacles to compromise is when the quality of the argumentation flounders. In the words of van Osch,

A military representative may use an argument that seems irrelevant but doesn't want to say that it is. It starts if someone feels [that the reasoning] is crazy and it happens always. Of course it weakens the argument if you don't believe in it yourself.[49]

Sometimes a military representative who is obligated to state his case in a certain way ends up fighting an uphill battle against the twin forces of his nation's hidden agenda and his personal lack of support for what he must say. The military representatives know each other well enough to be able to discern if the argument is empty, and this knowledge undermines the would-be persuader's ability to be convincing.

A third shared professional norm that facilitates compromise among military representatives is the belief that they should not break the silence procedure. As stipulated by the formal rules of procedure of the Council, the silence procedure means that "the relevant text shall be deemed to be adopted at the end of the period laid down by the Presidency depending on the urgency of the matter, except where a member of the Council objects."[50] Given that decisions pertaining to CSDP—such as whether to engage in a particular operation—must be made unanimously, a strong norm against breaking the silence is significant and is intimately tied to a nation's reputation. Colonel Peter Kallert, the German deputy EUMC representative, said,

> Berlin might want to break the silence on a specific issue, but we in Brussels have the overall picture of all topics currently going on in the various fora. Therefore I might remind Berlin that we already broke silence on two other issues lately. At the same time, I might raise the question whether the topic is worth breaking silence a third time within a short period of time.[51]

At the same time, the silence procedure is also a means of enabling an operation to go forward without full participation. For example, the operation in Chad was very much spearheaded by France, but Greece had little interest: According to Greek admiral Kourkoulis Dimitrios, "I didn't block it, but I didn't participate."[52] All countries, regardless of whether they contribute soldiers or weapons, must contribute financially through the Athena Mechanism.

Military culture dictates that a solution is always there, and finding it determines success or failure. General van Osch said,

> We are not successful if we can't agree on a topic. And basically it's almost always the case that if we don't come to consensus, it's not because of a military argument. It's political interest. I can't think of an example without consensus on military issues. If we don't find consensus, it's a political issue.[53]

And although the milreps deal with political issues, too, they are first and foremost military experts charged with designing military solutions. If irreconcilable political obstruction exists, the matter boils down to whether the instructions coming from the capitals make it impossible to move forward. The strength of the common culture that binds military officials to each other in the EUMC is an important factor in whether the weight of their persuasiveness is strong.

Common Culture

The common culture among EU military representatives has historical, strategic, and social properties, some of which stretch back for centuries.

European states have often waged long and violent wars, but their contact with each other through battle, alliances, and purposeful emulation has resulted in a certain degree of convergence in both tactical and strategic expertise. Strategic culture is the civic, national, and historic context of military doctrine. It is based in part on public opinion about when it is appropriate to wage war and what is the appropriate level of force.[54] Military culture also has a social component, since it is "learned, broadly shared, adaptive, and symbolic"[55] and can adjust in various ways over time depending on national circumstances.[56] Training and experience contribute to this process.

By the time the milreps arrive in Brussels, they have followed very similar career paths and find they have much in common. They have an instant rapport. They know what it means to have been on the battlefield as a soldier, to be responsible for soldiers' lives, and they have usually spent time on the same operations. Many also have experience working on EU issues from their capitals, such as providing guidance to the EU Military Staff.[57] Even if their paths have not previously crossed, they have certainly served in the same locations at one point or another and immediately can draw on common experiences as a result. As van Osch put it,

> The main basis of our esprit de corps is our common background. We are military within a big diplomatic environment. We have the same language, same jargon, same kind of military thinking, and we read each other's military philosophers. Many of us knew each other before. At least we have been in the same missions or have common things to talk about.[58]

Given that they are clearly military officers in a diplomatic world, one way in which they show their solidarity is by wearing their uniforms to receptions, thereby enhancing their visibility as a collective and showing their shared identity.[59]

A broad military culture is common across EU member states and exists independently of the unique Brussels environment. This culture transcends even member states' individual goals in the international environment and differences brought about by the former Iron Curtain divide. The military representatives describe several qualities: efficiency, a can-do attitude, and the belief that no decision is a decision in itself.[60] All three are interrelated. Efficiency is first and foremost a part of European military culture. In many cases, soldiers' lives are on the line, and no matter what rank a military officer holds, he or she must be able to make decisions quickly. Doing so requires a can-do attitude, the idea that there is always a solution and that the main challenge is to identify it quickly. High-level military officers believe that making no decision at all is a decision because if those at the top are silent, events on the battlefield will still play out. Military officers fundamentally accept that inaction is still a kind of action. Graube believes that

> we are the most efficient EU committee; same for NATO because it's military. It comes from the blood, from military life, from when you were a lieutenant. If you don't make a decision, it's costly. If you don't make a decision, it's a decision. As you get more senior, there's more time for thinking. This is what unites us. Many know each other from previous missions or have been to the same places. What makes us more like a club is that we all have soldiers fighting together everywhere. This is a solid idea bringing us together.[61]

These military norms differ substantially from political or diplomatic approaches. If a group of diplomats is unable to reach agreement, they can decide that they have pushed the issue far enough and that it is time to set it aside. To be sure, a lack of consensus is considered a failed outcome for diplomatic negotiations, but it is not really a decision. As Graube expressed, however, the idea that a decision must be made as efficiently as possible is implicitly linked to a career in which lives are at risk whenever there is indecision at the top. One of the key characteristics of military thinking is that the group takes priority over the individuals who comprise it.[62] This overarching norm allows the others to fall into place.

These representatives also share a distinctive element brought into the mix when they begin their work in Brussels. After arriving in Brussels, milreps build on their immediate rapport during a period of socialization in their new setting. This socialization is not simultaneous for all individuals, as turnover is not coordinated across member states. Some are fairly new to the job, while others have been in their posts for three years and are near the end of their assignments (which may last as long as four years). Békési said,

> It's a tradition somehow inside the organization that if someone steps in, he has to follow the rules. In 1998, I attended the Army War College and had

to follow the rules and traditions. It was very different, and I had to figure out how to quickly follow. It was quite different when I first arrived here as well, and my colleagues were very helpful. I quickly learned what should be done.[63]

The milreps' shared background, language, and experiences certainly help in establishing a common culture that is in some ways unique to the EU-NATO environment. Those within the group are adept at helping new members learn the new aspects of their professional norms.

This process of socialization is important because milreps face contextual challenges that go beyond what they might have experienced in the past. First, they find themselves in a multilateral setting in which politics is a part of the job. According to Graube,

> At our level, you can't separate the political and military. You have to know how to understand another country's other aspects. This is a strategic environment. The operational environment is more about following orders.[64]

General van Osch concurred:

> Both the military aspects and other aspects are important at our level. We always think of the population. Factors of influence are numerous. There are clearly military, political, and economic arguments.

Thus, while there is a tendency to imagine that military officers simply follow orders and that doing so is fundamental to military culture, at the level of the EUMC representatives, the chain of command is no longer part of the job. They are at the top of the hierarchy. As experts with decades of exposure to different aspects of military-defense strategies, they are now in the driver's seat, and it is a seat they share with 26 others.

Second, the atmosphere at NATO headquarters is not only multilateral but multihatted. The military representatives typically spend all but one day per week at their NATO offices, even when working on EU issues. The idea that they answer to two different institutions with separate hierarchies and goals is not typical of a military environment. While some spend a significant majority of their time dealing with NATO issues,[65] others report that they work equally on both, depending on what is most pressing. "We don't want to fail because we are very visible," said van Osch. "We are walking around in uniform in a diplomatic world. The civilian staff is four times bigger than the military staff at NATO."[66] And their previous postings generally do not prepare them for this distinctive institutional aspect of the NATO environment. Military principles usually involve leadership of only one hierarchy of personnel, not two. Some comedic situations can result: van Osch noted, "Formally, I'm sometimes not allowed to give a document to myself. Eighteen of us are in the same position."[67]

To add even more complexity to the situation, when the military representatives have their NATO hats on, in a way they acquire more status than when they are wearing their EU hats. Graube said,

> We play a higher role in NATO. We're the highest level that reports to the NAC. In the EU, the military committee is one part. The EU also engages in state building; it can have Civcom involved. We are more focused in NATO. In the EU, we are part of a larger picture. Our role is a little lower.[68]

Structurally, the EUMC is placed below the PSC, on a par with the Civilian Committee for Crisis Management (Civcom). The PSC, in turn, formally answers to Coreper II. In NATO, the same military representatives are just below the NAC, the highest level. This status differential is recognized within the Council of the European Union. Quentin Weiler, French chargé de mission for the PSC, said, "EUMC is very high-ranking but still subordinate to the PSC."[69] Even though the EUMC is at the same level in the hierarchy as Civcom, the members of the latter are midranking diplomats, of lower status, and far earlier in their careers than the military representatives. Without a strong common culture holding them together, the milreps might find the tension between their NATO and EU roles quite distracting. Instead, they handle both of their hats quite smoothly and effectively.

Third, the EU side of their work is distinctive in that it embodies a more encompassing interpretation of security than one usually finds in more traditional military cultures. Military representatives more often bring up the civilian side of their work on planning EU operations. For example, during discussions to establish NAVFOR Atalanta, which deals with the problem of pirates off the coast of Somalia, many interviewees described how they were quite occupied with developing a legal framework that would determine what would happen to pirates after they were arrested at sea, arguing that the problem could not be resolved only at sea but must also be tackled on land, especially in terms of dismantling the financial system on which the pirates rely. There was a general understanding that "the EU could get involved in civil dimensions," and the milreps sought a way to do so.[70] The EU is more comprehensive in its approach to security, and it is not primarily a political-military organization, as NATO is.[71] Altogether, these three contextual factors might have hindered the milreps' effective operation in an unfamiliar environment, but with the strong backbone of a common military culture alongside quick socialization, they excel.

Like their diplomatic counterparts, military representatives also share certain substantive norms about security that are a crucial part of their common culture. The example of NAVFOR Atalanta hints at one major substantive norm: the belief that it is appropriate to think of security in terms of both its civil and political dimensions to have successful CSDP operations. Swedish admiral Stefan Engdahl said,

> There's no development without security, and no security without development. You can't just put in the military. You have to help a country to develop. If you make a plan, you need to see both sides. There's a need for structures, policy, judges, hospitals. . . . The whole concept needs to hang together. . . . If you make a plan, all the factors need to be part of the plan. The military part is easy. But how to develop a country that is Muslim when you're not from that country—it's extremely difficult.[72]

Britain's Bill concurred, arguing that the main difference between NATO and CSDP is that the latter must take into account civil-military coordination.[73] Indeed, a new directorate within the Council Secretariat, the Civil-Military Planning Directorate, was an initiative drafted by France, the UK, and Germany and enjoys wide support in the military committee.

Another substantive norm holds that it is necessary to increase the EU's hard power so that the organization can act effectively in the international environment. This belief is significant given that hard power would seemingly not constitute a major area of advantage for the EU, which is typically known for its soft or civilian power. Spanish admiral José M. Treviño-Ruiz compared the NATO Response Force (NRF) to the EU's battle groups: Whereas the EU has 2,500 well-trained, well-equipped soldiers waiting to go into action in the event of a crisis, the NRF has 25,000 at the ready. He said, "We need to try to preserve a reserve corps reaching the highest ambition level in order to interfere. We have more than 1,200,000 troops with a lot of assets, but no structure."[74] The milreps believe that the EU can and should be capable of engaging in significant military action.

Another substantive norm is the belief that long-term capabilities planning should lead to integration. With one or two exceptions, interviewees described themselves as very prointegration. Treviño-Ruiz even expressed a hope for the creation of a European army.[75] Ioan supported the need for more security integration to achieve a common security identity:

> It's a necessity to have the same type of capabilities. Capabilities to cover the entire spectrum of military forces, not only mechanized or combat, but also other sorts—intelligence. . . . These forces must be compatible and interoperable. If you're not interoperable, you at least should be compatible. This involves integration. . . . The EU should have a common security identity.[76]

Similarly, de Rousiers said, "No one is in a position of not agreeing with the overall idea that we should work together in operations and capabilities build-up."[77] The logic for the long-term development of a common defense is well understood and agreed upon within the military committee, but it still lacks the full political backing necessary for such a move.[78] Most EUMC members also feel that the EU needs a permanent operational headquarters to facilitate planning of preventive operations. The UK firmly opposes such a headquarters, seeing it as overlapping too much with NATO, but most other member states favor it. Coelmont argued that the lack of a permanent operational headquarters "goes against all military logic. There's no arguing about the principle because coming from NATO, they have already agreed to its importance." He further insisted that all members of the military committee technically agree to the establishment of a permanent headquarters but said that they are held back by their political instructions.[79] In this area, the norm for long-term security integration is strong, and given the strength of the military epistemic community, they may yet persuade their capitals to move further in this direction.

To some extent, they members of EUMC have already achieved a degree of success, as the creation and normalization of the concept of battle groups illustrates. Multinational military formations—despite the complications that come with integrating command structure and capabilities—have become an accepted form of hard power exercise among EU member states. The military committee played an important role in convincing EU capitals that this idea was the appropriate way forward. The idea of permanent, multinational forces has now become much less revolutionary or controversial.[80]

With all of these qualities and norms coming together to create a surprisingly cohesive whole, it is still important to ask whether there is any source of division among military representatives. EUMC representatives tend to emphasize that they possess an esprit de corps, but several brought up the possibility of an East-West divide among member states. In this view, military representatives from Eastern Europe seem to focus more on purely military matters than on both political and military issues. This approach may be a legacy of military service during the Soviet era and subsequently being more focused on NATO.[81] Representatives of western countries tend to see their national safety as fundamentally tied to the existence of NATO and support for the United States.[82] However, this perspective is slowly changing. Explained Belgium's Coelmont,

> What I've seen with enlargement is that the milreps from new countries believe that the military *is* NATO. Coming from these countries and seeing the fall of the Berlin Wall, the U.S. and NATO played a very important role. Gradually, that has changed. In the beginning, they were a little silent, not intervening much. In the beginning, military operations were not that big, and newer countries were not as involved. It has been a natural process for them to get more involved. If you put the military around the table, whatever country they come from, they have the same logic of thinking, and they come to the same results.

Thus, the common military culture that binds these officials together despite their somewhat different starting positions is helping them to overcome their past experiences. In addition, the military representatives from older member states strive to minimize this feeling of dissimilarity. When they hold working dinners at their homes, de Rousiers said, "All of us balance our guests in order to not have just Western Europe and next week Eastern Europe."[83] Although the organization remains in a period of transition, the older member states, even if smaller or less powerful, remain more heavily invested in the EU and are usually more eager to come up with new ideas.

Another division can be found at the level of the representatives themselves rather than the member states. There is a feeling of separation between the single-hatted representatives to the EU and double-hatted representatives to both the EU and NATO. Most milreps wear both hats—among countries belonging to both organizations, only France and Belgium have separate representation. How do countries decide whether to have double- or single-hatted representatives? Belgium made a concerted effort in the 1980s to treat EU security as something important and thus for historical and political reasons appointed a dedicated military official for CSDP issues.[84] Both the EU and NATO military representatives deal with a single chief of defense, so a high level of coordination exists between the two. France's reasoning is similar. French officials felt that because CSDP was so much newer than NATO, a dedicated team of experts was necessary from the beginning.[85] Both approaches have strengths as well as weaknesses. The main strength of having two representatives is that one can spend all of his time dealing with EU security issues rather than having to allocate some time to NATO matters. The main strength of a double-hatted military representative is that it is easier to create links between EU and NATO and to eliminate any information gap.[86] With French president Nicolas Sarkozy's recent decision to rejoin NATO's military structure, officials in the country are now considering transitioning to a double-hatted general in EUMC.

For neutral countries such as Sweden, the disparity is more pronounced. According to Engdahl,

> There's a big difference not being a member [of NATO]. There are a lot of issues that will go simultaneously in the discussion in NATO and the EU. I don't know where they're going unless I get information from somebody. . . . NATO milreps have the advantage of other activities. . . . Not being a member of NATO means you're not into the same kind of issues.[87]

Still, only Austria, Malta, Cyprus, Finland, and Ireland occupy the same position as Sweden—that is, with membership in CSDP but not NATO. One possible conclusion is that cohesion within the EU military epistemic community might be improved if these five countries were to join NATO.

Finally, in the military environment, where hard power capabilities are paramount, some feeling of division exists between more and less powerful member states. Scholarly works that focus on the role of states in the EU often argue that the Big Three—the UK, France, and Germany—dominate decision making. But the milreps argue that it is important not to exaggerate the power of the Big Three or of any other grouping.[88] While it is true that if France, Germany, and the UK are on the same page, others are also likely to agree, the same is also true for other member states. There is a sense that if the same member states always band together to push for initiatives, they risk annoying the others. Germany is in a somewhat special position in this respect because it is one of the Big Three and is regarded as an honest broker country. In many instances, smaller countries expect and want Germany to take the lead, as, for example, with the initiative to synchronize and harmonize the capability development of the EU and NATO.[89]

The common background and culture of the military epistemic community are part of what makes the EUMC more than simply a Council committee. A natural allegiance exists before the generals arrive in Brussels, paving the way for them to exercise agency beyond their instructions, to act as more than the sum of their parts, and to go beyond simple calculations of rationalist bargaining. A sense of camaraderie and willingness to help each other maintains a common culture and adds a new, distinctive layer to it. This culture reflects traditional military norms as well as the realities of an emerging, postmodern era of military expertise where national borders, interests, and suspicions are less relevant than was previously the case.

Persuading the Capitals

The relationship between each military representative and his capital demonstrates the added value of the committee. As Germany's Kallert explained, capitals can and do negotiate directly with each other but can only do so with 2 or 3 other capitals: Communicating directly with 26 others is simply impossible.[90] Thus, the final compromise rests with the committee. Adam Sambrook, the UK head of military-defense CSDP, said, "The experts discuss the issues in Brussels. On occasion there might be capital-to-capital talks. But talking directly to capitals to resolve problems is the exception, not the rule."[91] Having all 27 voices around the table at the same time is important. Each member state is on equal footing when it comes to CSDP issues, as each has the ability to block the others. In this forum, even a small member state can ask for a change in the wording of a document, and the other member states can find themselves agreeing to something they had not foreseen.[92]

So where are decisions actually made? Formally, capitals—specifically, ministries of defense—provide instructions to milreps. But informally, the process involves two-way communication in which milreps can persuade their government officials and have thus achieved quite a bit of flexibility with what they can do. According to Sambrook,

In London, we're further away from the formal communication in Brussels. It is not that there is a division between those who negotiate and those who formulate policy. The decisions are made somewhere in between. Policy formulation happens somewhere in the space between Brussels and London. . . . The distinction between the center doing policy-making and the embassy doing implementation is a myth. . . . It is not the case that they have to consult London every time they do something.[93]

Portugal places an even greater emphasis on Brussels decision makers because there are very few in the capital who are working on CSDP issues and even fewer who can fully grasp what is going on.[94] The Portuguese Ministry of Foreign Affairs has around 450 diplomats, half of whom are abroad at any given time. Thus, leaving a thin layer of individuals in Lisbon must cover all aspects of foreign policy. CSDP, in particular, is regarded as technical and detailed. The Portuguese director for security and defense affairs, João Pedro Antunes, said, "In the end, it's not very easy to have people in each place with the right background. I have three heads of division, and none have worked in Brussels."[95] The Hague is more on the other side of the spectrum: With a complex system of interministerial coordination and frequent preparation of formal instructions, the capital tries closely to monitor and control what its agents do in Brussels. But the Dutch foreign ministry views the EUMC as having a special role. Henrick van Asch of the Dutch ministry's Security Policy Department said, "The EUMC has to give independent military advice. Officially, they shouldn't really be instructed in a sense. Otherwise, you get the national perspective. Mostly, they write their instructions themselves."[96] He recognized that good expert advice has political implications but is not politicized. Kallert said, "Our three-star general . . . gets guidance from Berlin, it's not an order; it's *guidance*. If necessary, he can be flexible. . . . He also may dispense with an intervention. He can do this due to his experience. Afterwards, he might call Berlin and explain why he didn't follow the guidance."[97] The frequency of the dialogue between the capitals and Brussels also varies among member states. Some are in constant interaction, while others may not interact even every week.[98]

It is not part of EUMC members' modus operandi to escalate issues to their chiefs of defense or ambassadors. Formally, the decisions are made by the CHODs, but each military representative frequently informs his CHOD or his staff of what is possible and how negotiations are playing out. The milreps know more about the issues at stake, dealing with them on a daily basis. Moreover, if a chief of defense or ambassador takes a different line than the milrep, the discrepancy can reflect negatively on the delegation. According to Kallert, representatives seek to avoid situations in which a member state's general sticks to a hard-line position but the ambassador takes a different position if he or she becomes involved.[99]

The interaction between military representatives and CHODs parallels the relationship between ministers and Coreper II members. In effect, even though the EUMC is technically two levels below Coreper in the Council hierarchy, the two bodies have similar status and influence vis-à-vis their capitals. One ambassador said that on occasion, a minister would be sent to Brussels to negotiate particularly important components of treaties but would not show up at the relevant meetings.

> I have seen how they have flown in ministers or deputy ministers, and they did not show up for meetings because their permanent representative went for them. . . . They are very intelligent, high-profile, and able men, but it is difficult for them to do it if they are not used to negotiating or do not know the treaty. Even those who have chosen others rely on their personal representative.[100]

Similarly, when the CHODs come to Brussels, they rely heavily on their EUMC representatives. In Békési's words,

> I understand issues better [than the capital]. During preparation, I try to give [the CHOD] necessary information, but they're busy all the time, so we have to separate what type of information to bring to his attention. It is a short brief.[101]

A personal presence in Brussels is a necessary prerequisite to understanding ongoing formal and informal deliberations and to keeping abreast of the intricate policymaking environment.

The CSDP operation NAVFOR Atalanta illustrates how the EUMC has shaped policy outcomes and has found agreement despite member states' different starting points. Since roughly 2005, piracy has increased in the southern Red Sea area, the southern coast of Somalia, the Gulf of Aden, and the area around the Seychelles Islands. The growth in piracy has resulted primarily from ongoing political instability and unrest on land, rapid increases in marine traffic, smaller-sized merchant crews on sea vessels, and more readily available low-cost arms.[102] Perhaps the biggest shift came as pirates' financial resources grew as they developed a steady and sizable income through collecting large ransoms. Piracy consequently became quite a profitable organized crime industry in the region.

As the largest donor and provider of humanitarian aid to Somalia, the EU was particularly concerned about the safety of World Food Program (WFP) ships transporting much-needed food to the people of Somalia.[103] In addition, more than 30 percent of EU oil is transported by ship through this region, and about 25,000 ships per year representing 15 percent of the annual global trade pass through the Gulf of Aden and Suez Canal.[104] But the protection of WFP ships has been the EU's top priority, with merchant shipping coming in second.

NAVFOR Atalanta, launched on November 10, 2008, was initially somewhat controversial because it constituted the first time that CSDP executed a naval operation. Not all member states were on board. Moreover, NATO ships were already in the region, as were those of non-EU nations. At the same time, some observers believed that action against piracy could be taken without a formal CSDP operation. Many milreps, however, felt that the details of a potential operation had not been studied properly but that having a formal operation would eventually be preferable for a variety of reasons. After some deliberation, the committee came to a consensus: They could advise moving forward with the operation if they could establish a coordination network that would enable ships to communicate with sources on the ground as well as with ships from non-EU nations, including China, Russia, and India. By pushing for a wider mission—including the coordination network and agreements with nearby countries on what to do with captured pirates—member states reached agreement. They could see the benefit of a formal operation under EU leadership.

Altogether, the EU operation consisted of 2,000 personnel from 19 member states as well as from Croatia and Norway; 12 ships; three full-time maritime patrol and reconnaissance aircraft; and eight helicopters. In addition, in accordance with the EUMC's recommendations, legal instruments were put into place—specifically, rules governing the capture and transfer of piracy suspects to be tried by judicial authorities on land. Member states provided judicial experts to deal with the legal enforcement dimension. From 2008 to 2010, the EU spent around 400 million per year to maintain the operation.[105] More than two dozen international vessels and ships from more than 20 countries are seeking to prevent piracy in the region, with these resources coming not only from Atalanta but also from NATO and from a U.S.-led coalition, the Combined Maritime Forces. The EUMC's plan for a coordination network has resulted in monthly meetings among the major players and direct consultations between EU ships and other fleets. An Internet-based platform, Mercury, allows chatting, information exchange, and real-time images of ships as they cross the Gulf of Aden.[106] Again, these various initiatives were spearheaded by the military committee and were based on military logic. After the political mandate was in place, the military needed only a few days to launch the operation at sea.[107]

Atalanta has been a challenging operation, given that the sea area under EU protection is 1.4 million square nautical miles.[108] Nevertheless, since the launching of the operation, EU ships have responded to every WFP ship's request for safe escort into Somalia, and no humanitarian ships have been lost to pirates.[109] From November 2008 to August 2009, EU forces captured and transferred 68 pirates to Kenyan authorities. They have also instituted a system of group transit for merchant ships and help manage the Internationally Recommended Transit Corridor to facilitate the protection of these ships. Thus, Atalanta could boast early results. While the operation was initially intended to last for one year, in light of earlier reluctance to launch such an operation, member states agreed to extend it for at least another year.

Another illustrative example is the case of EUFOR Chad, a humanitarian mission to bring security and relief to refugees. Chad has been at war since 1964 and has suffered from numerous internal political crises. In more recent years, violence between different ethnic groups and armed militia has centered on the borders separating Chad, Sudan, and the Central African Republic. In 2003, the humanitarian crisis in Darfur resulted in massive flows of refugees across the border into Chad. France is the main EU member state with political interests in the country as a consequence of former colonial ties. With 400,000 Darfur refugees in Chad, French leaders wanted to find a way to provide assistance in the form of a CSDP operation.

Controversy initially arose from the feeling that the problems in Chad were too far removed from EU nations' commercial, national, and political interests. At the same time, EU members found it politically difficult to reject a humanitarian mission that would clearly help alleviate a desperate situation. While complex historical, political, and international issues were at stake, when the French proposal to launch a military operation in Chad reached the EU milreps' table, their main concern was whether an EU operation could achieve successful results. The situation was more tenuous than in the case of Atalanta because of member states' seeming unwillingness to contribute enough troops, even after several attempts to gain further commitments. In the end, 23 EU member states and three nonmember states (Russia, Albania, and Croatia) participated in the operation, generating a total of 3,700 personnel. Despite an initial shortfall of 2,000 troops, the military committee found enough reserves to satisfy the operation's requirements and felt that if the UN took over as planned, the operation could do well. This information was critical to the EUMC's final decision. To reach a compromise, those more skeptical about the operation remained silent without blocking the initiative and made financial contributions. France made up some of the troop shortfall. The military committee's process of dialogue and ability to agree on common advice, which included the risks involved in the operation, was crucial to the outcome.

EUFOR Chad's ultimate success rested on the strategy that it would complement the UN's mandate by protecting civilians and refugees, ensuring humanitarian workers' safety and ability to provide aid, and helping to secure UN facilities and equipment in the area. The mission would not address the core causes of the conflicts, since that goal did not represent the ideal use of military force. The operation lasted one year starting on March 15, 2008, and cost €120 million from the common budget—a total of €1 billion including member states' contributions.[110] When EUFOR Chad came to an end and operational leaders handed over control to the UN Mission to Central African Republic and Chad (MINURCAT), the European Commission became involved on a more long-term basis and is central to the international effort to bring about necessary political and economic reforms.

These two examples illustrate how the milreps sometimes find military solutions that contribute to overcoming political obstacles stemming from the capitals. EUMC can also put an operation into place quickly once the political dimension is complete. General van Osch said,

> The military starts to work around it, and there you see a difference. . . . If the decision is there, the military is quick in implementing. We anticipate everything which is necessary. Formally, there's no consensus—we can't have coordination between NATO and EU forces in Kosovo, for example. Of course, we are coordinating, and the military just makes it happen. They play the game at the political level, and we go forward.[111]

The milreps affect the process of persuasion, engaging in a constant dialogue with their capitals and seeking to influence PSC ambassadors even in informal settings. According to van Osch,

> Solutions are never found in formal meetings. They're always found in the evenings, . . . and it's the whole community. I invite diplomats to come to dinners as well so we can try to understand and influence them. We cannot explain in formal meetings how to get agreement. We are very much influencing the political level.[112]

The three or four informal dinners per week clearly provide an opportunity for milreps to socialize with diplomats—in particular, PSC ambassadors. In fact, military representatives often interact with diplomats on a daily basis at all levels.[113] Of course, milreps have varying degrees of flexibility from their capitals, and thus the level of autonomous influence also differs. In some cases, the delegate feels he is in the driver's seat, constantly aware of broader national positions and informing his superior of agreements already made. This process requires a great deal of trust and experience.

In sum, the EUMC representatives are experts at a kind of military art. They are driven by their shared expert knowledge and by a culture that pushes them toward finding solutions. Their expertise provides them with clear-cut solutions to political obstacles. In fact, they find that they rarely even disagree on the nuances of military planning. Rather, the main obstacles to cooperation arise from their political red lines. Their high status and experience as well as their strong rapport with their capitals enable them to persuade others of their compromise solutions.

THE LONG-TERM VISION FOR EUROPEAN DEFENCE CAPABILITY AND CAPACITY NEEDS

The Long-Term Vision (LTV) is an example of the military representatives' involvement in security integration on the more conceptual side. It is essentially a military-defense strategy that accounts for demographic, economic, political, and security strategies that Europe will face 20 years in the future and prescribes solutions to long-term military capability and capacity needs. Access to EUMC negotiations is very limited; indeed, most negotiations occur either verbally or via classified documents. But because this policy initiative was partially debated in an outside forum, the Security and Defence Agenda, it is possible to observe some of the LTV's development over time. Moreover, interviews also reveal the motivations and norms underlying the LTV. The milreps were not the only contributors to the LTV, however. They worked on part of it, while experts in other areas provided input regarding other facets of the plan. Since the members of this wider network shared the same overall policy goals despite their different types of expertise, the network can be said to have constituted an epistemic coalition.[114]

An Epistemic Coalition

In the lead-up to the LTV's creation, the epistemic coalition comprised (1) members of the EUMC, (2) security experts from the EU Institute for Security Studies (EUISS) in Paris,[115] and (3) a network of European scientists, technology experts, and academics.[116] While some interaction took place among the three groups, they can be characterized as more or less distinct, their own separate characteristics. They were from different professions but had a synergistic kind of expertise.

While the milreps were experts at planning defensive and offensive strategies in the field, the researchers and academics were able to draw important generalizations about these strategies, including big picture, sociopolitical implications. The technology experts had worked closely with the milreps to develop and provide the weapons and logistical equipment necessary for successful operations (see chapter 6) and thus knew what was possible in terms of future weapons systems, information technology, and potential costs. Each of these groups alone might have been able to tackle only a piece of the puzzle, but together they had a powerful knowledge base on which to build a multifaceted agenda.

The EDA was instrumental in bringing this military-defense epistemic coalition together, through its request for research on the LTV and its broader agenda of fostering strong, supportive networks.[117] Since member states agreed to establish the EDA at the June 2003 European Council in Thessaloniki, the agency's specific aim has been to look for ways to achieve long-term integration in the area of defense equipment procurement.[118] To this end, in March 2005, the EDA's Steering Board, comprised of participating member states' defense ministers (excluding Denmark) and Javier Solana, decided to establish by the end of the year "a voluntary intergovernmental approach to opening up defence procurement within Europe."[119] As head of the EDA, Solana called for member state input and an outward-looking organizational culture:

> Extensive networks with national experts in various disciplines have been created, allowing for direct interaction between the Agency and capitals on a day-to-day basis. . . . The Agency is also building an effective external communication strategy, supported by good media and other contacts, a website and appropriate information materials. The level of public affairs and media interest in the Agency is now consistently high.[120]

Seppo Kääriäinen, Finnish defense minister at the founding of the EDA, said, "We need interoperable and reliable solutions that can support both homeland defence and the requirements of working CSDP cooperation."[121] Thus, the EDA created the broad context in which a policy such as the LTV could emerge, but the experts bore responsibility for shaping it into tangible goals. The military experts in particular were critical to this process, since they serve as a bridge between the chiefs of defense and the EDA, connecting together the different philosophies of the former to deliver common positions to the latter.[122]

Discussions about how to enhance interoperability and deal with future challenges through the LTV began in April 2005. Seven months into the process, the EDA Steering Board conveyed to the Council the urgent need to plan ahead.[123] Ministers of defense are well aware of the fact that to achieve any change in defense capabilities requires decades of advance preparation. As Solana described,

> It is vital to have this kind of 20-year perspective, given the lead times typically involved in developing defence capability. Decisions we take, or fail to take, today will affect whether we have the right military capabilities, and the right capacities in Europe's defence technological and industrial base, in the third decade of this century.[124]

On October 3, 2006, after eleven more months experts' deliberation, the steering board endorsed the completed LTV document.[125] The endorsement process is vital to understanding this epistemic coalition's important role in fostering shared security norms and launching the first major steps toward a plan for long-term security integration.

Development of Norms

In the months preceding the submission of the LTV to the EDA's Steering Board, a process of deliberation and clarification of shared causal norms occurred. On June 13, 2006, key members of the epistemic coalition attended an expert seminar hosted by the Security and Defence Agenda (SDA), an independent, nongovernmental think tank based in Brussels. In attendance were nine research and security experts, eight high-ranking military officials, seven EDA officials, and four EU officials.[126] SDA's membership primarily includes EU and military officials as well as defense, security, and industry experts. One of its ongoing goals is to follow the U.S. model of linking government to think tanks.[127] Thus, SDA represented a forum in which the epistemic coalition could meet, deliberate regarding the future of security policy in Europe, and coalesce around a common goal. A summary of the expert seminar's proceedings, *Europe's Long-Term Vision of the Defence Environment in 2025: Sharp or Fuzzy?*, provides a record of the process of deliberation and clarification of shared norms that occurred.[128]

According to the published proceedings, at the beginning of the meeting, the EDA's chief executive, Nick Witney, summarized some of the initial findings of the military-defense epistemic coalition. He emphasized that in 2025, globalization would continue, but Europe's population would also be declining and aging. Europeans would comprise only 6 percent of the world's population, and the average age of the European population would be 45. Such demographics would pose a challenge for maintaining defense budgets and recruitment into the armed forces.[129] Witney said that Europe would likely have a lower share of wealth relative to other countries and would have to devote a greater portion of public budgets to pensions.[130] To counter these developments, Europeans would have to anticipate the evolving nature of threats in the information age and create economies of scale in the military sector.

The key causal norm expressed repeatedly during the meeting was that budgetary pressures necessitated integration of member state resources to achieve security aims. Member states clearly saw a trade-off between maintaining national sovereignty over security policy and achieving efficiency. EDA deputy chief executive Hilmar Linnenkamp concluded that a good strategy would entail "the blurring of distinctions between intergovernmental and common decision-making processes with respect to a range of issues; for instance, research and technology, industrial matters, crisis management and humanitarian policy."[131] By the end of the seminar, members of the epistemic coalition were stressing efficiency through integration over national sovereignty for the sake of ensuring security 20 years down the road.

On June 29, 2006, a grand seminar took place, with representatives of the participating member states in attendance. The epistemic coalition used this venue to persuade member states of its conclusions and to ensure that everyone was on the same page.[132] The LTV was emerging as a three-strand document based on the specific knowledge-based groupings within the epistemic coalition. The July 2006 *EDA Bulletin* summarized,

> **Strand 1** discusses developments in the global context such as trends in demography, economy and global governance. The EUISS has supported this exercise by developing an excellent paper, compiling the collective wisdom of "futurologists" from all over.[133]
> **Strand 2** addresses the future military environment. Here, the EU Military Committee is in the lead. Initial EUMC considerations include a wide spectrum of potential future capability profiles.
> **Strand 3** evaluates of Science & Technology (S&T) trends both in the light of challenges and of opportunities. The EDA's R&T director is leading this work.[134]

Since this chapter focuses on the role of the military epistemic community embedded in the larger epistemic coalition, it is important to highlight the norms and motivations of the EUMC with respect to the LTV and, in particular, to Strand 2.

EUMC Motivations

The norm that emerged among EUMC representatives was that to deal with mounting economic pressures, security integration was the necessary path forward. A key way that security integration could be achieved, according to the milreps, was to integrate research and development of military technology. Romania's Ioan said,

> I can't see any company from the military-defense industry working alone. You have to start with R&D, and you can't have military research done on its own. You have to put the money together. . . . This is beneficial for each

country. They can be sure that delivery will work, and products won't be stuck in their own market. You start every program from research, and research is very costly. It is better to be part of a research program.[135]

Spain's EUMC representative, Treviño-Ruiz, agreed, arguing that in comparison to the United States, the EU is extremely inefficient.[136] While the United States might have one or two companies producing a particular military resource—for example, aircraft—the EU will have five or six, producing the same resource at a higher price. The milreps agreed that that the EDA is the appropriate entity to ensure that R&D integration and interoperability are carried out effectively among the member states. The EDA reports to the EUMC, so by emphasizing the EDA's role in running this process, the milreps can also keep their fingers on the pulse of future developments.

The milreps' belief about the need to integrate military research is significant, since states typically strive to guard the development of new defense technology to enhance their relative advantage over other countries. Nonetheless, the milreps saw integration as a necessary step to take in the name of European security overall. General Ioan sees the main obstacle to procurement and research integration as EU legislation itself and believes that the armaments market should have the same principles as the common market. Instead, special legislation creates a separate category for armaments that excludes it from the regulations governing the common market. Békési also focused on the economic rationale:

> The biggest problem for the EU and NATO is the economic crisis, the financial burden for transforming our countries, and not being able to spend as much money as is required. . . . We need to not duplicate, to be more focused, and to have a common effort to improve—the EDA, Military Committee, and member states.[137]

Similarly, Graube said,

> Procurement is about market protections. It's really about the EU vs. the U.S., like Lockheed Martin. We can't organize with different weapons. You can't deliver seven different bullets or shells to the middle of nowhere. . . . It's a strange body, Europe. In the U.S., there are two large companies en-

gaged in defense procurement, and there could be 5, 6, 7, 10 in the EU doing the same research because of national interest. Each country believes
that if it develops the product, it will have economic benefits. It's a strange
situation, because all want to be stronger.[138]

Again, the military experts clearly separated themselves from the traditional aims of states, which is to focus on national defense spending and
national procurement. In addition, in the shorter term, EUMC representatives agreed that member states should buy only military equipment that is
interoperable, a feature that is more important than price.[139] Their specific
expertise in the nature of defense spending and the present need to embrace multinational forces in the battlefield led them to prioritize the need
for interoperability and the long-term perspective of eventual integration.
Admiral Engdahl said, "These are difficult decisions. We can't influence directly what happens, but the lack of results can influence [outcomes] when
we bring it up." One of the EUMC members' main conclusions was that interoperability is central to the EU's and each member state's future individual military capacity.

Again, these arguments are striking because traditional military generals would not typically be expected to support the integration of military
R&D. However, in light of the postmodern EU environment, in which protecting national borders and upholding purely national interests are no
longer the only concerns, the norms shaped by the EUMC make sense. The
group's top priority is to secure Europe, and if military-defense capabilities
can be maximized through integration, then this is the route to take.

Outcomes and Implementation

In the end, the members of the military epistemic community presented
the product of their research and deliberations to the EDA's Steering Board,
where it faced strong intergovernmental scrutiny. After accepting the document, Solana succinctly expressed the key conclusion in a press release:

> The best way to prepare for this future is through greater mutual trans-
> parency about medium- to long-term defence planning, so we can identify
> all those areas where the pooling of efforts and resources promises better
> value for money from tight defence budgets.[140]

In short, efficiency and expediency required security integration. The key words were *interoperability, consolidation,* and *increasing investment.*

When the document was presented to the defense ministers, not all approved of it in its entirety, but there was general agreement.[141] Even United Kingdom, which has traditionally opposed security integration, hailed the LTV's findings:

> The UK believes that the Long Term Vision is a valuable piece of work that sets out a coherent view of the challenges we will face and the capabilities we will need. No-one knows whether the vision will turn out to be accurate. But we need a long term aiming point to guide the future development of our defence capabilities. We believe that the Long Term Vision provides a reasonable foundation upon which the EDA's medium to long term agenda can be based. Furthermore, we strongly support the ongoing work to establish the [C]SDP Capability Development Plan.[142]

The Council immediately supported the LTV. Five weeks after the document's public release, the Council issued its guidelines for the EDA's 2007 work. Focusing on the medium- to long-term, the Council first instructed the EDA to start developing a Capability Development Plan that incorporated the LTV's analysis. This process would require member states to disclose their national security plans to facilitate cooperation and interoperability. Second, the Council asked the EDA to develop an initial European Defence R&T Strategy with the aim of maximizing efficiency and setting up collective spending on defense research and technology. Third, the Council charged the EDA with investigating what an "ideal" defense technological and industrial base would look like, again incorporating the LTV's findings.[143]

It is still too early to see the LTV's full practical impact, which will have to be evaluated in 2025. To date, ministries of defense have tended to be more reluctant to embrace these reforms than have the milreps in Brussels, but this phenomenon is slowly changing. Portugal's Antunes, said, "The oversight of the EU is not strong. The ministry of defense does not take seriously the overview of EU resources." The ministries of foreign affairs, however, tend to be more in favor of integration.[144] For example, Rochus Pronk of the Political Affairs Department of the Dutch Ministry of Foreign Affairs believes that "in the long run, we will require a lot more investment in joint EU capacity to sustain and make these missions effective. We need to be careful not to undermine [C]SDP by not delivering."[145] As is typical in many member states, the Dutch ministry tends to be much more oriented toward CSDP, while the ministry of defense has traditionally been more oriented toward NATO. In various member states, however, evidence has indicated that the ministries of defense are gradually becoming more open to the goals of CSDP, EDA guidance, and the various elements of the LTV.[146] This process was triggered in part by the Capability Development Plan that resulted from the LTV as well as an increased understanding that the absence of a single defense market is a serious disadvantage.[147] Going forward, the EUMC milreps will need to continue this process of persuasion in various member states, with particular attention to ministries of defense.

Despite the fact that EU military power remains a relatively new aspect of EU security integration, the impact of the military epistemic community on the trajectory of security integration has been quite strong and is likely to grow. The professional norms, culture, and worldview of the military epistemic community indicate that it is a highly cohesive transnational network of experts. In particular, for all intents and purposes, members have the same tactical expertise, which enables them to come to agreement very quickly. An important contributing factor to this group's esprit de corps and common culture is the fact that most milreps are also double-hatted to NATO, so they share a distinctive identity in a kind of hybrid environment as well as have the opportunity to foster closer relationships.

The EUMC will be an important actor in coming years as works with the EDA to review and update the goals of the LTV and persuades member states of its advantages. The EUMC's responsibilities extend beyond long-term interoperability and integration to CSDP operations, EU-NATO synergies, and day-to-day military planning. Perhaps unexpectedly, EU military experts as a community are taking on a kind of postmodern character as the scope of European security policy promises much more to its citizens than traditional military goals. The milreps not only have taken on this challenge but are breaking new ground with their keen understanding of the connections between the internal and external as well as civilian and military aspects of security. This case shows that while knowledge-based networks are transforming the course of security integration, their efforts are also helping them remake themselves.

CHAPTER 6

Loose and Nascent Communities

WITHIN THE EU BORDERS, a number of epistemic communities are not quite as established, cohesive, or prominent as those discussed thus far. While they may often appear weak, they are not necessarily failed actors. Some may be loose epistemic communities in which members come from a variety of professions and have different types of expertise. For example, they might not meet often, or they might share only broad policy goals. Others may be nascent, with the raw ingredients for a future epistemic community present but not yet coalesced into a body that can exercise agency. These groups are important because they may contain the seeds of future EU decision making. If competitive selection, rigorous training, frequent meetings, a strong body of shared professional norms, and a common culture are what give some epistemic communities high status, cohesiveness, and influence, one or more of these factors would have to be missing or weak to undermine the influence of a potential epistemic community. Alternatively, if the members of a network have policy preferences that derive not from their expert knowledge but from some other motivation—that is, they are not fully behaving like an epistemic community—this situation can undermine their neutral status and ability to be persuasive.

By observing the inner workings of two key cases—the Group of Personalities in the Field of Security Research (GofP) and the Civilian Crisis Management Committee (Civcom)—I show why epistemic communities may ultimately be loose or nascent. In both cases, members of the network have varying types of expertise, with the GofP having a much more diverse membership than Civcom but both lacking homogeneity relative to the other case studies. The GofP was a loose epistemic community whose members came from a variety of different backgrounds. They were not held together by a strong body of shared professional norms, and the level of cohesiveness thus was low. Indeed, when the group reached the end of its mandate, the network fell apart.[1] In contrast, members of Civcom grapple with a relatively new policy area that does not yet have a strong body of knowledge on which to draw. They must gain their experience and expertise on the job. Overall, when compared to a strong epistemic community such as the European Union Military Committee (EUMC), Civcom falls a bit short. It does not have a well-defined common culture or meet frequently in informal settings. The GofP was a short-lived epistemic community that lasted only a few years, while Civcom is a nascent epistemic community that will likely strengthen in the future.

This chapter first examines the case of the GofP and its impact on the Preparatory Action on Security Research (PASR). This initiative, designed to spark integration of civilian security research, eventually led to the creation in 2007 of the European Security Research Program, which guides the EU's medium- to long-term strategy to support common research on security technology. In addition to being a good example of how and why groups of scientists can affect security integration in Europe, the GofP adds a new dimension to this study. It is an epistemic community that no longer exists. Thus, this case addresses the question of why an epistemic community might lack staying power. While this is an important question, one constraint in the research of a disbanded epistemic community is that it is more difficult to interview its members, who have moved on to different activities and are spread out geographically. However, one benefit of this case in particular is that it is a rare example of a scientific community for which there is some available documentation, shedding light on the nature of members' dialogue and subsequent development of shared norms and policy goals.

Subsequently, I examine the role of Civcom in influencing civilian crisis missions under the European Security and Defence Policy. Along with the EUMC, Civcom provides the Political and Security Committee (PSC) with advice on how to proceed with Common Security and Defence Policy (CSDP) planning. While Civcom mostly comprises midranking diplomats, it also includes a number of police experts. The growing trend, however, has been a gradual shift in favor of diplomats rather than police, so a homogenization of the group is likely to occur over time. This case study analyzes Civcom's role in shaping civilian missions under CSDP. One challenge in investigating a group like Civcom is that much of the documentation of its discussions remains classified because many CSDP missions are ongoing. It is thus necessary to rely more on anecdotal evidence and interviews.

The two case studies look at different aspects of security integration: technology research and civilian crisis management. While the former deals more with internal, civilian security, the latter focuses on external, third-country security. Both are excellent examples of the highly interconnected nature of internal and external security. The manufacturers of civilian security technology in the GofP case are often the same as those who produce military technology, so they are inclined to find dual-use technologies to take advantage of potential synergies and economies of scale. The Commission wrote, "Today, many technologies are 'dual-use': civil developments adding to defense capabilities, developments originally made for defense purposes leading to major innovations and benefits in the day to day life of citizens."[2] Integration of technology research and development (R&D) on the civilian side can lead to similar progress on the military side. The overall process leads to integration of scientific research across member states, an important part of security integration more generally. Similarly, experts in civilian crisis response are managing processes in third countries that use the same techniques that police, judges, legal experts, and others use domestically. Staffing these missions relies on seconding these national experts to other parts of the world. Lessons learned from these external experiences may be applied domestically, and vice versa. Each CSDP mission thus directly affects internal security.

THE RESEARCH AND TECHNOLOGY COMMUNITY

Of the transnational networks examined in this study, the various groups of scientists involved in the R&D of security technology most closely conform to the original interpretation of the concept of epistemic community. Their knowledge is scientific in the traditional sense. However, scientific expertise in the EU tends to be so specialized that the membership in any particular epistemic community is usually quite small.[3] At the same time, not all scientists belong to an epistemic community, as many do not share any particular policy goals related to their expert knowledge. If they do, they typically meet together with other types of professionals, such as diplomats, industry suppliers, think-tank researchers, emergency personnel, and parliamentarians. Altogether, those involved in European civilian security research who also share an interest in shaping EU policy tend to form loose groupings of experts from different professional backgrounds. These groups may be more properly described as epistemic coalitions.

The GofP provides some insight into the intimate relationship between security and technology in today's world and into the civilian technology dimension in particular. This relationship is both economic and political. European governments' acquisition of defense equipment relies on the efficiency of industrial suppliers. Militaries are much more effective when they have a strong base of suppliers reliably providing the latest technology and equipment. The central nature of the relationship between defense and technology prompted six EU countries—France, Germany, Italy, Spain, Sweden, and the UK—to sign a July 6, 1998, letter of intent to "facilitate cross-border restructuring of defence industries."[4] Member states subsequently have struggled to accomplish this goal on an EU-wide scale.

Different actors can influence the development of security policy as it pertains to technology research at a number of levels.[5] First, as the only customers, governments could change the nature of their demand for defense equipment, thereby forcing industries to change accordingly. Governments make decisions about their needs based on whether they would like to focus more on internal or external security or defense or third-country operations and on the size of the overall defense budget. Since governments are accountable to their citizens, they must take into account considerations other than the direction they would like to take policy. In spending taxpayer dollars, governments must respect the public interest, spending in ways that create jobs, favor national industries, and support technology research. Second, military officials and domestic law enforcement request certain technologies and equipment. Militaries, for their part, must consider factors such as whether future operations will be multilateral, the types of equipment that need to be updated, and desired degree of interoperability with other states. Third, industrial suppliers must fulfill government demand but are also motivated by profit, long-term contract commitments, and procurement programs in which they participate. In an effort to increase profits and chances for survival, defense companies have begun a process of mergers and acquisitions, diversification of production, and joint ventures with other suppliers.[6] Finally, the scientists who develop the technology must win large sums of research funding, grapple with ever-changing demand, and deal with lag times between the request for new research, the feasibility studies they must conduct, the development of the new technology, and the production of new equipment.

The GofP had significant influence in light of the ongoing challenges that exist at multiple levels with respect to the integration of security technology research. Europe has virtually no chance of catching up with the United States any time soon in terms of the development of new military technology, but the GofP's strength was that its members focused on civil technology and on the protection of the European "homeland." Europe has a comparative advantage in this arena; indeed, civil technology is ahead of military technology. But a focus on civil technology has secondary benefits for the military side. Many technologies have dual-application capability, and defense companies have been working on both.[7] The PASR in particular was an important step toward EU-level support for security research and the funding of projects whose implementation leads to security integration. The GofP paved the way for additional developments in the design of medium- to long-term security research at the European level.

Norm Development and Policy Goals

EU Commissioners Philippe Busquin (Research) and Erkki Liikanen (Enterprise and Information Society) first convened the 27 EU officials, high-level strategists, academics, industry professionals, and researchers known as the Group of Personalities in the Field of Security Research in October 2003.[8] The group had a mandate from the Commission to propose policy as a formal body,[9] but the members accomplished more. Their expertise and shared norms effectively shaped the direction of security integration in the area of technology research and arguably continued to do so even in the absence of the GofP itself. The group received a broad mandate but put forward precise policy goals rather than simply echoing what the Commission wanted to hear. At the time, they would seem to have had the properties of an emerging epistemic community. The height of the GofP's influence lasted from 2003 to 2006, when it was tasked with creating priorities for the European Security Research Program. Although the role of the GofP was formally designated to last from 2003 to 2004, its direct influence continued through the duration of the PASR, which lasted from 2004 to 2006.

So what substantive norms, or shared causal beliefs, did the GofP members develop? Throughout their deliberations, the group produced a small number of publications documenting its findings. Each relied on the argument that terrorism in the form of an attack on borders, infrastructure, and people posed a serious security threat to the foundations of European society.[10] First, the GofP saw borders—including points of entry at airports, land borders, harbors, coasts, and waterways—as particular areas of vulnerability. Second, members saw threats to infrastructure in the form of disruption to the electrical grid, information technology, oil and gas, and transportation systems as a major cause for concern. And third, they judged that European citizens were at significant risk from hostage taking; chemical, biological, radiological, and nuclear (CBRN) weapons; and conventional arms. All of these views stemmed from members shared belief that terrorism posed the biggest threat to European security.

After membership in the GofP was established in October 2003, the group spent six months deliberating and clarifying their shared norms, with the results documented in a March 2004 report, *Research for a Secure Europe*.[11] The report enabled the GofP to put forward its arguments about what strategies should be adopted in Europe to deal with the new and dangerous security threat posed by terrorism. The report argued that the EU needed to integrate the internal and external foci of the security agenda, share knowledge between the civilian and military dimensions of security, establish a European Security Research Advisory Board (ESRAB) to oversee the European research agenda, implement goals though the European Security Research Program (ESRP), and strive to coordinate national, community, and intergovernmental responses. In addition to advocating the immediate implementation of these measures, the group carefully emphasized that these goals should not supersede the EU's duty to protect and uphold individual rights and democratic values.[12] Finally, the report recommended financing of at least €1 billion per year for the ESRP to accomplish these initiatives. The Commission was persuaded by these arguments and gave approval to pursue these policies as well as provided the requested funding.

Also in March 2004, the commission launched the three-year PASR with a total budget of €65 million—€15 million for 2004 and €25 million for 2005 and 2006 each—in line with the GofP's recommendations. This initiative sought to allow Europeans at large to apply for funding to engage in security research as a lead-up to the ESRP. In 2007, after PASR was completed, funding of security research would be fully launched as part of the Seventh Research Framework Program (FP7), from 2007 to 2013, with a budget of €1.4 billion.[13] The first call for applications stated that PASR proposals should encapsulate the goal of Community-level security action and should "research, validate and integrate security-oriented technologies."[14] In particular, the GofP wanted new research under the PASR to address new kinds of diverse threats, writing that "this diversity presents a major challenge for the formation of security policies and calls for common European answers."[15] PASR fulfilled this demand for a common approach by requiring multicountry participation and hence cross-border collaboration on each funded project.

Just days after the release of the first report, terrorist attacks on Madrid's commuter train system killed 191 people and injured 1,800. These real-world events launched a new phase of deliberations among the 27. By February 2006, they emphasized the overarching substantive norm that technology made security possible. At a conference in Vienna,[16] participants reiterated the belief that "technology itself cannot guarantee security, but security without the support of technology is impossible."[17] When the members of the GofP spoke about technology, they meant not simply an upgrading of current systems but a whole new era of technological advancement, with such innovations as microwave feed systems, microfluidic scanners, and space-based communication. Moreover, such technological advancement firmly set the stage for security integration since it required implementation at the community level to work.

The GofP's shared causal belief that new technology would provide security is crucial, since the resulting policy goal was not necessarily obvious. The 27 might instead have advocated providing development aid to third countries to alleviate poverty, creating a training program or supplying equipment to local groups, running risk assessment, or reexamining budget allocations and legislation. The U.S. strategy, for example, emphasized combating terrorism using conventional military means over tackling direct and credible threats.[18] The development of new technology, while important, was not the main focus for the United States.

The GofP played a key role in moving the EU in a different direction. The 27 experts sought to persuade others, especially the Commission, of the norm that technology innovation was the answer to the question of how to deal with its major vulnerabilities—borders, critical infrastructure, and CBRN disasters. Based on their expertise, they specifically outlined the technologies they believed necessary to reduce these threats, including a variety of laser, thermal, and infrared sensors, Earth observation from space, advanced information technology systems, firewalling, encryption, and CBRN neutralizers.[19] This technology would enable the EU to detect and prevent CBRN attacks, improve surveillance and monitoring, ensure systems interoperability, secure against cyberattack, provide digital communication, protect network hardware, and decontaminate in the event of a CBRN attack. The GofP's technology norm had the added potential of promoting security integration through a less politically sensitive approach. In many ways, it is more palatable to offer European-level funding for research on security technology than, for example, to require member states to become militarily interoperable.

Did the GofP's deliberations and publications affect outcomes? Since the group clearly influenced the results of PASR, which ultimately paved the way for ESRP, one method of observing outcomes is to look at the kinds of proposals that were funded under PASR to see whether they conformed to the criteria set by the 27 and then to examine whether or not their beliefs continued to shape the policy dialogue. With the first call for proposals, PASR immediately attracted a large and diverse pool of applicants. The first deadline, June 23, 2004, resulted in 173 applications from all 25 member states.[20] Of these, 12 were selected and launched in December 2004. They lasted between six months and three years.[21] The second call for proposals, with a deadline of May 3, 2005, drew 156 proposals, of which 13 were accepted.[22] The final call, ending on May 10, 2006, attracted 165 proposals, of which 15 received funding.[23] Although the PASR required scientists from only two different member states to participate in each project, the average number in the first two rounds was six, dropping slightly to five for the last round. Tables 4, 5, and 6, describe the technology research that resulted from the three-year program.

The first round of PASR projects, shown in table 4, strongly reflected the GofP's beliefs that terrorism posed the biggest danger to security, that technology helped overcome this danger, and that threats to borders, infrastructure, and people were the most crucial areas of vulnerability. In particular, group members believed that huge leaps in technological capabilities were necessary. The research projects selected for PASR funding provided just such leaps, and their implementation necessitated further security integration among member states. Any weak link would be an obvious target, so all member states would need to implement the new measures. TERASEC, for example, would require all member states to use the same technology to detect weapons on people or in the mail. Similarly, ISCAPS, a project researching new surveillance technology for monitoring crowded areas and critical infrastructure, would be particularly useful at borders, requiring universal adoption. SUPHICE, which developed on-demand secure communications between member states, was inherently multistate. CRIMSON was a supporting project that effectively spread norms about crisis response within Europe through the development of a 3D virtual-reality simulation of a CBRN attack on the EU. As with any actor that seeks to influence through persuasion, spreading norms about policy goals is crucial. In effect, member states could simulate responding to a European threat in an integrated fashion, thus making doing so in real life more acceptable.

The second round of funding, summarized in table 5, also possessed an

TABLE 4.   Preparatory Action on Security Research 2004

Name	Method of Preventing Terrorism—PASR 2004	Implications for Security Integration[a]
ASTRO	Develop Europe space industry	High
CRIMSON	Create 3D virtual reality crisis-simulation technology	Potentially High
ESSTRT	Analyze threats and recommend new cooperative measures	High
GEOCREW	Research early detection system for manmade crises	Potentially High
IMPACT	Build foundation for integrated CBRN counterterrorism plan	High
ISCAPS	Institute integrated surveillance of crowded areas	Potentially High
SeNTRE	Consult a network of technology experts for integrated security	High
SUPHICE	Create a common EU crypto not owned by any member-state	High
TERASEC	Develop terahertz radiation and laser for remote and nearby detection of CBR and explosive weapons on people or in the mail	High
TIARA	Constitute an EU network for treatment after radiological accidents	High
VITA	Assess threat to highly transnational networks of infrastructure	Potentially High

Source: European Union Enterprise and Industry, *Preparatory Action for Security Research 2004 Funded Activities,* http://europa.eu.int/comm/enterprise/security/articles/article_2164_en.htm (accessed May 7, 2007). This table previously appeared in Mai'a K. Davis Cross, "An EU Homeland Security? Sovereignty vs. Supranational Order," *European Security* 16 (1): 79–97.

[a]"High" denotes necessary security integration if member-states implement the project. "Potentially High" indicates that the project is likely to lead to supranational coordination but may also be used purely at the domestic level.

inherent integrative drive behind its projects. Effective implementation required adoption and standardization across member states. TRIPS and SOBCAH, for example, led to new surveillance technology aimed at railroads, land, and coastal borders. Given the realities of the Schengen zone, implementation would necessitate EU-wide participation. PRISE was simi-

TABLE 5. Preparatory Action on Security Research 2005

Name	Method of Preventing Terrorism—PASR 2005	Implications for Security Integration
TRIPS	Improve protection of rail passengers with scanners, cameras, ground penetrating radars, etc.	High
SOBCAH	Create surveillance across Europe of 6,000 km of land borders and 85,000 km of coastline by increasing connectivity	High
ROBIN	Secure computers linked to networks	Potentially High
PATIN	Institute multilayered system networks to protect air transportation from CBRN attacks	High
MARIUS	Build a "Demonstrator": an autonomous command post, with IT to monitor crisis situations	Potentially High
PALMA	Protect commercial aircraft against man-portable air defense systems	Potentially High
HiTS/ISAC	Gain superior situation awareness and cross-border interoperability. Make information available across EU.	High
PROBANT	Research sensors and biometric and pulsed signal techniques to visualize and track people inside buildings	Potentially High
PETRA.NET	Network the security research community with public authority users	High
SECCOND	Standardize technical interface between a secure container and data reader at port/border	High
BSUAV	Build unmanned aerial vehicles for peacetime security of borders	High
PRISE	Encourage public acceptance of security protection; privacy and human rights guidelines	High
USE IT	Exchange sensitive information among all European bodies	High

Source: European Union Press Releases, *13 New Security Research Projects to Combat Terrorism,* MEMO/05/277, Brussels, August 2, 2005. This table previously appeared in Mai'a K. Davis Cross, "An EU Homeland Security? Sovereignty vs. Supranational Order," *European Security* 16 (1): 79–97.

TABLE 6. Preparatory Action on Security Research 2006

Name	Method of Preventing Terrorism—PASR 2006	Implications for Security Integration
ISOTREX	Improve technologies to detect particle/vapor trace explosives, including liquids, at border check points	High
CITRINE	Develop integrated information tools to implement emergency services for humanitarian and rescue tasks	High
WATERSAFE	Use nanotechnologies to sense and decontaminate networked drinking water distribution systems	High
BODE	Assess need for biological weapons detection apparatus and propose a detection demonstrator device for manufacture	Potentially High
i-TRACS	Develop an enhanced tracking and surveillance system with multiple data sources while protecting civil liberties	Potentially High
WINTSEC	Explore wireless interoperability across member-states' security agencies and find acceptable federal solutions	High
GATE	Study modeling techniques to detect money laundering and terrorism financing and deploy models within banks	Potentially High
AEROBACTICS	Design models to distinguish natural occurrences of airborne microorganisms from real attacks	Potentially High
STABORSEC	Investigate the interoperability and standardization of technologies that enhance border security	High
SECURESME	Help integrate small and medium enterprises and encourage their participation in EU security research	High
BIO3R	Study scenarios and assess social responses to bioterrorism in the EU and reinforce capabilities	High
EUROCOP	Improve efficiency, access to information, and intelligence reporting of pedestrian police officers	Potentially High
STACCATO	Define methods and solutions for the overall integration of the security market and supply chain	High
BioTesting Europe	Establish network for testing and certification of biometric technology like the new electronic passports	High
HAMLeT	Improve chemical sensors to track potentially suspicious people	Potentially High

Source: European Union Press Releases, *PASR 2006: 15 New Security Research Projects to Combat Terrorism,* MEMO/06/375, Brussels, October 13, 2006. This table previously appeared in Mai'a K. Davis Cross, "An EU Homeland Security? Sovereignty vs. Supranational Order," *European Security* 16 (1): 79–97.

lar to CRIMSON in that it sought to spread norms about security research. It was designed to inform and persuade the general public of the merits of Europe's security research agenda and to ensure the protection of human rights and civil liberties, as per the GofP objective.

The final preparatory round, shown in table 6, sought to fill some of the gaps remaining after the first two rounds. Both STABORSEC and STAC-CATO, for example, augmented security by finding areas for better interoperability, standardization, and market access. They were essentially aimed at ensuring a path to integration for the other PASR projects. ISOTREX and BioTesting Europe, like many of the previously funded proposals, dealt with the priority area of border security, seeking new technology to counter the use of liquid explosives and to certify electronic passports. ISOTREX, in particular, reflected a response to real-world events. On August 10, 2006, British police arrested twenty-four terrorist suspects planning to smuggle liquid explosives onto aircraft in an attempt to repeat the devastation of 9/11. Thus, ISOTREX sought to improve weapons detection technology at border checkpoints. i-TRACS, WINTSEC, EUROCOP, and HAMLeT concerned federalizing and sharing information about dangerous individuals through tracking and surveillance technology that would be Europeanized. Overall, PASR's three rounds provide evidence that the GofP's norms and subsequent policy goals were reflected in funded scientific research.

Outcomes and Implications

Looking beyond the PASR, did the GofP have a lasting impact on security integration more generally? Yes, but its impact has become increasingly indirect over time, in large part because it ceased to convene after its last formal meeting in 2004. Despite its dissolution, the work of the GofP has left a lasting imprint on the permanent EU program for security research. On December 22, 2006, the Commission launched the FP7 as planned, with its €1.4 billion earmarked for security-themed projects during 2007–13. These multiyear research framework programs have been designed to achieve the main priority of the March 2000 Lisbon Agenda: making the EU "the most competitive and dynamic knowledge-based economy" in the world as well as bridging the gap between civil and national or intergovernmental security research.[24] Framework programs provide EU funding for a wide variety of activities, but the one launched in 2007 was the first to include security research (previously PASR), and it was housed under the cooperation rubric, largely a result of the GofP's persuasiveness and the success of PASR. Thus, 2007 marked the institutionalization of security research into an EU-level agenda item supported by EU funding.

The incorporation of PASR into the EU's Framework Program structure shows the GofP's ultimate normative influence in the process of security integration as it pertains to the key area of technology research. It also brought security research into the mainstream EU research and governance agenda. One shortcoming is that the GofP had recommended a budget of at least €1 billion per year, and FP7 offered €1.4 billion over seven years. But to boost this amount, the Commission also established the EU Framework Program on Security and Safeguarding Liberties, which brought the total funding up to €2.135 billion.[25]

In addition to bringing security research into the Commission's Framework Program, the 27 convinced other actors of their shared norms, thereby affecting longer-term processes. European Commission officials were so convinced by the group's initial report that they released a response, *Security Research: The Next Steps*, in which they fully accepted all of the GofP's recommendations. According to this document,

> In addressing the new security challenges, technology plays a key role. The European potential to research, develop and deploy a wide range of security technologies exists. However, in facing the new diversity of threats, Europe needs to surmount current structural and functional deficiencies: reducing fragmentation and duplication of effort, increasing cooperation and achieving standardization and interoperability.[26]

Much of this document reiterates the GofP's *Research for a Secure Europe*. With regard to the PASR and ESRP, the Commission followed the GofP's advice in selecting and implementing research proposals. The Commission put into place officials at the level of head of unit (middle management) to oversee the process.

The GofP's substantive norms were also echoed in the aspirations of the European Defence Agency (EDA), which provides a forum for defense ministers. In addition to pushing for technology research, the group argued that ESRP representatives needed to develop synergies and connections with officials from the EDA, including sharing research results and meeting regularly. On November 13, 2006, the EDA agreed to a new defense fund that explicitly sought to enhance the development of new security technology. The GofP had emphasized throughout the course of its deliberations that the EU spends less than half of what the United States spends on defense and that the EU should aim to spend between 1.9 percent and 3 percent of average GDP on defense by 2010.[27] Defense ministers hoped that the new defense fund would help alleviate the discrepancy between U.S. and EU spending.[28] The results were not perfect. Some member states hesitated to fully and equally participate because of its implications for maintaining independent national foreign policies: The French, German, and Polish governments became the largest contributors to the fund, but the British refused to participate.[29] Nonetheless, the EDA's role in the procurement of defense equipment for external security is growing, and thanks to the GofP, the applications for dual-use technology and information sharing fall within the purview of Framework Program discussions.

Finally, the GofP's legacy was quite visible in its successor, ESRAB, which it created in March 2005. The advisory board was intended to bring together a broad spectrum of stakeholders from the EDA, academia, industry, and science and to bridge the divide between private and public strategists and those involved on both the supply (performers of security research) and demand (end users of security research) sides.[30] As the GofP stipulated, membership in the advisory board consisted of 50 high-ranking strategists, although more than 300 individuals participated in crafting ESRAB's output.[31] The GofP, by contrast, had consisted of a more select body of experts. ESRAB's mandate differed somewhat from that of the GofP, which advocated specific policy goals based on a broad mandate. ESRAB focused more narrowly on implementation, especially meeting the demands of end users and increasing the competitiveness of Europe's technology research. The advisory board's main report, *Meeting the Challenge: The European Security Research Agenda,* shows that board members followed the main principles of the GofP but came up with less specific goals.[32] For example, ESRAB's strategic framework covers both technological and nontechnological research; its rules on implementation of research both rely on EU regulation governing sensitive information and enhance the role of member states' authorities; and the board calls for national funding alongside EU funding. The advisory board did not comprise an epistemic community as its membership was too broad ranging and its basis for shared knowledge too weak, as its results reflected. It neither conceived of new and specific causal beliefs based on shared expertise nor pushed to see these norms expressed in policies.

ESRAB decided to replace itself with the European Security Research and Innovation Forum, created on September 11, 2007. The forum is a public-private network designed to develop medium- to long-term civil security research strategy. While the forum continues to express some of the basic causal beliefs set forth by the GofP, its members are now two steps removed from the original epistemic community whose discussions consolidated these knowledge-based norms. ESRAB stipulated that the forum should comprise all relevant stakeholders in Europe's security agenda from the public and private sectors, that membership should number between 50 and 70 individuals, and that member states should nominate individuals to participate. In addition, forum members could select between 200 and 300 people to form supportive working groups. Once established, the forum included 64 members from 31 countries (some of which were not EU members) as well as more than 600 experts.[33] While their work is ongoing, the members of the forum have emphasized most the need to achieve "an interoperable, trust-embedded, and resilient society."[34] Technological innovation remained a theme in the forum's final report, but the social aspects of security and the need for trust, education, interoperability, and a broadly shared vision were paramount. This second degree of separation from the GofP clearly demonstrates even wider membership, broader goals, diverse types of expertise, and a lowest-common-denominator approach. It is more difficult to say that the impact of the GofP's more specific norms and goals remain first and foremost within the forum.

As a new epistemic community, the GofP's of 27 experts demonstrated their facility to agree on shared norms that coalesced into common policy goals. Their ability to persuade other actors was significant, and thus their policy goals very clearly reached fruition through the PASR, ESRP, and FP7. Evidence also shows that the GofP contributed to longer-term policy change through the EDA's defense fund and through the diffusion of norms through other actors. Despite these successes, the GofP was ultimately a very short-lived epistemic community. The norms it set forth had a lasting influence, but the 27 no longer meet and do not continue to push for the same policy outcomes. Rather, they have put into place other actors who have gradually relinquished the GofP's specific aims.

The last official meeting of the GofP took place in 2004, although nothing prevented participants from continuing their network on a more informal level. Why does an epistemic community disband? At least three explanations exist. First, if an epistemic community is relatively loose because its members do not share the same types of expertise, there is no professional incentive to hold them together. That this explanation applies to the GofP is evidenced by the fact that all of its members have gone on to different professional occupations. Without a similar basis of understanding, a common language, and shared professional norms, it is difficult for real relationships based on shared goals to hold together in the longer term.

Second, if members of an epistemic community are not purely driven by their expert knowledge, they are not likely to be fully invested in their network. Numerous members of the GofP, especially the industry suppliers, stood to profit financially from the collective decision to focus on technology development, so there is some question about whether their goals were based purely on professional expertise or whether they had other motives.

Third, as a result of the first two factors, epistemic communities with loose ties and weak cohesion are not likely to exercise agency beyond their stated mandate. The GofP, while more successful and effective than its successors, was not driven to push for truly groundbreaking advances. The Commission had some funding to allocate and left its terms open to the influence of this knowledge-based group. The GofP fulfilled its mandate but did not really go beyond it.

Whether or not the GofP had official reason to meet is not central to their existence as a knowledge-based network. Epistemic communities can exist within or outside of formal structures and may initially come together formally or informally. What really matters is what its members make of their grouping and what they bring to the table collectively. The GofP members could have continued to seek shared policy goals with or without the official sanction of the Commission. But the heterogeneity of their expertise, lack of shared professional norms, and subsequent low incentive to exercise agency kept them from reaching fruition as an epistemic community. Europe still possesses a strong desire to move forward with security integration in the area of research, but the articulation of these goals is somewhat weak on the civilian side. Rather, the EDA, with its focus on external security, is becoming more prominent and concrete in its achievements, in no small part because of the strong cohesiveness and growing influence of the EUMC.

THE CIVILIAN CRISIS MANAGEMENT COMMUNITY

The Civilian Crisis Management Committee is an example of a nascent epistemic community that holds more long-term promise than the GofP did
during its existence. Like the EUMC, Civcom was established to provide advice and policy recommendations to PSC ambassadors, but Civcom's area
of responsibility is civilian missions and priorities rather than military
ones.[35] Both groups are positioned at the middle of the Council hierarchy,
both represent all the member states, and both receive regular instructions
from their capitals. But despite their similarities and the fact that they were
created within one year of each other, Civcom's shared professional norms
and common culture are significantly less defined than those of the EUMC.
However, the field of civilian crisis management is a relatively new policy
area for member states. Civcom members clearly arrive at the table with
less of a common background and collective memory than their military
counterparts.

On a day-to-day basis, Civcom keeps track of progress in ongoing civilian missions and plans future CSDP missions, including the determination
of available resources. It typically works on the basis of discussion papers
first generated by the Council Secretariat. Member states did not anticipate
how many civilian missions in third countries Civcom would oversee.
Nearly three-quarters of the 23 CSDP operations have been civilian. In addition, Civcom is responsible for civilian capability management. The Feira
European Council of June 2000 and Civilian Headline Goals 2008 (established in 2004) and 2010 (established in 2007) framed Civcom's priority areas in this respect. Among Civcom's responsibilities are developing a database of personnel available for crisis management, maintaining deployable
target numbers, and creating civilian response teams.[36]

Civilian capacity building for overseas missions is arguably just as crucial for the future of EU security integration as is military capacity building,
and member states are not yet on the same page. First and foremost, civilian crisis management does not yet benefit from efficient national structures to support the activities emanating from Brussels. Daniel Korski and
Richard Gowan argue that member states can be divided into four groups
with regard to their willingness and ability to contribute well-trained civilian forces to CSDP missions: the Professionals (Denmark, Finland, Germany, the Netherlands, Sweden, and the UK), the Strivers (Austria, Belgium, France, Ireland, Italy, and Romania), the Agnostics (the Czech

Republic, Hungary, Poland, Portugal, Slovakia, Slovenia, and Spain), and the Indifferents (Bulgaria, Cyprus, Estonia, Greece, Latvia, Lithuania, Luxembourg, and Malta).[37] Some member states have taken the lead on civilian capacity building by requiring training before deployment, debriefing personnel after their return to garner lessons learned, and putting into place a government-wide planning process. Other member states have not yet begun.

Given the EU's consolidated image as a civilian power, the need for Civcom to become even more visible, effective, and expertise driven is mounting. The EU's 2007–10 police mission in Afghanistan was a step in the right direction. Its high visibility has enabled the EU to demonstrate to the international community its integrated capacity and political will to be engaged in one of the world's most pressing issues. Indeed, the EU's contribution to reconstruction and stabilization in Afghanistan has been crucial although somewhat underrecognized. One of the main reasons that civilian CSDP has grown so rapidly over the past ten years is Civcom's ability to reach compromise on the details of civilian missions. Civcom's status as a nascent epistemic community bodes well for the future of civilian CSDP, as the group has significant room in which to build a higher degree of cohesion and a stronger sense of shared causal beliefs about what this area of security policy needs. If Civcom flourishes as an epistemic community, it can begin to push for medium- to long-term integration of civilian capacity management across member states, inevitably leading to more efficient and effective missions. Civcom currently tends to focus on the needs of the moment, but a higher level of expertise that can bring to light a more comprehensive perspective is sorely needed.

Selection and Training

Civcom is populated with experts from national ministries of foreign affairs, interior, and justice, many of them low- to mid-ranking diplomats. Technical expertise in EU affairs or civilian crisis management and experience in the diplomatic art of compromise are important qualities for a potential civilian crisis community. Except for the police officials, most Civcom delegates do not come to Brussels with experience in either civilian crisis management or EU affairs. Rather, they gain this technical knowledge by learning on the job. Over time, Civcom's purview has evolved from more conceptual to more operational, but the number of delegates with operational expertise has not increased. As one delegate said, "There are problems because some areas are very technical, like in [civilian crisis management], and experts are needed. This presents a problem for postings like this one: the lack of expertise."[38] Those diplomats who have no experience in Common Foreign and Security Policy and who come from countries with little structure to deal with these issues are more likely to simply support whatever the Secretariat proposes.

Civcom clearly would benefit from a stronger presence of those with specific civilian crisis expertise. However, the committee mitigates this disadvantage in several ways. First, Civcom delegates are replaced one at time, so relative novices in EU or civilian crisis management can benefit from the support of their colleagues when they arrive in Brussels. A high learning curve confronts new delegates. One Civcom delegate said, "Formal qualifications rarely tell all the truth about a person. . . . It takes diplomats with enough expertise or experts with enough diplomatic skills."[39] Civcom delegates are more likely than EUMC members to learn from those in their permanent representation rather than from their counterparts. As a result, the learning process itself does not promote as much transnational socialization within Civcom as it does in the EUMC. Nonetheless, in-house support, a high learning curve, and quick socialization into the group can go some distance in helping new delegates catch up.

Second, in situations where technical expertise is lacking, Civcom representatives can rely on various groups within the Council, including the Civilian Planning and Conduct Capability (CPCC) and DG E9, the directorate on civilian crisis management. CPCC was created in August 2007 as a group of 70 experts within the Council Secretariat. It provides Civcom with advice on police, rule of law, finance, procurement, and logistical matters.[40] On occasion, those with police expertise in Civcom can be quite crucial in persuading other members. For example, in discussing the mandate on EU-POL Afghanistan, some police experts saw the need to create an interlinkage between the police and rule-of-law sections of the mission. They argued that police work relies on prosecutors. When the whole committee agreed, the linkage was included in Civcom's advice to PSC. As a result, all subsequent missions have had rule of law as a component of police work.[41]

Third, although most Civcom members do not tend to come to their posts with specific expertise, they, like most career diplomats, arrive with experience in how to conduct negotiations and find compromise solutions. They have usually served in at least two previous postings and thus are not new to the more general techniques of negotiation. For example, Irish Civcom delegate Tim Harrington described the technique of overemphasizing opposition to a capital's red lines to gain flexibility with his instructions. The justification for this strategy is that those in Brussels often have a better grasp of what is possible in negotiations than do their counterparts in the capitals.[42] The style in which delegates choose to put forward their points within Civcom also requires a particular kind of expertise. One delegate described how experienced diplomats may simply state what they want without giving reasons, leaving it to those opposed to give reasons for their case instead.[43] Holding "pre-meetings" and finding "pre-agreements" are also important, especially to influence the Council Secretariat. If diplomats keep their fingers on the secretariat's pulse, they can ensure that their countries' input is wrapped into the discussion document before it is even circulated.

Thus, despite the fact that a large proportion of Civcom members are not experts in civilian crisis management or EU processes, they are budding experts at negotiation procedures and the art of compromise. With gradual turnover of Civcom members, the ability to learn quickly on the job, and the Council Secretariat as a resource, lack of technical expertise is mitigated.

Meetings and Shared Professional Norms

Political decisions usually are not made in formal meetings because stuffy procedure and protocol get in the way of real deliberation. Civcom is somewhat of an exception to this rule, as its formal meetings, held on Mondays and Wednesdays, are conducted in an informal fashion. Delegates describe a relaxed atmosphere and an informal approach. These meetings often run hours longer than scheduled. At the beginning of the meeting, everyone must agree on the agenda, which is circulated a couple of days in advance, and highlight any points for further discussion. The committee then listens to briefings about the latest developments in the field, often from the Secretariat. Any group that provides a briefing will leave the room after taking questions from the delegates. Civcom representatives with specific expertise sometimes rotate as well, depending on the issue. Certain member states have several diplomats, typically with different geographic knowledge, posted to Civcom. Interviewees describe a lot of coming and going of representatives during these meetings, which makes it is more difficult to rely on cultivated relationships and shared understandings.

Civcom meetings are governed by certain shared professional norms that help to smooth interactions and create certain expectations. These professional norms range from appropriate behavior in the conduct of meetings to notions of how consensus is best reached. During formal meetings, Civcom representatives often find themselves talking in the corridors, making phone calls to their capitals, or even text-messaging each other across the table to informally resolve conflicts before they are formally aired. Participants generally want to avoid sharp confrontation in the open, a desire that distinguishes the group from other committees, particularly in light of the fact that Civcom often deals with controversial subjects.

There is a common expectation that some type of consensus should be found by the end of the proceedings. Interviewees report that the means are not as important as the ends. When delegates speak, they express their positions and misgivings frankly as a means of facilitating mutual understanding. One professional norm that governs Civcom meetings is the decision about when to speak. This choice is part of the skill required of delegates and clearly depends on the degree of their respective countries' involvement in or commitment to specific issues.[44] With 27 people in the room, meetings would drag on for hours if a *tour de table* were commonplace, even if everyone kept their remarks to three minutes. At that rate, one *tour de table* would take 80 minutes, with additional time required for the contributions from the Commission and Secretariat, and without any real discussion taking place. Consequently, Civcom delegates have developed a sense of when it is appropriate to intervene in the negotiations and when it is better to abstain. According to one delegate, if a country is not going to participate in a mission, a delegate should not block agreement but instead should remain silent and let the others go forward.[45] There is pride in achieving implementation of missions and in always leaving the room with a paper ready.

In addition, Civcom delegates avoid putting one or two member states on the spot even if they are the primary obstruction to accomplishing the majority's goals.[46] Instead, delegates who are skeptical of a particular idea may not take issue with it if the matter is not consequential from their standpoint. EUMC and Civcom share this sense of when to let something pass and when to tackle it head-on. In other words, the dynamic involves always keeping in mind the big picture, the shared goal of moving CSDP forward. Ultimately, this determination to leave the room with a compromise in hand affects what happens in the CSDP missions. Interviewees observed that PSC nearly always accepts Civcom's agreed positions.

Finally, as in all multilateral settings, Civcom members have a keen understanding that everyone must work with some degree of instruction from their capitals. A kind of empathy consequently arises: At any given point in time, any of them could find themselves in a tough situation, trying to find the middle ground between their capitals and the collective will of the group. They deal with this inherent aspect of the job professionally. Said one Civcom delegate, "There's a certain personal detachment from the content. You don't always identify the person with what he says."[47] As a general rule, in Civcom, esprit de corps and shared professional norms have less of an impact when instructions contain red lines and the issues are controversial. This phenomenon indicates the nascent quality of this epistemic community.

EULEX Kosovo, for example, was a tough case for Civcom delegates. They sought to put together a rule-of-law mission in Kosovo that would become the largest civilian CSDP mission to date. But five member states—Cyprus, Greece, Romania, Slovakia, and Spain—opposed Kosovo's bid for independence and gave their Brussels representatives very specific instructions about what they could say during the deliberations. Civcom collectively navigated rough waters to find consensus in two ways. First, members agreed to adopt the planning documents for the rule of law mission before Kosovo formally declared independence. In so doing, Civcom used status-neutral language in the documents in an unproblematic way. As Belgian Civcom representative Koenraad Dassen put it, it was "a *technique du non-dit*. We don't say it, but it's there."[48] If Civcom had waited until after the declaration of independence, delegates would have had to deal with the question of what to label Kosovo, its leadership, and its government. Consensus on a mission would have become unlikely. Second, those from the five member states against the recognition of Kosovo also did their part to rationalize compromise at Civcom's level. One delegate said, "We considered it a technical job that should be done to create capacity for a functioning, lawful administration respecting the rule of law and Western traditions."[49] Committee members found that by taking a more technical approach, they could leave aside the independence issue. While this example shows skilled diplomatic maneuvering, it also reveals that Civcom members chose to find ways to avoid addressing the central controversy head-on. They found a solution, but it did not involve persuading the capitals to change their positions.

Civcom representatives do not meet frequently outside of regular meetings. They report having a particularly heavy workload as a consequence of their group's central position in CSDP decision making. Delegates attend biweekly meetings and sit in on any PSC meetings pertaining to points they have made. After these meetings, they then write up reports and read hundreds of pages in preparation for the next meeting.[50] Civcom delegates must be knowledgeable on fewer issues than PSC members but discuss them in greater detail, sometimes spending hours debating a single line or even word in a document. Twelve-hour work days are typical.

Despite this overload, Civcom members participate in two types of regular, informal meetings: biannual visits to the capital of the rotating presidency and field visits to specific civilian CSDP missions. This time away from the office builds relationships among delegates. The field missions in particular are also directly useful for their work. They can see firsthand problems on the ground rather than relying solely on mission reports. They also often welcome new Civcom delegates by inviting them to bilateral lunches. In general, however, Civcom emphasizes formal meetings conducted in a relaxed atmosphere rather than informal gatherings as are more common in EUMC or Coreper.

Common Culture

Given the variety of delegates' experience and professional backgrounds, the bulk of Civcom's culture lies mainly in its esprit de corps. Common culture can be far richer than esprit de corps, which is often thought of as a sense of camaraderie and devotion to group goals. Common culture is a bit more encompassing as it is typically a key part of the identity, heritage, symbolism, and sense of purpose shared by a group of individuals. Civcom has not yet developed a tangible common culture that is much more than its esprit de corps, although the latter does add to its cohesion as a group.

Civcom's esprit de corps consists first of pride in what it is accomplishing. Many interviewees describe how they accomplish tasks that are politically important and practical. Their pride also stems from the feeling that their ambassadors and political masters at home recognize their achievements and that they are dealing with issues that are fundamentally new. Italian Civcom representative Gabriele Altana described feeling that the group is "blazing new trails."[51] And even when negotiations do not always run smoothly, members of Civcom find that their esprit de corps can even spring from internal professional rivalry and competition. Just because they sometimes must represent opposing positions does not mean that they have personal hostilities.

The second main element of Civcom's esprit de corps is the legacy from its predecessors—how committee members shaped the group's dynamic from the start. Esprit de corps can be somewhat path dependent.[52] After a certain norm of interaction becomes entrenched within an institution like Civcom, it becomes self-reinforcing. Since Civcom is repopulated piecemeal, each new member is socialized into the existing culture, and it is difficult for any one member to change it. This situation holds true for all Council committees; as a result, each now has a distinguishable culture. A Civcom delegate described his committee as possessing "a common understanding that in the end, apart from the concrete questions, there's a common desire to move the EU forward. The spirit of consensus is there."[53]

Third, it follows that Civcom's esprit de corps is determined to some extent by the type of people who populate it. If a group's members have a similar professional background, they will find they have similar worldviews, experiences on which to draw, and working methods. They can hit the ground running. From this standpoint, Civcom is not as homogeneous as the EUMC, nor is it as heterogeneous as the GofP. Its members are both diplomats and nondiplomats, and they are at different stages in their careers. According to Dutch representative Marc Bentinck, Civcom is "a happy mix of younger and older diplomats and policemen. Somehow it works well."[54] But several delegates are on only their second or third assignments;[55] because they are not diplomats of high seniority, a posting in Civcom is a career bonus for them. Bentinck said, "Age is a factor. Most of us are younger, and very happy to be in this position. . . . It's considered an interesting step to be here. You feel privileged, enthusiastic."[56]

At the same time, Civcom's heterogeneity results in some fragmentation within the overarching esprit de corps. On the one hand, Civcom is like a club in that everyone recognizes the other members as equals. On the other hand, some delegates form a kind of separate clique. One particular subcommunity encompasses those who have served together longer in Civcom. Because they have known each other for more time, they share a deeper trust and common points of view, which enable them to work things out among themselves separately and more easily. Other subcommunities within Civcom reflect certain consistent, normative values. The Nordic countries and and neutral countries such as Austria, for example, find they have more in common.[57] France, Italy, Germany, and the UK also often find a common niche, separate from the others, in that they often contribute more resources or personnel to civilian CSDP missions and thus have similar stakes in the outcome. They may communicate more frequently to determine their shared interests. A subcommunity of Central and Eastern European countries (CEECs) is less manifest than might be expected, however.[58] Although CEECs are relatively new to the EU, their Civcom delegates tend to have served on the committee for about the same amount of time as the older member states' delegates. Postings average between three and four years. It is more common to find a shared subcommunity among longer-standing delegates than longer-standing member states.

In addition, coalitions also form within Civcom based on certain issues, but these groupings are fluid over the long run. For example, the EU member states that did not recognize Kosovo's independence stood together on certain aspects of EULEX Kosovo but have little reason to form an automatic coalition with regard to other CSDP missions. National interest still trumps the ties of esprit de corps if member states have a lot at stake. Delegates with experience in geographically focused working groups say that they would not describe Civcom as like-minded. Unlike in other committees, Civcom has a horizontal mandate, dealing with many areas of the world, which often makes it more difficult to "pre-agree" negotiations. By contrast, even though military representatives similarly deal with horizontal issues, their high degree of shared expertise makes them remarkably like-minded when it comes to military advice, regardless of the geographic region involved. The milreps report more instances of coming to agreement and then persuading political players even when national interests are at stake. Nonetheless, Civcom's esprit de corps as it stands may evolve into a stronger bond over time, especially as members' expertise grows to match the importance of their work.[59]

The Capital-Civcom Dynamic

Instructions are conveyed to Civcom delegates in a variety of ways, and the means indicate the level of importance of the matter and flexibility of the capital. For day-to-day work, Civcom delegates play an important role in shaping their instructions. After all, they are more knowledgeable than those at home about developments in Brussels and have a keener sense of what can be agreed to and where they might become isolated. Civcom delegates occasionally get instructions by telegram, immediately indicating that their capitals have certain red lines that cannot be crossed. Other delegates, however, never receive instructions by telegram. Instructions by phone or e-mail tend to indicate that the member state's position is less fixed and usually that the Civcom delegate has played a strong role in preparing them. Finally, instructions by text message are the least formal type, and there is always the possibility that delegates will have no instructions at all. One representative said that in two-thirds of the cases, his capital provides no particular indication of what to say.[60]

In general, smaller member states tend not to have formal instructions, while bigger member states are more invested in CSDP and thus try to control events more from their capitals. Representatives from smaller countries will always have some instructions for more politically important issues, but on occasion they take the initiative, asking for instructions to ensure that they have backing from their capitals. Smaller countries lack the administrative resources to follow everything that is happening in Brussels. In fact, one delegate explained that only the biggest countries and the Commission can really follow everything that the Secretariat produces.[61] Expertise among Civcom delegates thus becomes more at a premium for small and medium-sized member states.

A Civcom delegate's relationship with his capital also reflects how policy is made domestically. In Ireland, the International Secretariat Division of the Irish Foreign Ministry comprises four diplomats, and only one works full time on CSDP. By comparison, the foreign ministries of France, the UK, and Germany count on vast resources. The fact that bigger member states also have larger and more complex security interests adds to the potential rigidity of their instructions. Further complicating matters is the fact that multilateral civilian crisis management remains relatively new in some member states, and many are in the process of setting up structures to better handle them in the future.

Many Civcom delegates strongly believe that instructions are important for two reasons. First, instructions tell them what to do. Second, they ensure capitals' support. Without instructions, delegates take on personal risk that whatever they agree to will not be accepted by their capitals or that they will be unable to persuade officials at home that the right stance was taken. Capitals must take a certain degree of ownership of the Civcom process, but going too far in terms of detailed instructions causes harm. Some delegates prefer flexible instructions so that they have room to argue a certain position well. Just as with EU ambassadors and generals, the level of autonomy within these instructions is determined to some extent by the delegate's specific relationship with the capital. Delegates must feed back to their capitals a real sense of the proceedings in Brussels to gain some room in which to maneuver and make compromise possible. Ultimately, the capitals take tougher stances than their Civcom representatives, potentially frustrating the delegates, who hope to find workable compromises. But even when instructions get in the way or Civcom members personally disagree with their instructions, the delegates believe that it would not be professional to express that frustration.[62] They prefer to convey the impression that they are united with their capitals. This is a classic example of how Civcom more closely resembles a transmission belt than does Coreper or EUMC. A reluctance to exercise agency separate from state preferences indicates a nascent epistemic community.

In sum, Civcom delegates come from a variety of backgrounds and levels of experience, and their common culture is less defined than is the case in other networks. As a result, Civcom experiences longer negotiations, delegates have varying amounts of room in which to maneuver, and delegates are more strongly tied to domestic circumstances. The emphasis is more on knowing when to keep quiet on an issue and picking the battles that are most important to a delegate's member state. In contrast to those epistemic communities that tend to resolve issues in informal settings, often relying on relationships built over a career of interactions and similar experiences, Civcom's main forum is formal meetings. Nonetheless, Civcom's work has resulted in an unexpected number of civilian CSDP missions, signaling that the group is off to a good start. Delegates have convinced member states to participate, thereby enhancing the EU's image overseas. Delegates have a sense of newness about what they are doing that has fostered a natural esprit de corps. They keep their meetings relaxed and avoid sharp exchanges. Their day-to-day tasks can be quite technical, involving hours of negotiations over every line in a document. But they are driven to leave the room only with a completed paper in hand. PSC ambassadors rarely reject Civcom's advice, so in that sense they are able to carve out compromise solutions against the backdrop of competing interests.

Civcom currently only has quite limited ability to encourage meaningful steps forward in providing security integration in the field of civilian crisis management. The main way the group might accomplish this is by targeting medium- to long-term perspectives on civilian capabilities alongside a more comprehensive approach. But Civcom's ability to achieve integration in this policy area faces several obstacles. In addition to Civcom's lack of persuasive power as a nascent knowledge-based network, it cannot push for the same kinds of integration patterns that exist on the military side. Civilian missions cannot benefit much from R&D and procurement. It is also not possible to have a standing European corps of police officers and experts in rule of law, administration, and civil protection. Finally, the availability of these civilian personnel is highly constrained, since all have important roles to play domestically. This state of affairs hampers what Civcom can do in the long term to encourage member states to take a permanently integrative approach to civilian crisis management.

Again, for many member states, civilian crisis management does not yet firmly constitute a key part of their foreign policy agendas. As long as this is the case, representatives will find it somewhat difficult to come to Brussels with a high level of experience and expertise in this area. The caliber of Civcom as an epistemic community will likely grow in tandem with the continued evolution of the civilian aspect of CSDP. Civcom representatives can certainly encourage member states to get on the same page and even to harmonize their approaches to developing structures that will assist in the generation and training of civilian personnel for CSDP missions. They can also put into a place a better system for analyzing lessons learned.

When epistemic communities possess a high level of expertise and tangible common culture, they are more readily able to reach compromise, exercise agency beyond their mandate or instructions, and persuade political actors of their shared norms. The two networks examined in this chapter, however, possess varied expertise and have not developed a strong common culture. In the case of Civcom, the newness of the policy area means that no strong body of knowledge yet exists, and thus these delegates must nurture the knowledge and thereby enhance the strength of their community. With the dismantling of the GofP, the norms behind its policy goals have become significantly diluted, leading to a weakening of its aims. The integration of civilian technology research has progressed little in the past few years. For Civcom's part, despite the high visibility and seeming success of civilian CSDP, a lack of expert knowledge has not helped the longer-term challenges of declining resources, limited numbers of crisis personnel, and weak domestic structures.

Conclusion

THERE IS NO QUESTION that the security of a state's borders, infrastructure, and people is as fundamental to sovereignty as a state's "monopoly of legitimate physical violence."[1] Nevertheless, this study reveals an unexpected phenomenon: knowledge-based networks are redefining the meaning of sovereignty and security in Europe. These networks are creating an environment of thick diplomacy through their multilayered and expertise-driven interaction. Integration begins with dialogue, persuasion, and shifting worldviews before leading to policy change and implementation. Thus, this study peels back the formal layers of decision making to expose this policy environment and to show how epistemic communities are constructing a unique European conception of security.

Moreover, these achievements clearly are not the result of a coincidence of national interests—a desire to maximize material gain. Integration inherently requires states to give up some part of their sovereignty over policies that affect their material resources. By agreeing to integrate security research, for example, member states lose exclusive ownership of certain technologies and the potential economic benefit such ownership might bring. Similarly, by investing together in long-term military interoperability and capabilities development, member states increasingly conceive of operations in a multilateral framework, a view that brings constraints. Thus, the EU's recent security developments cannot be explained through combining the various national interests of the member states to see where they converge. Indeed, even if such an approach could work, it would miss the most important part of the story. As one journalist writes, "As ever with the EU it is not just a question of agreeing ambitious goals, but creating instruments to realise them."[2] Epistemic communities are doing both.

A close examination of the most central actors in this dialogue—ambassadors, military generals, technology researchers, and civilian crisis ex-perts—shows that security integration is surprisingly robust. In such areas as strategies for tackling the root causes of radicalization and recruitment, civil and military capacity building, and common technology research, security integration is clearly moving forward, albeit faster in some areas than in others. Furthermore, the line between internal and external dimensions is rapidly dissolving. In the corridors of Brussels, decisions are often arrived at informally by those who really understand the issues at stake; collectively, these individuals can be highly persuasive. Without consideration of these seemingly quiet but certainly powerful actors, it would be difficult to explain how the EU holds together and what future role it is likely to play in the world. At the same time, because there is room to improve the expertise, cohesion, and common culture within some of these epistemic communities, the possibility for increasing levels of integration exists. However likely, it is not inevitable, and a few words of caution are in order.

To the extent that political will is needed to move integration forward, that will does not emanate primarily from member states. Rather, explaining European security integration requires looking to the group dynamics, relationships, procedural norms, identities, and worldviews within these key epistemic communities. They are persuading states to go further in directions that states tend not to want to go. States are not acting against their national interests; rather, epistemic communities are gradually persuading states to redefine the meaning of national interests with regard to security. To begin with, national interests cannot typically be reduced to a calculation of material benefit. More generally, states can aim to achieve economic power as an end in itself or can strategically choose to demilitarize as a means of boosting civilian power. Soft power—the ability to attract others to a society and foreign policy—is receiving increasing emphasis as a strategic aim for states and nonstate actors alike.[3] In the case of the EU, national interest is increasingly tied to collective interest: the idea that more can be gained for each individual member state by working together than by working separately, especially in the longer term. This idea is manifested in a growing European security space. The definition of strategic national interest ultimately must be considered in these broader terms, meaning that the norms espoused by epistemic communities are not mutually exclusive.[4]

Explaining why and to what degree epistemic communities matter requires examining the key properties that characterize the internal dynamics of these communities: selection, training, meeting frequency, shared professional norms, and common culture. A given epistemic community is likely to be more cohesive if selection and training are competitive, a high level of expertise is required, and meetings are frequent and informal. These features enable the growth of a strong body of shared professional norms, the evolution of a well-defined common culture, and a shared worldview. Cohesion, in turn, translates into a better ability to persuade others of shared norms and to achieve policy goals. Epistemic communities are in a privileged position because of their high status and unique knowledge.

Even though epistemic communities are held together in part by shared norms and seek to convince others of these norms, they also exist in a larger normative context. The EU as an aggregate actor embodies certain socially embedded norms, and members of epistemic communities—along with everyone else—are products of this environment. Community members can benefit from the existing structure as well as work within it to shape new norms. For example, there is a widespread belief that the EU's image should be based on civilian power. Since the basis of civilian power is the desire to take into account voices of nonmilitary actors, epistemic communities benefit from this norm: Policy leaders are more likely to listen to them and to take them seriously. Four of the epistemic communities covered in this study are nonmilitary, and all have affected how leaders and society understand and implement civilian power. Similarly, there is the widespread belief within the EU that terrorism is a police rather than military issue. Epistemic communities operate within these parameters and push the boundaries of the norm. Epistemic communities argue that terrorism must be tackled with both internal and external security strategies and that the technology to detect terrorist threats benefits most from an integrated approach.

Epistemic communities are key norm entrepreneurs within the greater social context of the EU.[5] As they engage in persuasion and implement policies, they gradually shape the nature of these socially embedded norms. And if their policies ultimately fail, epistemic communities learn from on-the-ground experiences and gain further expertise in achieving their goals. In effect, epistemic community norms and broader contextual norms are mutually constitutive. Overall, epistemic communities do not exist within a contextual vacuum but are contained within a structure. However, on its own, the structure of any system, whether it is material or normative, has no intrinsic ability to shape outcomes and thus cannot explain changes over time. Influential actors such as epistemic communities set into motion the dynamics of integration within this structure.

In this concluding chapter, I first summarize my main findings before highlighting some of the implications of the argument that knowledge-based networks are transforming the EU. I address a number of key questions. How do these epistemic communities fit together or interact with one another? Are they complementary or competing? What picture do they paint for security policy as a whole? Given their elite status, do they contribute to a democratic deficit? Do they ultimately enable the EU to become a stronger global player? And finally, I return to the question posed at the beginning: What will the end of integration look like? Will member states embrace a new supranational order?

SUMMARY OF FINDINGS

The most powerful and promising epistemic communities in the security area are those of professional diplomats in the Committee of Permanent Representatives (Coreper) and the three-star military officers in the European Union Military Committee (EUMC). The former has had more of an impact on concrete policy outcomes than the latter, but both nonetheless have high levels of influence by virtue of their expertise and strong internal cohesion. EUMC remains somewhat underutilized when it comes to Common Security and Defence Policy (CSDP), and as the policy area grows, the military committee will likely become a more significant player.

Coreper works like a well-oiled machine. Its ambassadors are among the most qualified that member states can offer. They are experts at the art of negotiation and possess an intimate understanding of the EU. They have the trust and respect of the decision makers in their capitals. Most important, they have well-developed substantive norms: beliefs that more integration is better, that the common good is best served through a focus on the common constituency of European citizens rather than on national interests, and that they can achieve more by operating in the gray area between technical and political decision making. The permanent representatives are heavily involved in internal security integration, and the case of the Strategy on Radicalization and Recruitment shows how their norms have translated directly into policy. They have Europeanized the strategy, infused it with protections of fundamental rights, engaged members of civil society, and provided a legal framework. Through subsequent revisions to the strategy, the Coreper ambassadors have pushed integration in this area even further.

The military representatives of the EUMC also share a wealth of expertise, particularly at the tactical level. In fact, their expertise is often described as a kind of military art. This knowledge is so uniform across member states that milreps rarely find reason to disagree, even on the nuances of military planning. If disagreement arises, it stems from political red lines instead of from any fundamental difference of opinion within the group. A natural allegiance, camaraderie, and common background exist before the generals even arrive in Brussels. A willingness to put the interests of Europe above the individual member states maintains this common culture and adds a distinctive layer specific to the new environment they occupy. Most milreps are double-hatted to both the EU and NATO. While it is not typical for military officials to answer to more than one hierarchy, this situation affords them more time to build relationships and develop shared worldviews on a number of issues. They frequently have working lunches and dinners together and are keenly aware of their distinctiveness as officers in the midst of a diplomatic world. Their high level of professionalism, objectivity, status, and experience gives them a great advantage in influencing outcomes. They often have flexibility in carrying out their instructions and in persuading capitals of their goals. The case of the 2006 Long-Term Vision for European Defence Capability and Capacity Needs reflects the EUMC's evolving identity in an emerging postmodern military era where national capabilities, borders, and interests are no longer as paramount as they were in the past.

The most powerful networks are those with the richest backgrounds of historical professionalization as well as those whose motivations derive from their expert knowledge rather than from some other factor. The dynamic within these groups does not simply mirror state power. The case studies show that members of these epistemic communities gain respect and are listened to because of their personal qualities. Ability, knowledge, and experience can matter more than country of origin. Representatives from smaller member states can play a strong role as mediators and often have special involvement in particular issues. Given the nature of EU external security goals, smaller states can sometimes provide much-needed resources when bigger member states have already made commitments elsewhere. The members of these networks are driven to find compromise and to follow through with it. However, historical professionalization is not enough to guarantee a strong epistemic community today, as the Political and Security Committee (PSC) demonstrates. The dynamic within a network seeking to influence policy goals is vital and could undermine a potentially powerful group.

PSC shows the utility of the epistemic community framework. While PSC ambassadors share many of the same qualities as Coreper ambassadors and appear to comprise a very similar type of group, the PSC ambassadors, as an epistemic community of moderate strength, are more limited in their collective influence. PSC members work as quickly as possible to find the areas of overlap within their instructions, and outcomes sometimes reflect lowest-common-denominator decision making. The key variables of meeting frequency and quality, shared professional norms, and common culture are weaker than in Coreper and EUMC, allowing only a moderate level of cohesion and persuasive power. The fact that PSC meetings are often thronged by more than 100 attendees and the ambassadors at the core of the group have difficulty scheduling informal meetings does nothing to help cohesion. As a result, despite benefitting from an extensive jurisdiction under the Nice Treaty, PSC has relegated itself to a relatively narrow focus on CSDP crisis management. Even within the area of crisis management, PSC does not work toward longer-term goals, such as improving the overall CSDP apparatus and promoting integration where it could benefit outcomes. The PSC tends to operate on a case-by-case basis, and the range of flexibility across member states varies sharply according to national circumstances and what is at stake. As long as PSC ambassadors meet relatively infrequently in informal settings, are not able to cultivate a stronger and more specialized set of professional norms, and continue to shy away from embracing a rich, tangible common culture with clear substantive norms for policy development, their potential as an epistemic community is unlikely to grow.

The loosest knowledge-based network, the now disbanded Group of Personalities in the Field of Security Research (GofP), conformed most closely to the original conception of epistemic communities as scientific experts. Yet it faced a number of challenges. First, scientific knowledge tends to be so specialized that it is difficult to form a critical mass unless nonscientists with related expertise are part of the network. Second, motivations may not fully derive from expert knowledge when members of the network stand to gain monetarily from the policy outcomes, as was certainly the case for the industrial suppliers who were part of the GofP. Finally, if significant variation in professional backgrounds exists, shared professional norms and esprit de corps suffer. In the end, the GofP had a notable influence on the integration of security research in the EU but did not push far beyond its mandate. Furthermore, the network was short-lived because little tied together its members over the long run. Thus, a big gap exists between what the GofP actually accomplished and what it might have accomplished. Nevertheless, it had important effects the integration of security research through the Preparatory Action on Security Research, European Security Research Program, and eventually Seventh Research Framework Program. By initiating EU-level funding for multicountry civil security research to help secure borders, infrastructure, and people (through the Preparatory Action) as well as by calling for the institutionalization of security research as a permanent item on the EU governance agenda (through the Seventh Research Framework Program), the GofP initiated a major step toward integrated security research with long-term implications for both the internal and external dimensions. Unfortunately, however, the group's norms were not sustained after it disbanded. Its ultimate goals may not be achieved unless it is replaced by a more cohesive epistemic community.

Finally, in the case of the Civilian Crisis Management Community (Civcom), a nascent epistemic community, the lack of a high degree of specific, technical knowledge currently hampers the group's ability to exert agency as well as the development of a common culture with a strong body of shared norms. Members of the group spend much of their time in formal meetings or reading documents to prepare for meetings. Informal meetings are relatively rare. Civcom has an esprit de corps based on members' feeling that they are breaking new ground in their work and on a common desire to see CSDP progress. The more junior diplomats, in particular, have a sense that they are really contributing to an important new project. But Civcom has not yet transcended this esprit de corps to develop a tangible common culture with a sense of common identity, heritage, symbolism, and sense of purpose. Despite these shortcomings—Civcom and EU civilian crisis management are very new—this network of civilian crisis experts accomplishes a great deal in terms of fostering security cooperation. Indeed, this group is likely to rise in status and caliber, especially as member states begin more fully to develop their domestic structures in support of civilian crisis management, thus providing training that will prepare diplomats and others to serve as experts in Brussels.

These five epistemic communities have contributed to EU security cooperation and integration in significant ways. For some time, Coreper has hammered out agreements in the realm of Justice and Home Affairs and has been responsible for an array of policies that have led to the integration of nearly every aspect of internal security integration. Although less influential, PSC has played a strong oversight role in bringing together the various aspects of CSDP crisis management. After member states agree to a certain civilian mission or military operation, PSC is indispensible as a manager overseeing coordination and cooperation. The military experts have been very instrumental in planning long-term defense interoperability and integration of research and procurement. The research and technology community has also affected the trajectory of security research on the civilian side. Civcom has shown potential in the area of civilian crisis management. The group frequently confronts situations that seemingly have no common solution—the rule of law mission in Kosovo is one example—and has nonetheless navigated through these obstacles to achieve cooperation. If civilian CSDP is to continue to thrive as it has over the past few years, specific expertise is essential to guide it forward and achieve integration in key areas. Indeed, while EUMC may be underutilized, Civcom may be overutilized. Some catch-up time is needed. In sum, without the knowledge-based, persuasive influence of these epistemic communities, the EU would probably fall far short of where it is today in terms of security integration.

Epistemic communities can serve as the impetus for security integration because they are distinctive from other actors. They have (1) larger policy objectives that involve decisions about the degree of security integration and not simply the quality of the agreed-upon measures; (2) the potential to exercise agency; and (3) shared norms that give momentum to their policy goals. Member states are fully involved in their own foreign and security policies in a range of areas. Chiefs of state sign treaties, attend European Councils, and take part in determining the EU's overall political direction. They are judged by their electorate on what EU policy they endorse. Member states often shape the context within which epistemic communities act but are also heavily constrained in a way that those in Brussels are not: Those in capitals do not regularly sit at the same table with 26 other dignitaries, cannot feel the climate in Brussels as it shifts on a day-to-day basis, and are mainly concerned with their electorate at home. Thus, while member states' preferences are crucial, they are only a part of the story. Without a close examination and understanding of these knowledge-based networks, tracing the key processes that drive security policy forward would be impossible.

A DEMOCRATIC DEFICIT?

Epistemic communities are very influential in the EU setting, but could their agency contribute to a democratic deficit? Several scholars suggest that the democratic accountability present at the domestic level has not been properly translated to the supranational level as the EU takes on new areas of decision-making power.[6] In other words, citizens cannot participate as they would if decision making had been maintained at the domestic level. In these accounts, EU institutions are to blame for lacking transparency and democratic structure. Decisions are made behind closed doors, and EU citizens suffer from a knowledge deficit. Is it possible that the elite nature of epistemic communities may exacerbate the situation amid these calls for increased transparency and accountability of EU institutions?

Good governance requires experts of various kinds, whether they are supreme court judges, economists, or engineers. Elected representatives cannot possess expertise in everything. But an authoritative claim on knowledge is not enough to allow expert groups to make decisions without some kind of democratic accountability. In the case of the EU, there is no mistaking the fact that epistemic communities are not elected and typically do not participate in public discourses at the national level about their policy goals. At the level of EU governance, they are even more removed from publics than are the experts who advise national-level governments.

At least thus far, however, epistemic communities have not contributed to a democratic deficit. First and foremost, they must get approval from elected officials at home before moving forward with their internal compromises. Although they do spend much of their time persuading officials at home and often get their way, they still cannot implement policies independently. They need the backing of those at home. Ambassadors and military generals are directly appointed by elected officials based on careful deliberation and meritocratic criteria. Members of the epistemic communities described here are thus not far removed from national accountability, and they can always be removed from their positions if they abuse their power.

Second, security epistemic communities' target audience is quite specific—officials in the ministries of defense, foreign affairs, interior, and justice—but the dialogue should not stop there. These officials bear responsibility for encouraging broader democratic processes at home and for ensuring that citizens' will is adequately represented. This is the way of representative democracy. Direct societal influence in decision making is neither possible nor desirable in all policy areas, especially those that are more technical or lack public interest to begin with. Issues that do not affect citizens on an everyday basis—in particular, certain aspects of foreign policy—may not resonate with them. The general public is often more concerned with issues such as unemployment, health care, and education than with issues such as border surveillance technology, prison radicalization, and humanitarian missions in Africa.

Third, epistemic communities embody a respect for democratic values. They rely on their expertise, objectivity, status, and knowledge to be persuasive. They respect the process of deliberation, cultivate the ability to reach a reasoned compromise, and value pluralism. They do not simply reflect the relative power of their respective countries. They do not force each other's hands with coercion and hard bargaining. Rather, they tend to treat each other as equals and to rely on good arguments. These internal qualities represent what is typically most valued in democracies: informed and open debate. Thus, not only do epistemic communities fulfill an essential role in providing valuable expertise in key processes of EU governance, but their power is constrained by the elected officials who delegate authority to them as well as by their own professional norms.

A NETWORK OF NETWORKS?

Another important implication of this study is that epistemic communities in the same policy area do not tend to compete with each other. This finding supports one of John Gerard Ruggie's original arguments that each epistemic community will find its own niche rather than competing with others over issues.[7] So how do security epistemic communities fit together overall? If they are complementary rather than competing, do they form a kind of network of networks? Yes and no. On the one hand, members of different epistemic communities in the EU do not meet with each other and instead treat issues in a very sectoral way. Cross-issue dialogue is thus rare, and as a whole, policy discussions end up being quite fragmented. On the other hand, it is hard to ignore Coreper's key role in pulling together the various pieces to form a coherent picture of European security.

Coreper is central to this story of thick diplomacy in Europe. In a sense, it is a common thread tying together this network of networks. In its deliberations, Coreper often reflects on the intimate connection between the internal and external dimensions of security and continuously calls for a more comprehensive approach. As Romanian Antici diplomat Alina Padeanu said, "Coreper puts the pieces together."[8] Most security issue areas—research and technology, border protection, Common Foreign and Security Policy (CFSP), interoperability, and so on—pass across Coreper's table. In the process, the committee both gains and embraces a more global perspective. It is uniquely positioned to ensure that policies remain compatible and that progress in any one area is maximized across the board. The fact that these ambassadors focus more concretely on internal security aspects is also useful for the goal of integration, as more has been achieved in this area. Internal security policies often affect external security, pulling it along.

While Coreper holds much promise as the network of networks, recent trends indicate that its continued centrality and influence may be threatened. In particular, increasing policy segmentation, burgeoning meeting agendas, and divisions of Coreper (into Coreper I, II, and PSC) are leading to a general weakening of its influence. The roots of this transformation go back to the early 1990s, just after the implementation of the Maastricht Treaty. At the same time that these high-ranking ambassadors have been making ever more important decisions, their ability to influence the overarching trajectory of EU integration has gradually eroded as other groups have siphoned off issues. A kind of paradox exists in that the more power Coreper gains, the more its members suffer from overload, necessitating the creation of more committees and working groups to lessen the burden and ultimately diminishing their power. While the product of these subordinate bodies still passes through Coreper, it has less and less time to deliberate on the issues. If this process continues, Coreper's ability to oversee security integration from a big-picture perspective may become lost in the shuffle.

THE END OF INTEGRATION: SOVEREIGNTY VERSUS
SUPRANATIONAL ORDER

So what is the prognosis for security integration in Europe? Will the EU become a credible security actor with the ability not only to protect its common borders but also to contribute to global security? Many scholars argue that it is unclear what security integration would actually look like. Michael E. Smith writes,

> Unlike many economic goals, such as a single market or single currency, there is no clear "end product" to be achieved with a "common" foreign and security policy. Such a common policy, like political "integration" and political "union," implies a final stage when the mechanism, in actual practice, can mean only a continuing process of action that evolves over time.[9]

Thus, political or security integration may always be a continuing process. However, this in-depth study of five critical epistemic communities and their impact on major areas of security policy suggests a vision of what the end point of security integration might look like.

To take the best-case scenario, initiatives such as the Long-Term Vision and Seventh Research Framework Program mean that internal and external security integration will likely go hand in hand. For the aim of efficiency, interoperability, and economies of scale, integrated research and development will increasingly produce technology and weaponry that can be employed for both defense of the homeland and external missions and for both civilian and military uses. Transnational epistemic communities of technology and scientific experts will become more cohesive as they compete for common resources from the European Defence Agency, Commission, and other sources.[10] The EU will likely have full integration of border control, transportation networks, surveillance of people, secure and encrypted communication, and space technology. In addition, visa, immigration, and asylum policy as well as laws protecting individual rights will likely achieve full harmonization. Because internal security integration is occurring much more rapidly than its external counterpart, we are likely to observe some spillover from one to the other in the form of cross-pillarization. As internal security increasingly moves into the Community Method of decision making, hybrid internal-external issues will increasingly be resolved quickly under the Community Method, making external security de facto more integrated.

The future of external security, especially CFSP and CSDP, will rest on military and civilian crisis expertise. As military CSDP moves forward, it is likely that planning, capabilities, and interoperability will fall into place rather quickly. EU member states will easily contribute to multinational, integrated forces, and operations will run relatively smoothly, especially with the benefit of lessons learned. CSDP will probably use battle groups or at least transform them to be more usable, whether or not the crisis is time sensitive in nature. The civilian side of CSDP will continue to grow in visibility but will become more integrated with the military side. It will be increasingly common to see combined civil-military missions under CSDP, instead of one or the other. Over time, Civcom will likely have a better idea of what resources and personnel are available to the EU at any given point. When member states finish putting into place domestic structures to support civil crisis management, many more resources will be readily available, but a certain limit will always exist to what is possible, given the need for police, judges, and legal experts to serve at home. A European army that encompasses all member states' armies is unlikely, but complete interoperability of these armies is highly likely. Member states may choose which areas are their strengths and focus investments and efforts accordingly.

If the best-case scenario does not play out, it will likely occur because internal and external security policies do not develop in tandem. No matter what happens, internal security integration is likely to be realized, but a lesser outcome would mean that external security is left behind. This outcome is a possibility if Coreper (or perhaps another future expert body) does not oversee the variety of processes happening at many levels and therefore cannot ensure that they create a coherent whole. It may also occur if current knowledge-based networks fail to persuade their capitals of policy goals. More than one kind of expertise will be needed to move these issues forward, but diplomatic influence will be critical to tying everything together. The end point of integration would thus be quite similar to what exists today on the external side. A constant struggle to generate force contributions would take place, CSDP operations would remain relatively small, and the process of managing them would remain quite fragmented and overly complicated. In terms of internal security, while harmonization of border security and its accompanying legal provisions would still be achieved, member states would continue to guard national intelligence and restrict their police from fully cooperating. The end result would be harmonized borders without maximized protection.

The security policies covered in depth in this volume show that at minimum, member states' heads of government are somewhat flexible in how they see the concept of sovereignty. They have been willing to succumb to persuasion from the epistemic communities in Brussels and gradually to adopt new norms. These developments fly in the face of more restricted views on the nature of sovereignty, especially with regard to the core security functions of states. In a more general sense, Robert Keohane was right when he suggested that "with respect to sovereignty over security issues, it is all too evident that there is no universal consensus in favor of such limitations to sovereignty."[11] The possible creation of a European security space would certainly be unprecedented and would mark a major transformation in the meaning of state sovereignty. But such a transformation is quite probable given epistemic communities' ability and political will to overcome traditional assumptions. Step by step, they are forging a new kind of supranational order whose beginnings can already be observed.

Notes

Introduction

1. In January 2010, the EU announced its decision to launch a new military operation, EUTM Somalia.

2. European Defence Agency, "Defence Data 2009," 2.

3. A wealth of literature supports this approach. See, for example, Finnemore and Sikkink, "International Norm Dynamics"; Acharya, "How Ideas Spread"; Gheciu, "Security Institutions"; Ciută, "End(s) of NATO."

4. Cortell and Davis, "Understanding," 70.

5. Ibid., 71. In this respect, Cortell and Davis cite Bachrach and Baratz, "Decisions and Nondecisions."

6. See, for example, Lindberg, *Political Dynamics;* Rosamond, *Theories;* Pollack, "Theorizing"; Jupille, Caporaso, and Checkel, "Integrating Institutions."

7. Moravcsik, "New Statecraft?"

8. Checkel, "'Going Native'"; Risse, "Euro"; Caporaso, Cowles, and Risse, *Transforming Europe.*

9. Pistone, "Altiero Spinelli."

10. Wallstrom, "Public Diplomacy"; Fiske de Gouveia with Plumridge, *European Infopolitik.*

11. Haas, "Introduction," 3.

12. For recent examples of studies that address the identity question, see Checkel and Katzenstein, "European Identity"; Favell, "Eurostars and Eurocities"; Fligstein, "Euroclash"; and Risse, "A Community of Europeans."

13. For a shorter work suggesting the importance of looking at internal and external security together in the context of the EU, see Pastore, "Reconciling." The topic has subsequently been little explored.

14. The 2005–10 Hague Programme, soon to be revised as the Stockholm Programme, outlines the priority areas for the internal security in the EU. See *Hague Programme.*

15. These Commission delegations are being turned into EU delegations, some with the status of embassies, to prepare for the launch of the European External Action Service, effectively a European-level diplomatic foreign service.

16. The Community Method is how decisions are made in the first pillar. The Commission has the sole right of initiative, the Council votes through qualified majority voting, the Parliament legislates with the Council, and the Court of Justice ensures that Community law is interpreted uniformly across the EU.

17. Bigo, "When Two Become One."

18. For research on this topic, see Duke and Ojanen, "Bridging"; Rees, "Inside Out."

19. *Secure Europe.*

20. Clemens and Cook, "Politics and Institutionalism," 446.

21. Whether a non-European actor could exert such influence on the trajectory of EU security integration remains unknown, though the only contender would be U.S. president Barack Obama.

Chapter 1

1. The first book systematically to grapple with this approach is Christiansen, Jorgensen, and Wiener, *Social Construction.*

2. Wendt, "Anarchy"; Ruggie, "What Makes the World Hang Together?," 856. Ruggie cites the sociological works of Emile Durkheim and Max Weber as providing the roots of the argument that social facts are as important as material facts.

3. Fierke and Wiener, "Constructing."

4. Schimmelfennig and Sedelmeier, *Europeanization.*

5. Howorth, "Discourse," provides a concise history of the birth of CSDP and the importance of certain individuals, ideas, and communicative discourse.

6. Mérand, "Social Representations," 133–34.

7. Moravcsik, "Quiet Superpower."

8. Moravcsik, "Europe."

9. Jachtenfuchs, Diez, and Jung, "Which Europe?," puts forward a good framework with which to analyze both interests and ideas.

10. Checkel, "International Institutions."

11. Keck and Sikkink, *Activists.*

12. Slaughter, *New World Order.* Slaughter also examines transgovernmental networks of regulators and judges.

13. See, for example, Risse, *Community.*

14. A similar concept is that of thought communities. See Antoniades, "Epistemic Communities."

15. Thomas, "Public Management," 223. For details on issue networks, Thomas cites Heclo, "Issue Networks," 102–4.

16. Keck and Sikkink, *Activists,* introduction.

17. Ibid., 2.

18. Keohane and Nye, "Transgovernmental Relations."

19. See Slaughter, *New World Order;* Grevi, "ESDP Institutions."

20. Thurner and Binder, "European Union Transgovernmental Networks."

21. Cross, *The European Diplomatic Corps,* chapter 2, provides a more in-depth explanation of this point.

22. Deutsch, Burrell, and Kahn, *Political Community.*

23. Krebs, "Limits of Alliance," 219.

24. Adler and Barnett, *Security Communities;* Adler, "Spreading of Security Community."

25. Haas, "Introduction," 3.

26. Kuhn, *Structure.*

27. Ibid.

28. Ruggie, "International Responses," 569, citing Foucault, *Order of Things.*

29. Ibid., 557.

30. Ibid., 558.

31. Ibid., 570.

32. Ibid. Ruggie also cites Holzner, *Reality Construction.*

33. Haas, "Introduction," 3.

34. Ibid.

35. Verdun, "Role."

36. Radaelli, "Public Policy," 762.

37. Ibid., 763.

38. Haas, *Saving the Mediterranean,* 55.

39. Thomas, "Public Management."

40. Zito, "Epistemic Communities," 586.

41. Ibid., 600.

42. Haas argues that the main exception to this rule is when the available data do not support the epistemic community's previously held causal beliefs. In other words, when the epistemic community no longer seems to hold its monopoly on expertise because the shared knowledge of its members has been proven false, they will not affect policy outcomes (*Saving the Mediterranean,* 55).

43. Dunlop, "Epistemic Communities," 141.

44. Toke, "Epistemic Communities"; Krebs, "Limits of Alliance," 225–26.

45. Toke, "Epistemic Communities."

46. Krebs, "Limits of Alliance," 225–26.

47. Sebenius, "Challenging Conventional Explanations"; Dunlop, "Epistemic Communities."

48. Dunlop, "Epistemic Communities."

49. Krebs, "Limits of Alliance," 225–26.

50. Dunlop, "Epistemic Communities."

51. Krebs, "Limits of Alliance," 225–26.

52. Ibid.

53. Haas, "Policy Knowledge," 11580.

54. Krebs, "Limits of Alliance," 220–22.

55. Pouliot, "Logic."

56. Cortell and Davis, "Understanding the Domestic Impact of International Norms," 69.

57. Gough and Shackley, "Respectable Politics," 332.

58. Haas, "Introduction," 3.

59. Ibid.

60. Antoniades, "Epistemic Communities," 27.

61. Moravcsik, "Quiet Superpower."

62. Haas, "Banning Chlorofluorocarbons," 187.

63. Ibid., 190.

64. Zito conducts a similar study on EU policy on acid rain. While his independent variable is the epistemic community's activities and ideas, his dependent variable is "actor preferences, both fundamental policy strategies and more typically secondary, instrumental concerns that inform the core policy positions." He is also interested in how these preferences are manifested in actual implementation of policies, although this is not his main focus. His emphases, however, are directed at a more advanced stage in the policy process than this study, since EU environmental policy is much more mature than EU security policy ("Epistemic Communities," 586).

65. Zürn and Checkel, "Getting Socialized," 1048.

66. Hooghe, "Several Roads," 865.

67. Ibid., 866. The exceptions include primacy and novelty. Young people will often be socialized more quickly since they have not had a lot of time in alternative social contexts (primacy), and newcomers to a social group will be more influenced by earlier experiences than later ones (novelty).

68. Gourevitch, "Second Image Reversed."

69. Acharya, "How Ideas Spread," 241.

70. Evangelista, "Paradox."

71. Risse, "'Let's Argue!'"; Checkel, "International Institutions"; Legro, "Which Norms Matter?"

72. Cortell and Davis, "Understanding," 69.

73. Dunlop, "Epistemic Communities," 141.

74. Rathbun, "Interviewing," 690.

75. Ibid., 689.

76. Ibid., 692.

77. Ibid.

78. Risse, "Transnational Actors."

79. While the analysis is wide ranging and generally takes a broad definition of security, certain issues with potential security ramifications that are somewhat secondary to direct processes of security integration are not included. For example, enlargement and Turkey's bid for membership or dependence on Russia for energy are not central to the analysis.

80. For example, Zito is explicit about his decision to examine an issue where epistemic communities are more likely to have a successful impact on policy outcomes. He seeks, however, to emphasize the institutional constraints that epistemic communities face and thus tries to find any evidence for impact ("Epistemic Communities," 586).

81. Many of the policies described in chapter 2 are also the result of epistemic community initiative. Further research could be conducted on these other examples to test my argument even further, especially as more EU documents are declassified.

Chapter 2

1. *EU Counter-Terrorism Strategy.*

2. Den Boer, *9/11*, 1–2.

3. Howorth and Keeler, *Defending Europe.*

4. For a full account of the importance of security, see Mitsilegas, Monar, and Rees, *European Union and Internal Security*, 7–10.

5. Kirchner and Sperling, *EU Security Governance.*

6. Ekengren, "Terrorism and the EU," 36.

7. Malcolm Anderson, "Internal and External Security," 33–34.

8. Jones, *Rise.*

9. Smith, *Europe's Foreign and Security Policy*, 1.

10. Ibid., 2.

11. Treaty on European Union, Article J, Official Journal, C 191, July 29, 1992.

12. Petersberg Declaration, adopted at the Ministerial Council of the Western European Union, June 1992.

13. Howorth, *Security and Defence Policy*, 98.

14. Rees, *Transatlantic Counter-Terrorism Cooperation*, 5.

15. The story behind this agreement is well told in Howorth, "Discourse"; Mérand, "Pierre Bourdieu."

16. Franco-British Summit Joint Declaration on European Defence, Saint-Malo, December 4, 1998.

17. Lindley-French, *Chronology*, 247.

18. Jones, *Rise*, 4.

19. Mitsilegas, Monar, and Rees, *European Union and Internal Security*, chapter 1.

20. EU Document 5330/04. Between January and June 2004, Committee members dealt with issues as diverse as the establishment of a European asylum system, a directive on compensation for crime victims, a border management agency, a second-generation Schengen information system, and a visa information system.

21. For a concise history of JHA, see Donnelly, "Justice and Home Affairs."

22. Martenczuk and van Thiel, "External Dimension."

23. Mitsilegas, Monar, and Rees, *European Union and Internal Security*, 84.

24. Ibid., 6.

25. *JHA External Relations Multi Presidency Work Programme*, 8.

26. The priorities are (1) fundamental rights and citizenship, (2) the fight against terrorism, (3) migration management, (4) internal and external borders and visas, (5) a common asylum area, (6) integration and the positive impact of

migration on society and economy, (7) privacy and security in sharing information, (8) the fight against organized crime, (9) civil and criminal justice, and (10) freedom, security, and justice.

27. Howorth, *Security and Defence Policy;* Gänzle and Sens, *Changing Politics;* Smith, *Europe's Foreign and Security Policy;* Jones, *Rise;* Telò, *Europe;* Cottey, *Security;* Meyer, *Quest.*

28. Cottey, *Security,* 16–21.

29. Soft integration is not simply an intermediary step between cooperation and hard integration. Since it can be just as binding as hard integration, it is often an alternative to the latter.

30. Schmitt, *From Cooperation to Integration.*

31. Jones, *Rise,* 5. See also Tardy, *European Security.*

32. Jones, *Rise.*

33. Smith, *Europe's Foreign and Security Policy.*

34. Mitsilegas, Monar, and Rees, *European Union and Internal Security,* 11–15.

35. Howorth, *Security and Defence Policy,* 100.

36. Staffan Ocusto, Swedish Civcom representative, interview by author, March 2009.

37. Given the sensitive nature of many of these issues and the ongoing nature of their development, interviewees can discuss only certain policies, and declassified documentation is limited to specific areas.

38. Kirchner and Sperling, *EU Security Governance,* 120–84.

39. Cottey, *Security,* 178.

40. Rees, *Transatlantic Counter-Terrorism Cooperation,* 88.

41. Frattini, "Keynote Address."

42. Data from Europol website, www.europol.europa.eu. The personnel data is from 2008, the budget is from 2010.

43. Rees, *Transatlantic Counter-Terrorism Cooperation,* 83–84.

44. Malcolm Anderson, "Internal and External Security," 40–41.

45. Rees, *Transatlantic Counter-Terrorism Cooperation,* 84.

46. *European Union Counter-Terrorism Strategy.*

47. Spence, *European Union and Terrorism,* 25.

48. Rees, *Transatlantic Counter-Terrorism Cooperation,* 86.

49. Lindstrom, "EU's Approach," 118–19.

50. For an excellent overview of these institutions, see Lindstrom, *Protecting,* 39–56.

51. Ibid., 40–41.

52. Rhinard, Boin, and Ekengren, "Managing Terrorism," 95–96.

53. Kirchner and Sperling, *EU Security Governance,* 124.

54. Rees, *Transatlantic Counter-Terrorism Cooperation,* 87.

55. Spence, *European Union and Terrorism,* 12–14.

56. Cottey, *Security,* 178; Garlick and Kumin, "Seeking Asylum," 131.

57. Garlick and Kumin, "Seeking Asylum," 132.

58. Rees, *Transatlantic Counter-Terrorism Cooperation,* 98.

59. Garlick and Kumin, "Seeking Asylum," 127.

60. Mitsilegas, Monar, and Rees, *European Union and Internal Security,* 87–88.

61. Martenczuk, "Visa Policy," 53–88.

62. Ibid., 28.

63. Peers, "EU Migration Law," 53.

64. Garlick and Kumin, "Seeking Asylum," 112–14.

65. Ibid., 124–26.

66. Givens and Luedtke, "EU Immigration Policy," 292.

67. Lindstrom, "EU's Approach," 127.

68. Ibid., 130.

69. Garlick and Kumin, "Seeking Asylum," 128–29.

70. Ibid., 126.

71. Nilsson, "Judicial Cooperation," 83.

72. Ibid., 80.

73. Rhinard, Boin, and Ekengren, "Managing Terrorism," 93.

74. Kelemen, "EU Rights Revolution," 221.

75. *European Military Capabilities,* 5.

76. European Defence Agency, "Defence Data 2009," 2, 11, 18.

77. Grevi, Helly, and Keohane, *European Security,* 20.

78. *European Military Capabilities,* 9.

79. Ibid., 27.

80. Ibid., 28.

81. General Jo Coelmont, former Belgian EU Military Committee representative, interview by author, June 2009.

82. *European Military Capabilities,* 99–100.

83. European Defence Agency, "Defence Data 2009," 7.

84. Ibid.

85. Stumbaum, *Risky Business?,* 21.

86. *Code of Conduct.*

87. *European Military Capabilities,* 113–14.

88. Darnis et al., *Lessons,* 3.

89. Duchêne, "Europe's Role"; Manners, "Normative Power Europe."

90. For a comprehensive overview of ESDP (now CSDP), see Howorth, *Security and Defence Policy.*

91. Salmon, "European Union."

92. Rhinard, Boin, and Ekengren, "Managing Terrorism," 96.

93. Ibid., 98.

94. Also, as Keukeleire points out, even when the EU fails to exert influence externally, member states may still feel that they have succeeded internally by achieving, through strong diplomacy, some degree of mutual solidarity ("European Union," 34).

95. Thornhill, "EU Struggles."

96. French Delegation, *Guide,* 19.

97. In January 2010, the EU decided to launch its twenty-fourth operation, EUTM Somalia, a military mission to train Somali security forces.

98. Admiral José M. Treviño-Ruiz, Spanish EUMC representative, interview by author, June 2009.

99. Coelmont, interview; General David Bill, British EUMC representative, interview by author, June 2009.

100. EU Council Secretariat, "EU Operations Centre."

101. French Delegation, *Guide,* 21.

102. European Security and Defence Assembly, "Assembly Factsheet."

103. French Delegation, *Guide,* 69.

104. Howorth, *Security and Defence Policy,* chapter 4.

105. Pastore, "Reconciling," 2.

106. Cottey, *Security,* 180.

107. Rees, *Transatlantic Counter-Terrorism Cooperation,* 89.

108. *European Military Capabilities,* 94.

109. Ibid.

110. European Defence Agency, "Defence Data 2009," 7.

111. *European Military Capabilities,* 95.

112. Another avenue of research is the Transatlantic epistemic community between intelligence officials. The EU's new intelligence agency is the Joint Situation Centre (Sitcen).

113. Mitsilegas, Monar, and Rees, *European Union and Internal Security,* 9–10.

114. Spence, *European Union and Terrorism,* 15.

Chapter 3

1. Jan Store, Finnish Coreper II ambassador, interview by author, January 2009.

2. For a full analysis, see Cross, *European Diplomatic Corps.* Spence first put forward the suggestion that EU diplomats comprise an epistemic community in 2002. Spence, "The Evolving Role of Foreign Ministries," 33.

3. The data in this chapter is based on semistructured interviews of ambassadors in Coreper II, Coreper I, and the Political and Security Committee in 2009. The interviews lasted an average of 45 minutes, while some went as long as an hour. I also conducted interviews of several Antici diplomats for additional background.

4. See M. S. Anderson, *Rise;* Mattingly, *Renaissance Diplomacy;* Osiander, *States System;* Hamilton and Langhorne, *Practice;* Berridge, *Diplomacy;* Croxton, *Peacemaking.*

5. Cross, *European Diplomatic Corps.*

6. Merger Treaty, Article 4, April 8, 1965.

7. European Economic Community Council, *Provisional Rules of Procedure.*

8. The EU consists of a multitude of institutions, but at the center lies the

power triangle—the Council, the Commission, and the Parliament. Observers debate whether the Council or Commission has more power. The Commission has the power to initiate legislation, while the Council is supposed to be the main intergovernmental body representing the member states. The Parliament is the only democratically elected body, but it has a formal role only in setting the EU budget and in approving legislation under the codecision procedure.

9. Valls, "Origin and Development."

10. Heinisch and Mesner, "COREPER," 1.

11. Store, interview.

12. Claus Grube, Danish Coreper II ambassador, former deputy Coreper I ambassador, interview by author.

13. Store, interview.

14. The study of Coreper I as a possible epistemic community is beyond the scope of this book.

15. Ulrika Larsson, Swedish deputy Coreper I ambassador, interview by author, January 2009.

16. Anonymous Coreper I ambassador, interview by author, January 2009.

17. Interview with former Polish deputy Coreper I ambassador Andrzej Babuchowski, February 2009.

18. Christian Braun, Luxembourgian Coreper II ambassador, interview by author, February 2009.

19. Anonymous Coreper I ambassador, interview by author, January 2009.

20. Braun, interview.

21. Grube, interview.

22. Larsson, interview.

23. Treaty on European Union, Article 13, paragraph 3.

24. *Official Journal*, "Council Decision of 22 January 2001 Setting Up the Political and Security Committee."

25. Foreign ministry officials, the Hague, the Netherlands, interview by author, May 27, 2009.

26. Normunds Popens, Latvian Coreper II ambassador, interview by author, January 2009.

27. Duke, "Preparing."

28. Bruter, "Diplomacy."

29. Pop, "No 'Big Bang.'"

30. Andreas Mavroyiannis, Cypriot Coreper II ambassador, interview by author, January 2009.

31. See, for example, Verdun, "Role"; Haas, "Banning Chlorofluorocarbons."

32. Hans-Dietmar Schweisgut, Austrian Coreper II ambassador, interview by author, January 2009.

33. Grube, interview.

34. Joannis Vrailas, Greek deputy Coreper II ambassador, interview by author, February 2009.

35. Braun, interview.

36. Darius Jonas Semaška, Lithuanian PSC ambassador, interview by author, February 2009.

37. Braun, interview.

38. Popens, interview.

39. Jeffrey Lodermeier, public affairs officer, U.S. Embassy, Luxembourg, interview by author, March 2009.

40. Best, Christiansen, and Settembri, *Institutions*.

41. Risse, "'Let's Argue!'" The Paris Peace Conference is a good example of statesmen attempting negotiation on their own.

42. Igor Senčar, Slovenian Coreper II ambassador, interview by author, January 2009.

43. Much of the deliberation that takes place in Coreper is thus verbal. After the 2004 enlargement, the Council tried to require member states to submit written points of view, which the presidency could take into account, but this practice did not catch on. Ambassadors exchange e-mails as well as write explanatory notes regarding specific wording.

44. Maroš Šefčovič, Slovakian Coreper II ambassador, interview by author, January 2009.

45. Alina Padeanu, Romanian Antici, interview by author, January 2009.

46. Klen Jäärats, Estonian Antici delegate, interview by author, January 2009.

47. Raul Mälk, Estonian Coreper II ambassador, interview by author, January 2009.

48. Store, interview.

49. Jäärats, interview.

50. Ibid.

51. Šefčovič, interview.

52. Store, interview.

53. Ibid.

54. Grube, interview.

55. Šefčovič, interview.

56. Francisco Duarte Lopes, Portuguese Antici, interview by author, January 2009.

57. Šefčovič, interview.

58. Padeanu, interview.

59. Jäärats, interview.

60. Schweisgut, interview.

61. Ibid.

62. Ibid.

63. Mavroyiannis, interview.

64. Grube, interview.

65. Popens, interview.

66. Vrailas, interview.

67. Mihnea Motoc, Romanian Coreper II ambassador, interview by author, March 2009.

68. Braun interview.

69. Store, interview.

70. Senčar, interview.

71. Popens, interview.

72. Braun, interview.

73. Mavroyiannis, interview.

74. Motoc, interview.

75. Store, interview.

76. Jäärats, interview.

77. Duarte Lopes, interview.

78. Grube, interview.

79. Store, interview.

80. Mavroyiannis, interview.

81. Schweisgut, interview.

82. Šefčovič, interview.

83. Popens, interview.

84. Rogier Kok, policy officer, European and International Affairs Department, Dutch Ministry of Justice, interview by author, May 2009.

85. Emma Gibbons, EU Section, International Directorate, British Home Office, interview by author, May 2009.

86. Padeanu, interview.

87. Gibbons, interview.

88. Mavroyiannis, interview.

89. Kok, interview.

90. Pieter Jan Kleiweg, head of EU External Department, Director General for European Cooperation, Dutch Ministry of Foreign Affairs, interview by author, May 2009.

91. Rita Faden, Director General of Internal Affairs, Portuguese Ministry of Internal Affairs, interview by author, April 2009.

92. Peter Storr, director of the International Directorate, British Home Office, May 2009.

93. Faden, interview.

94. Popens, interview.

95. Jäärats, interview.

96. Cross, *European Diplomatic Corps*.

97. Mälk, interview.

98. Store, interview.

99. Andy Lebrecht, British Coreper I ambassador, interview by author, January 2009; Gibbons, interview; Storr, interview.

100. Pieter Jan Klewie de Zwaan, Head of EU External Department, Director General for European Cooperation, Ministry of Foreign Affairs, interview by author, May 2009.

101. Duarte Lopes, interview.

102. Šefčovič, interview.

103. Schweisgut, interview.

104. Duarte Lopes, interview.

105. For example, while Coreper ambassadors would like to see strong civil crisis management, they are not pushing for a European army, and they do not uniformly support capacity building through the European Defence Agency (Brussels diplomats, e-mails to author, August 2007).

106. Cross, *European Diplomatic Corps,* argues that Coreper II was largely responsible for negotiating and coming to agreement on the 1992 Maastricht Treaty.

107. *European Union Strategy.*

108. Ibid.

109. *From Coreper to Council.*

110. Rees, *Transatlantic Counter-Terrorism Cooperation,* 86.

111. *From Coreper to Council.*

112. Many branches of EU governance were involved in the revisions, especially the Commission, but Coreper did much of the preparatory work, which shaped the direction of the changes.

113. EU Action Plan on Combating Terrorism, May 24, 2006.

114. Mälk, interview.

115. Store, interview.

116. Anonymous Coreper II ambassador, interview by author, January 2009.

117. *Draft EU Strategy.*

118. The EU Action Plan on Combating Terrorism eventually evolved into the Counter-Terrorism Strategy.

119. *Implementation of the Strategy and Action Plan to Combat Terrorism,* 2006, 4.

120. Ibid.

121. *Implementation Report,* 2.

122. Ibid., 5.

123. *Implementation of the Strategy and Action Plan to Combat Terrorism,* 2007, 2–3.

124. *Addendum.*

125. Bossong, "Action Plan."

126. *Addendum.*

Chapter 4

1. In this chapter, Coreper refers only to Coreper II.

2. Howorth, *Security and Defence Policy,* 68.

3. Duke, *Linchpin COPS,* 1–34; Howorth, "Political and Security Committee and the Emergence."

4. Juncos and Reynolds, "Political and Security Committee."

5. Meyer, *Quest.*

6. Juncos and Reynolds, "Political and Security Committee," 131.

7. Ibid., 133.

8. *Official Journal,* "Treaty of Nice."

9. Annexes to the Presidency Conclusions, Nice European Council Meeting, December 7–9, 2000.

10. Meyer, *Quest,* 121; Missiroli, "ESDP," 64.

11. Howorth, "The Political and Security Committee."

12. Juncos and Reynolds, "Political and Security Committee," 139.

13. Ibid., 136.

14. Quentin Weiler, French Nicolaidis delegate, interview by author, January 2009.

15. Merger Treaty, Article 4, April 8, 1965.

16. Juncos and Reynolds, "Political and Security Committee," 135.

17. Howorth, "Political and Security Committee and the Emergence," 9.

18. Sander Soone, Estonian PSC ambassador, interview by author, January 2009.

19. Hans-Dietmar Schweisgut, Austrian Coreper II ambassador, interview by author, January 2009.

20. Rochus Pronk, Dutch Political Affairs Department MFA representative, interview by author, May 2009.

21. Darius Jonas Semaška, Lithuanian PSC ambassador, interview by author, February 2009.

22. Schweisgut, interview.

23. Howorth, "Political and Security Committee and the Emergence," 9.

24. Robert Milders, Dutch PSC ambassador, interview by author, January 2009.

25. Anne Sipiläinen, Finnish PSC ambassador, interview by author, February 2009.

26. Ibid.

27. Weiler, interview.

28. Juncos and Reynolds, "Political and Security Committee," 137.

29. Ibid., 138.

30. Ibid., 138.

31. Duke, *Linchpin COPS,* 20.

32. Meyer, *Quest,* 126.

33. Juncos and Reynolds, "Political and Security Committee," 143–44.

34. Duke, *Linchpin COPS,* 16.

35. Weiler, interview.

36. Ibid.

37. Alina Padeanu, Romanian Antici, interview by author, January 2009.

38. Meyer, *Quest,* 126.

39. Juncos and Reynolds, "Political and Security Committee," 142–43.

40. Joannis Vrailas, Greek deputy Coreper II ambassador, interview by author, February 2009.

41. Pronk, interview.

42. Sipiläinen, interview.

43. Meyer, *Quest*, 126.
44. Ibid., 127.
45. Semaška, interview.
46. Howorth, "Political and Security Committee and the Emergence," 26.
47. Soone, interview.
48. Juncos and Reynolds, "Political and Security Committee," 142.
49. Ibid., 144.
50. Klen Jäärats, Estonian Antici delegate, interview by author, January 2009.
51. Juncos and Reynolds, "Political and Security Committee," 143.
52. Milders, interview.
53. Soone, interview.
54. Howorth, "Political and Security Committee and the Emergence," 13–14.
55. Ibid., 25.
56. Juncos and Reynolds, "Political and Security Committee," 142.
57. Howorth, "Political and Security Committee and the Emergence," 22.
58. Sipiläinen, interview.
59. Milders, interview.
60. Didier Chabert, French deputy PSC ambassador, interview by author, January 2009.
61. Soone, interview.
62. Juncos and Reynolds, "Political and Security Committee," 142.
63. Sipiläinen, interview.
64. Meyer, *Quest,* chap. 5.
65. Howorth, "Political and Security Committee and the Emergence," 25.
66. Ibid., 21.
67. Juncos and Reynolds, "Political and Security Committee," 140.
68. Mirko Cigler, Slovenian deputy PSC ambassador, interview by author, March 2009.
69. Semaška, interview.
70. Chabert, interview.
71. Adam Sambrook, British team leader of the European Defence Policy and Institutions Team in the Security Policy Group of the Foreign and Commonwealth Office, interview by author, May 2009.
72. João Pedro Antunes, Portuguese Ministry of Foreign Affairs, Director for Security and Defence Affairs, interview by author, April 2009.
73. Ibid.
74. Ibid.
75. Pronk, interview.
76. Ibid.
77. Henrick van Asch, Dutch Ministry of Foreign Affairs Security Policy Department representative, interview by author, May 2009.
78. Semaška, interview.
79. Juncos and Reynolds, "Political and Security Committee," 144–45.
80. Korski and Gowan, *Can the EU Rebuild Failing States?,* 56–58.

81. Ibid., 56–57.

82. Chabert, interview.

83. Milders, interview.

84. Korski and Gowan, *Can the EU Rebuild Failing States?*, 22.

85. Juncos and Reynolds, "Political and Security Committee," 136.

86. Howorth, "Political and Security Committee and the Emergence," 7.

87. Padeanu, interview.

88. Schweisgut, interview.

Chapter 5

1. General Jo Coelmont, former Belgian EUMC representative, interview by author, June 2009.

2. Ibid.

3. Much of the following analysis of internal processes within the military epistemic community is based on thirteen interviews of EUMC military representatives from a total of twelve member states conducted between February and June 2009. Two of the interviewees were deputy EUMC representatives. Research into the internal workings of this epistemic community must rely on interviews because there are no transcripts of informal meetings, and formal summaries of meetings are classified and limited in what they can reveal.

4. Dunivin, "Military Culture," 533.

5. Cornish and Edwards, "Beyond the EU/NATO Dichotomy," 587.

6. Cross, *European Diplomatic Corps.*

7. Burk, "Military Culture."

8. In his *History of the Peloponnesian War,* Thucydides famously outlines the details of battle in 431 B.C.E.

9. Luvaas, "Great Military Historians and Philosophers," 63.

10. For an excellent account of this process, see Parker, *Military Revolution.*

11. Dorn, "'Military Revolution,'" 656–57.

12. Tertrais, "Changing Nature."

13. See, for example, Adler, "Spread of Security Communities"; Bellamy, *Security Communities.*

14. In this book, the EUMC refers to the permanent military representatives based in Brussels, rather than the chiefs of defense in the capitals they represent.

15. *Official Journal,* "Council Decision of 22 January 2001 Setting up the Military Committee of the European Union."

16. The Petersberg Tasks, constructed in 1992, are the underlying framework for CSDP. They outline the type and scope of military missions taken by the EU—humanitarian, rescue, peacekeeping, and crisis management.

17. The 2003 European Security Strategy outlines the EU's actions in the fight against terrorism, recognizing that military action alone will not diffuse the threat.

18. The EUMC may delegate to its working group certain matters that it cannot deal with quickly—usually issues that are more technical in nature.

19. EU member states that are not members of NATO do not have double-hatted milreps. The Belgian and French milreps are also not double-hatted.

20. General Raimonds Graube, Latvian EUMC representative, interview by author, March 2009.

21. Admiral Kourkoulis Dimitrios, Greek EUMC representative, interview by author, June 2009.

22. http://www.nato.int/cv/milrep/cv-mlrp.htm.

23. General Sorin Ioan, Romanian EUMC military representative, interview by author, February 2009.

24. Coelmont, interview.

25. At the same time, the EUMC does not have a monopoly on this knowledge. It is not uncommon for nonstate actors such as private military companies, militias, or rogue guerrillas, among others, to possess similar tactical expertise as well.

26. For a thorough overview of these three concepts, see Avant, "Institutional Sources."

27. Ibid., 410.

28. Ibid.

29. General David Bill, British EUMC representative, interview by author, June 2009.

30. Posen, *Sources*, discusses how states' military organizations create doctrines that enable success in battle and perpetuate their bureaucratic power. Posen argues that militaries gravitate toward offensive military doctrines for these reasons.

31. Snyder, *Ideology*; Sagan and Waltz, *Spread*; Miller, "Defense Policy."

32. Avant, "Institutional Sources."

33. Coelmont, interview.

34. Admiral Stefan Engdahl, Swedish EUMC military representative, interview by author, May 2009.

35. Interviews in Lisbon, London, and the Hague. In general, it is often observed that a member state's representatives in Brussels are more in favor of integration than those in the capitals, especially in the ministries of defense.

36. It is not possible to expose the informal processes of short-term operations planning within EUMC as the cases are ongoing and classified.

37. General Patrick de Rousiers, French EUMC representative, interview by author, May 2009.

38. General A. G. D. van Osch, Dutch EUMC military representative, interview by author, March 2009.

39. Ioan, interview.

40. Bill, interview.

41. Ioan, interview.

42. General István Békési, Hungarian EUMC representative, intervew by author, February 2009.

43. Graube, interview.

44. General Pier Paolo Lunelli, Italian deputy EUMC representative, interview by author, June 2009.

45. van Osch, interview.

46. Graube, interview.

47. van Osch, interview.

48. de Rousiers, interview.

49. van Osch, interview.

50. *Official Journal*, "Council's Rules."

51. Colonel Peter Kallert, German deputy EUMC representative, interview by author, June 2009.

52. Dimitrios, interview.

53. van Osch, interview.

54. Snyder, *Soviet Strategic Culture*, argues that U.S. and Soviet strategic culture explained the nuclear doctrines of the two powers.

55. Dunivin, "Military Culture," 533.

56. For an excellent literature review of strategic culture and how it has been researched as an independent variable, see Lantis, "Strategic Culture."

57. Ioan, interview.

58. van Osch, interview.

59. Lunelli, interview.

60. van Osch, interview.

61. Graube, interview.

62. Coelmont, interview.

63. Békési, interview.

64. Graube, interview.

65. Lunelli, interview.

66. van Osch, interview.

67. Ibid.

68. Graube, interview.

69. Quentin Weiler, French Nicolaidis delegate, interview by author, January 2009.

70. Bill, interview.

71. Engdahl, interview.

72. Ibid.

73. Bill, interview.

74. Admiral José M. Treviño-Ruiz, Spanish EUMC representative, interview by author, June 2009.

75. Ibid.

76. Ioan, interview.

77. de Rousiers, interview.

78. Coelmont, interview.

79. Ibid.

80. Ibid.

81. Engdahl, interview.

82. Dimitrios, interview.

83. de Rousiers, interview.

84. Coelmont, interview.

85. de Rousiers, interview.

86. Coelmont, interview.

87. Engdahl, interview.

88. Kallert, interview.

89. Ibid.

90. Ibid.

91. Adam Sambrook, British team leader of the European Defence Policy and Institutions Team in the Security Policy Group of the Foreign and Commonwealth Office, interview by author, May 2009.

92. Kallert, interview.

93. Sambrook, interview.

94. João Pedro Antunes, Portuguese Ministry of Foreign Affairs, Director for Security and Defence Affairs, interview by author, April 2009.

95. Ibid.

96. Henrick van Asch, Dutch MFA Security Policy Department representative, interview by author, May 2009.

97. Kallert, interview.

98. Lunelli, interview.

99. Kallert, interview.

100. Anonymous, interview by author, 2004.

101. Békési, interview.

102. *ESDP Newsletter* 8 (Summer 2009): 13.

103. Ibid., 15.

104. Ibid., 13; Grevi, Helly, and Keohane, *European Security,* 393–94.

105. Grevi, Helly, and Keohane, *European Security,* 395–96.

106. Ibid., 398–99.

107. Colonel Benedetto Liberace, Italian chief of the Operations and Exercises Branch, interview by author, June 2009.

108. Grevi, Helly, and Keohane, *European Security,* 395.

109. *ESDP Newsletter* 8 (Summer 2009): 16.

110. Grevi, Helly, and Keohane, *European Security,* 339–40.

111. van Osch, interview.

112. Ibid.

113. Lunelli, interview.

114. Gough and Shackley, "Respectable Politics," 332.

115. In 2001, the Council created the EUISS as an autonomous think tank that would research and develop the Common Foreign and Security Policy.

EUISS researchers refer extensively to academic and scientific work in the larger community as well as to official documentation.

116. Security and Defence Agenda, *Europe's Long-Term Vision.*

117. At the time, the EDA was working quickly to establish an extranet that would serve as a communication and discussion forum, allowing member states, experts, and EU institutions readily to participate in a more informal manner ("EDA's Relations with Key Stake-Holders," annex to *Report by the Head,* Document 14421/05).

118. *Report by the Head,* Document 8967/05.

119. Ibid., 4.

120. *Report by the Head,* Document 14421/05, 4.

121. "Assessing," 6.

122. Kallert, interview.

123. *Outcome.*

124. European Defence Agency, "EDA Steering Board News Conference," 1.

125. The steering board comprises member state defense ministers, who are political decision makers with the status of civilians. The new staff members of the EDA participated as part of the military-defense epistemic community.

126. Security and Defence Agenda, *Europe's Long-Term Vision,* list of participants.

127. Security and Defence Agenda, *Shaping.*

128. Security and Defence Agenda, *Europe's Long-Term Vision.*

129. In 2003, total defense expenditure of the 25 EU member states was €169 billion, or 1.7 percent of GDP (Hayes, *Arming,* 6).

130. European Defence Agency, "Initial Long-Term Vision," 10.

131. Security and Defence Agenda, *Europe's Long-Term Vision,* 11.

132. Public documentation of this meeting is not available.

133. EUISS alone consulted more than 650 studies related to the global context the EU might face in 20 years (Grevi and Schmitt, "Long Term Vision").

134. "Long Term Vision," 9.

135. Ioan, interview.

136. Treviño-Ruiz, interview.

137. Békési, interview.

138. Graube, interview.

139. Engdahl, interview.

140. European Defence Agency, "EU Defence Ministers."

141. European Defence Agency, "EDA Steering Board News Conference."

142. U.K. House of Commons, "Select Committee," 50.

143. *European Defence Agency.*

144. Antunes, interview.

145. Rochus Pronk, representative of the Political Affairs Department, Dutch Ministry of Foreign Affairs, interview by author, May 2009.

146. Rogier van der Pluijm, policy officer of the Security Policy Department, Dutch Ministry of Foreign Affairs, interview by author, May 2009.

147. van Asch, interview.

Chapter 6

1. Christian Rovsing, member of the European Parliament and former GofP, interview by author, April 2009.

2. *Security Research*, 4.

3. An exception would be the epistemic community of environmental scientists.

4. Lindley-French, *Chronology*, 245.

5. For a full account, see *European Military Capabilities*, 99–100.

6. Ibid., 101.

7. Ibid., 115.

8. This case study is drawn from Cross, "EU Homeland Security?"

9. The GofP is not simply a Commission committee and therefore does not have official authority to propose legislation.

10. Liem, *Brief Outlook*.

11. *Research for a Secure Europe*.

12. *Security Research*.

13. http://www.esrif.eu/background.html.

14. European Union Enterprise and Industry, *Strong Response*.

15. *Research for a Secure Europe*, 10.

16. Liem, *Brief Outlook*.

17. *Research for a Secure Europe*, 12.

18. U.S. General Accounting Office, *Combating Terrorism*.

19. Liem, *Brief Outlook*, 5.

20. European Union Research News Alert, *EU Blueprint*.

21. Projects were categorized as either major or supporting projects.

22. European Union Press Releases, *13 New Security Research Projects.* The U.S. Department of Homeland Security also mobilizes a variety of technological responses to border and internal security. Technology is certainly important, but it consumes nowhere near the amount of resources as are consumed in somewhat conventional wars in Iraq and Afghanistan.

23. European Union Press Releases, *PASR 2006*.

24. Nicole Fontaine, "Lisbon European Council 23 and 24 March 2000." Speech.

25. "European Security Research and Innovation Forum."

26. *Security Research*, 4.

27. European Union Research News Alert, *EU Blueprint*.

28. European Defence Agency, "Solana, Verheugen, Enders."

29. John, "UK Stays Out."

30. *Security Research*.

31. European Security Research Advisory Board, *Meeting the Challenge*, 6.

32. Ibid., 10.

33. *European Security Research and Innovation Forum Final Report*.

34. Ibid., 2.

35. *Official Journal*, "Council Decision of 22 May 2000." According to the Council decision, the committee's role is to "provide information, formulate recommendations and give advice on civilian aspects of crisis management."

36. Bono, "Implementing," 74; Meijer and Mateeva, "Training," 4.

37. Korski and Gowan, *Can the EU Rebuild Failing States?*, 13–14.

38. Anonymous Civcom delegate, interview by author, May 2009.

39. Ibid.

40. *ESDP Newsletter* 6 (July 2008): 24–25.

41. Leonardo Sanchez, Spanish Civcom delegate, interview by author, June 2009.

42. Tim Harrington, Irish Civcom delegate, interview by author, May 2009.

43. Anonymous Civcom delegate, interview by author, May 2009.

44. If a country devotes more resources to a particular mission, the Civcom delegate intervenes more.

45. Anonymous Civcom delegate, interview by author, May 2009.

46. Marc Bentinck, Dutch Civcom delegate, interview by author, March 2009.

47. Anonymous Civcom delegate, interview by author, May 2009.

48. Koenraad Dassen, Belgian Civcom delegate, interview by author, May 2009.

49. Anonymous Civcom delegate, interview by author, May 2009.

50. Ibid.

51. Gabriele Altana, Italian Civcom delegate, interview by author, March 2009.

52. Pierson, "Increasing Returns."

53. Anonymous Civcom delegate, interview by author, May 2009.

54. Bentinck, interview.

55. A diplomat who is between 40 and 45 would be appointed as a PSC or Coreper ambassador, although before the latest enlargement, the seniority was higher.

56. Bentinck, interview.

57. Harrington, interview.

58. Sanchez, interview.

59. All interviewees except one responded in the affirmative when asked about the presence of an esprit de corps.

60. Anonymous Civcom delegate, interview by author, May 2009.

61. Ibid.

62. Ibid.

Conclusion

1. Weber, *Politics*, 33.

2. Thornhill, "EU Struggles."

3. Nye, *Soft Power*.

4. Finnemore and Sikkink, "International Norm Dynamics," 911-12.

5. Ibid.

6. Hix, *Political System;* McCormick, *Understanding;* Hooghe, *European Commission;* Decker, "Governance."

7. Ruggie, "International Responses," 570.

8. Alina Padeanu, Romanian Antici delegate, interview by author, January 2009.

9. Smith, *Europe's Foreign and Security Policy,* 6.

10. Cross, "EU Homeland Security?"

11. Keohane, "Political Authority," 289.

Bibliography

Acharya, Amitav. "How Ideas Spread: Whose Norms Matter? Norm Localization and Institutional Change in Asian Regionalism." *International Organization* 58 (2004): 239–75.

Addendum to Note: Implementation of the Strategy and Action Plan to Combat Terrorism. Document 15912/08 ADD 1 REV 1. Brussels: Council of the European Union, 2008.

Adler, Emanuel. "The Spread of Security Communities: Communities of Practice, Self-Restraint, and NATO's Post–Cold War Transformation." *European Journal of International Relations* 14 (2008): 195–230.

Adler, Emanuel. "The Spreading of Security Community: Communities of Practice, Self Restraint, and NATO's Post–Cold War Transformation." Paper presented at the annual meeting of the International Studies Association, Chicago, February 28, 2007.

Adler, Emanuel, and Michael Barnett. *Security Communities.* Cambridge: Cambridge University Press, 1998.

Anderson, M. S. *The Rise of Modern Diplomacy, 1450–1919.* London: Longman, 1993.

Anderson, Malcolm. "Internal and External Security in the EU: Is There Any Longer a Distinction?" In *The Changing Politics of European Security,* ed. Stefan Gänzle and Allen G. Sens, 31–46. Basingstoke: Palgrave Macmillan, 2007.

Antoniades, Andreas. "Epistemic Communities, Epistemes, and the Construction of (World) Politics." *Global Society* 17 (2003): 21–38.

"Assessing the EDA's First Three Years." *European Defence Agency Bulletin* 5 (July 2007): 6.

Avant, Deborah D. "The Institutional Sources of Military Doctrine: Hegemons in Peripheral Wars." *International Studies Quarterly* 37 (1993): 409–30.

Bachrach, Peter, and Morton Baratz. "Decisions and Nondecisions: An Analytical Framework." *American Political Science Review* 57 (1963): 632–42.

Bátora, Jozef. "Does the European Union Transform the Institution of Diplomacy?" *Journal of European Public Policy* 12 (2005): 44–66.

Bellamy, Alex J. *Security Communities and Their Neighbours: Regional Fortresses or Global Integrators?* Basingstoke: Palgrave Macmillan, 2004.

Berridge, G. R. *Diplomacy: Theory and Practice.* Basingstoke: Palgrave Macmillan, 2005.

Best, Edward, Thomas Christiansen, and Pierpaolo Settembri. *The Institutions of the Enlarged EU: Continuity and Change.* Northampton, MA: Elgar, 2008.

Bigo, Didier. "When Two Become One: Internal and External Securitisations in Europe." In *International Relations Theory and the Politics of European Integration,* ed. Morten Kelstrup and Michael C. Williams, 171–204. London: Routledge, 2000.

Bono, Giovanna. "Implementing the Headline Goals: The Institutional Dimension." In *Unraveling the European Security and Defense Policy Conundrum,* ed. Joachim Krause, Lisa Watanabe, and Andreas Wenger, 67–91. Bern, Switzerland: Lang, 2003.

Bossong, Raphael. "The Action Plan on Combating Terrorism: A Flawed Instrument of EU Security Governance." *Journal of Common Market Studies* 46 (2008): 27–48.

Bruter, Michael. "Diplomacy without a State: The External Delegations of the European Commission." *Journal of European Public Policy* 6 (1999): 183–205.

Burk, James. "Military Culture." In *Encyclopedia of Violence, Peace, and Conflict,* ed. Lester R. Kurtz and Jennifer E. Turpin, 447–62. San Diego: Academic Press, 1999.

Caporaso, James, Maria Green Cowles, and Thomas Risse, eds. *Transforming Europe: Europeanization and Domestic Change.* Ithaca: Cornell University Press, 2001.

Checkel, Jeffrey. "'Going Native' in Europe? Theorizing Social Interaction in European Institutions." *Comparative Political Studies* 36 (2003): 209–31.

Checkel, Jeffrey. "International Institutions and Socialization in Europe: Introduction and Framework." *International Organization* 59 (2005): 801–26.

Checkel, Jeffrey, and Peter Katzenstein, eds. *European Identity.* New York: Cambridge University Press, 2009.

Christiansen, Thomas, ed. *The Role of Committees in the Policy Process of the European Union: Legislation, Implementation, and Deliberation.* Cheltenham: Elgar, 2007.

Christiansen, Thomas, Knud Erik Jorgensen, and Antje Wiener, eds. *The Social Construction of Europe.* London: Sage, 2001.

Ciută, Felix. "The End(s) of NATO: Security, Strategic Action, and Narrative Transformation." *Contemporary Security Policy* 23 (2002): 35–62.

Clemens, Elisabeth S., and James M. Cook. "Politics and Institutionalism: Explaining Durability and Change." *Annual Review of Sociology* 25 (1999): 441–66.

Code of Conduct on Defence Procurement. Brussels: European Defence Agency, 2005.

Cornish, Paul, and Geoffrey Edwards. "Beyond the EU/NATO Dichotomy: The

Beginnings of a European Strategic Culture." *International Affairs* 77 (2001): 587–603.

Cortell, Andrew, and James Davis. "Understanding the Domestic Impact of International Norms: A Research Agenda." *International Studies Review* 2 (2002): 65–87.

Cottey, Andrew. *Security in the New Europe.* New York: Palgrave, 2007.

Cross, Mai'a K. Davis. "An EU Homeland Security? Sovereignty vs. Supranational Order." *European Security* 16 (2007): 79–97.

Cross, Mai'a K. Davis. *The European Diplomatic Corps: Diplomats and International Cooperation from Westphalia to Maastricht.* Basingstoke: Palgrave Macmillan, 2007.

Croxton, Derek. *Peacemaking in Early Modern Europe: Cardinal Mazarin and the Congress of Westphalia, 1643–1648.* London: Associated University Presses, 1999.

Darnis, Jean-Pierre, Giovanni Gasparini, Christoph Grams, Daniel Keohane, Fabio Liberti, Jean-Pierre Maulny, and May-Britt Stumbaum. *Lessons Learned from European Defence Equipment Programmes.* Occasional Paper 69. Paris: EU Institute for Security Studies, 2007.

Decker, Frank. "Governance beyond the Nation-State: Reflections on the Democratic Deficit of the European Union." *Journal of European Public Policy* 9 (2002): 256–72.

Den Boer, Monica. *9/11 and the Europeanisation of Anti-Terrorism Policy: A Critical Assessment.* Policy Paper 6. Paris: Notre Europe, 2003.

Deutsch, Karl W., Sidney A. Burrell, and Robert A. Kahn. *Political Community and the North Atlantic Area: International Organization in the Light of Historical Experience.* Westport, CT: Greenwood, 1969.

Donnelly, Brendan. "Justice and Home Affairs in the Lisbon Treaty: A Constitutionalising Clarification?" *European Institute of Public Administration* 1 (2008): 1–5.

Dorn, Harold. "The 'Military Revolution': Military History or History of Europe?" *Technology and Culture* 32 (1991): 656–58.

Draft EU Strategy for Combating Radicalisation and Recruitment—Background Paper for Coreper Discussion. Document 12165/1/05. Brussels: Council of the European Union, 2006.

Drake, William, and Kalypso Nicolaidis. "Ideas, Interests, and Institutionalization: 'Trade in Services' and the Uruguay Round." *International Organization* 46 (1992): 37–100.

Duchêne, François. "Europe's Role in World Peace." In *Europe Tomorrow: Sixteen Europeans Look Ahead,* ed. Richard Mayne, 32–47. London: Fontana, 1972.

Duke, Simon. *The Linchpin COPS: Assessing the Workings and Institutional Relations of the Political and Security Committee.* European Institute of Public Administration Working Paper 2005/W/05. Maastricht: European Institute of Public Administration, 2005.

Duke, Simon. "Preparing for European Diplomacy?" *Journal of Common Market Studies* 40 (2002): 853–58.

Duke, Simon, and Hanna Ojanen. "Bridging Internal and External Security: Lessons from the European Security and Defence Policy." *Journal of European Integration* 28 (2006): 477–94.

Dunivin, Karen O. "Military Culture: Change and Continuity." *Armed Forces and Society* 20 (1994): 531–47.

Dunlop, Claire. "Epistemic Communities: A Reply to Toke." *Politics* 20 (2000): 137–44.

Ekengren, Markus. "Terrorism and the EU: The Internal-External Dimension of Security." In *The European Union and Terrorism,* ed. David Spence, 30–53. London: Harper, 2007.

EU Council Secretariat. "The EU Operations Centre." Press Office, Brussels, http://www.consilium.europa.eu/uedocs/cmsUpload/070228-EU_OpsCentre.pdf.

EU Counter-Terrorism Strategy—Discussion Paper. Document 15983/08. Brussels: Council of the European Union, 2008.

European Defence Agency. "EDA Steering Board News Conference: Opening Remarks by Head of Agency Javier Solana." Levi, Finland, October 3, 2006.

European Defence Agency. "EU Defence Ministers Welcome Long-Term Vision for European Capability Needs." Press Release. October 3, 2006. Levi, Finland.

European Defence Agency. "An Initial Long-Term Vision for European Defence Capability and Capacity Needs." Document SB MoDs. Levi, Finland, October 2, 2006.

European Defence Agency. "Defence Data 2009." Brussels: European Defence Agency, 2010.

European Defence Agency. "Solana, Verheugen, Enders Urge Boost for EU Spending and Collaboration on Defence R&T." Press Release. February 9, 2006. Brussels.

European Defence Agency—Council Guidelines for the EDA's Work in 2007. Document 15184/06. Brussels: Council of the European Union, 2006.

European Economic Community Council. *Provisional Rules of Procedure.* 1958.

European Military Capabilities: Building Armed Forces for Modern Operations. London: International Institute for Strategic Studies, 2008.

European Security and Defense Assembly of the Western European Union. "Assembly Factsheet No. 9." WEU Press and Information Office, November 2008.

European Security Research Advisory Board. *Meeting the Challenge: The European Security Research Agenda.* Luxembourg: Office for Official Publications of the European Communities, 2006.

European Security Research and Innovation Forum Final Report. Adopted by the ninth and tenth plenary meetings of ESRIF, September 3, 21, 2009.

"The European Security Research and Innovation Forum (ESRIF)—Public-Private Dialogue in Security Research." Europa Press Release, MEMO/07/346. Brussels, September 11, 2007.

The European Union Counter-Terrorism Strategy. Document 14469/4/05. Brussels: Council of the European Union, 2005.

European Union Enterprise and Industry. *Preparatory Action for Security Research 2004 Funded Activities.* 2005. http://europa.eu.int/comm/enterprise/secu rity/articles/article_2164_en.htm.

European Union Enterprise and Industry. *Strong Response to EU Call for Security Proposals,* August 3, 2004. http://europa.eu.int/comm/enterprise/security/ articles/article_1319_en.htm.

European Union Press Releases. *13 New Security Research Projects to Combat Terrorism.* MEMO/05/277. Brussels, August 2, 2005.

European Union Press Releases. *PASR 2006: 15 New Security Research Projects to Combat Terrorism.* MEMO/06/375. Brussels, October 13, 2006.

European Union Research News Alert. *EU Blueprint for Security Research Programme.* Document IP/04/1090. Brussels, September 9, 2004.

The European Union Strategy for Combating Radicalisation and Recruitment to Terrorism. Document 14781/1/05. Brussels: Council of the European Union, 2005.

Evangelista, Matthew. "The Paradox of State Strength: Transnational Relations, Domestic Structures, and Security Policy in Russia and the Soviet Union." *International Organization* 49 (1995): 1–38.

Favell, Adrian. *Eurostars and Eurocities: Free Movement and Mobility in an Integrating Europe.* Malden, MA: Blackwell, 2008.

Fierke, Karin, and Antje Wiener. "Constructing Institutional Interests: EU and NATO Enlargement." *Journal of European Public Policy* 6 (1999): 721–42.

Finnemore, Martha, and Kathryn Sikkink. "International Norm Dynamics and Political Change." *International Organizations* 52 (1998): 887–917.

Fiske de Gouveia, Philip, with Hester Plumridge. *European Infopolitik: Developing EU Public Diplomacy Strategy.* London: Foreign Policy Centre, 2005.

Fligstein, Neil. *Euroclash: The EU, European Identity, and the Future of Europe.* New York: Oxford University Press, 2008.

Fontaine, Nicole. "Lisbon European Council 23 and 24 March 2000." Speech.

Foucault, Michel. *The Order of Things.* New York: Vintage, 1973.

Frattini, Franco. " Keynote Address." Speech delivered at a conference organized by the Security and Defence Agenda, Brussels, October 18, 2007.

French Delegation to the EU Political and Security Committee. *Guide to the European Security and Defence Policy (ESDP).* November 2008.

From Coreper to Council; EU Action Plan on Combating Terrorism. Document 10010/3/04. Brussels: Council of the European Union, 2004.

Gänzle, Stefan, and Allen G. Sens, eds. *The Changing Politics of European Security: Europe Alone?* Basingstoke: Palgrave Macmillan, 2007.

Garlick, Madeline, and Judith Kumin. "Seeking Asylum in the EU: Disentangling Refugee Protection from Migration Control." In *Justice, Liberty, Security: New Challenges for EU External Relations,* ed. Bernd Martenczuk and Servaas van Thiel, 111–44. Brussels: Brussels University Press, 2008.

Gheciu, Alexandra. "Security Institutions as Agents of Socialization? NATO and the 'New Europe.'" *International Organization* 59 (2005): 973–1012.

Givens, Terri, and Adam Luedtke. "EU Immigration Policy: From Intergovernmentalism to Reluctant Harmonization." In *The State of the European Union,* Vol. 6, *Law, Politics, and Society,* ed. Tanja A. Börzel and Rachel A. Cichowski, 291–312. New York: Oxford University Press, 2003.

Gough, Clair, and Simon Shackley. "The Respectable Politics of Climate Change: The Epistemic Communities and NGOs." *International Affairs* 77 (2001): 329–45.

Gourevitch, Peter. "The Second Image Reversed: The International Sources of Domestic Politics." *International Organization* 32 (1978): 881–912.

Grant, Charles. "Making a Success of the EAS." May 21, 2009. http://centre foreuropeanreform.blogspot.com/2009/05/making-success-of-eas.html.

Grevi, Giovanni. "ESDP Institutions." In *European Security and Defence Policy: The First Ten Years (1999–2009),* ed. Giovanni Grevi, Damien Helly, and Daniel Keohane, 19–68. Paris: EU Institute for Security Studies, 2009.

Grevi, Giovanni, Damien Helly, and Daniel Keohane, eds. *European Security and Defence Policy: The First Ten Years (1999–2009).* Paris: EU Institute for Security Studies, 2009.

Grevi, Giovanni, and Burkard Schmitt. "Long Term Vision." *EUISS Newsletter* 18 (April 2006): 5.

Haas, Peter. "Banning Chlorofluorocarbons: Epistemic Community Efforts to Protect Stratospheric Ozone." *International Organization* 46 (1992): 187–224.

Haas, Peter. "Introduction: Epistemic Communities and International Policy Coordination." *International Organization* 46 (1992): 1–35.

Haas, Peter. "Policy Knowledge: Epistemic Communities." In *International Encyclopedia of the Social and Behavioral Sciences,* ed. Neil J. Smelser and Paul B. Baltes, 11578–86. Maryland Heights, MO: Elsevier Science, 2001.

Haas, Peter. *Saving the Mediterranean.* New York: Columbia University Press, 1990.

The Hague Programme: Ten Priorities for the Next Five Years: The Partnership for European Renewal in the Field of Freedom, Security, and Justice. Document COM(2005) 184 final—Official Journal C 236. Brussels: Commission of the European Communities, 2005.

Hall, Peter A. "Policy Paradigms, Social Learning, and the State: The Case of Economic Policymaking in Britain." *Comparative Politics* 25 (1993): 275–96.

Hamilton, Keith, and Richard Langhorne. *The Practice of Diplomacy: Its Evolution, Theory, and Administration.* London: Routledge, 1995.

Hayes, Ben. *Arming Big Brother: The EU's Security Research Program.* TNI Briefing Series 1. Amsterdam: Transnational Institute, 2006.

Heclo, Hugh. "Issue Networks and the Executive Establishment." In *The New American Political System,* ed. Anthony King, 87–124. Washington, DC: American Enterprise Institute, 1978.

Heinisch, Reinhard, and Simone Mesner. "COREPER: Stealthy Power Brokers or

Loyal Servants to their Government Masters? The Role of the Committee of Permanent Representatives in a Changing Union." Paper presented at the European Union Studies Association Conference, Austin, Texas, April 2, 2005.

Henrikson, Alan K. "Diplomacy's Possible Futures." *The Hague Journal of Diplomacy* 1 (2006): 3–27.

Hix, Simon. *The Political System of the European Union.* 2nd ed. London: Palgrave, 2005.

Holzner, Burkhart. *Reality Construction in Society.* Cambridge, MA: Schenkman, 1972.

Hocking, Brian, and David Spence, eds. *Foreign Ministries in the European Union: Integrating Diplomats.* Basingstoke: Palgrave, 2005.

Hooghe, Liesbet. *The European Commission and the Integration of Europe: Images of Governance.* Cambridge: Cambridge University Press, 2001.

Hooghe, Liesbet. "Several Roads Lead to International Norms, but Few via International Socialization: A Case Study of the European Commission." *International Organization* 59 (2005): 861–98.

Hopf, Ted. "The Promise of Constructivism in International Relations Theory." *International Security* 23 (1998): 171–200.

Howorth, Jolyon. "Discourse, Ideas, and Epistemic Communities in European Security and Defence Policy." *West European Politics* 27 (2004): 211–34.

Howorth, Jolyon. "The Political and Security Committee: A Case Study in 'Supranational Inter-Governmentalism.'" *Les Cahiers Européens, Sciences Po* 1 (2010): 1–24.

Howorth, Jolyon. "The Political and Security Committee and the Emergence of a European Security Identity." *IntUne: Integrated and United: A Quest for Citizenship in an "Ever Closer Europe."* MA/07/02 (2007): 1–30.

Howorth, Jolyon. *Security and Defence Policy in the European Union.* New York: Palgrave Macmillan, 2007.

Howorth, Jolyon, and John T. S. Keeler, eds. *Defending Europe: The EU, NATO, and the Question for European Autonomy.* New York: Palgrave Macmillan, 2003.

Implementation of the Strategy and Action Plan to Combat Terrorism. Document 15266/06. Brussels: Council of the European Union, 2006.

Implementation of the Strategy and Action Plan to Combat Terrorism. Document 9666/07. Brussels: Council of the European Union, 2007.

Implementation on the Strategy and Action Plan to Combat Terrorism. Document 15912/08. Brussels: Council of the European Union, 2008.

Implementation Report on the Radicalization and Recruitment Strategy and Action Plan. Document 15386/06. Brussels: Council of the European Union, 2006.

Jachtenfuchs, Markus, Thomas Diez, and Sabine Jung. "Which Europe? Conflicting Models of a Legitimate European Political Order." *European Journal of International Relations* 4 (1998): 409–45.

JHA External Relations Multi Presidency Work Programme. Document 10546/08. Brussels: Council of the European Union, 2008.

Jileva, Elena. "Do Norms Matter? The Principle of Solidarity and the EU's East-
ern Enlargement." *Journal of International Relations and Development* 7
(2004): 3–23.
John, Mark. "UK Stays Out as EU Launches Defence Research Fund." Reuters,
November 13, 2006.
Jones, Seth G. *The Rise of European Security Cooperation.* Cambridge: Cambridge
University Press, 2007.
Jönsson, Christer, and Richard Langhorne. *Diplomacy.* London: Sage, 2004.
Jordan, Andrew, and John Greenway. "Shifting Agendas, Changing Regulatory
Structures and the 'New' Politics of Environmental Pollution: British
Coastal Water Policy, 1955–1995." *Public Administration* 76 (1998): 669–94.
Juncos, Ana E., and Christopher Reynolds. "The Political and Security Commit-
tee: Governing in the Shadow." *European Foreign Affairs Review* 12 (2007):
127–47.
Jupille, Joseph, James A. Caporaso, and Jeffrey T. Checkel. "Integrating Institu-
tions: Rationalism, Constructivism, and the Study of the European Union."
Comparative Political Studies 36 (2003): 7–40.
Keck, Margaret, and Kathryn Sikkink. *Activists beyond Borders: Advocacy Networks
in International Politics.* Ithaca: Cornell University Press, 1998.
Kelemen, R. Daniel. "The EU Rights Revolution: Adversarial Legalism and European Integration." In *The State of the European Union,* vol. 6, *Law, Politics, and
Society,* ed. Tanja A. Börzel and Rachel A. Cichowski, 221–34. New York: Oxford University Press, 2003.
Keohane, Robert. "Political Authority after Intervention: Gradations in Sovereignty." In *Humanitarian Intervention: Ethical, Legal, and Political Dilemmas,*
ed. J. L. Holzgrefe and Robert Keohane, 275–98. Cambridge: Cambridge University Press, 2003.
Keohane, Robert, and Joseph S. Nye. "Transgovernmental Relations and International Organizations." *World Politics* 27 (1974): 39–62.
Keukeleire, Stephen. "The European Union as a Diplomatic Actor: Internal, Traditional, and Structural Diplomacy." *Diplomacy and Statecraft* 14 (2003):
31–56.
Kirchner, Emil, and James Sperling. *EU Security Governance.* Manchester: Manchester University Press, 2007.
Korski, Daniel, and Richard Gowan. *Can the EU Rebuild Failing States? A Review
of Europe's Civilian Capacities.* London: European Council on Foreign Rela-
tions, 2009.
Kratochwil, Friedrich V. "How Do Norms Matter?" In *International Law,* ed. Beth
A. Simmons, 264–98. London: Sage, 2008.
Krebs, Ronald R. "The Limits of Alliance: Conflict, Cooperation, and Collective
Identity." In *The Real and the Ideal: Essays on International Relations in Honor
of Richard H. Ullman,* ed. Anthony Lake and David Ochmanek, 207–36. Lan-
ham, MD: Rowman and Littlefield, 2001.
Kuhn, Thomas. *The Structure of Scientific Revolutions.* Chicago: University of
Chicago Press, 1962.

Lantis, Jeffrey S. "Strategic Culture: From Clausewitz to Constructivism." *Strategic Insights* 4 (October 2005). http://www.nps.edu/Academics/centers/ccc/publications/OnlineJournal/2005/Oct/lantisOct05.pdf.

Legro, Jeffrey W. "Which Norms Matter? Revisiting the 'Failure' of Internationalism." *International Organization* 51 (1997): 31–63.

Liem, Khoen. *Brief Outlook to Security Research in the 7th Framework Programme.* DG ENTR-H4. Vienna European Conference on Security Research, 2006.

Lindberg, Leon N. *The Political Dynamics of European Economic Integration.* Stanford: Stanford University Press, 1963.

Lindley-French, Julian. *A Chronology of European Security and Defence Policy, 1945–2007.* New York: Oxford University Press, 2007.

Lindstrom, Gustav. "The EU's Approach to Homeland Security: Balancing Safety and European Ideals." In *Transforming Homeland Security: U.S. and European Approaches,* ed. Esther Brimmer, 116–31. Washington, DC: Center for Transatlantic Relations, 2006.

Lindstrom, Gustav. *Protecting the European Homeland: The CBR Dimension.* Chaillot Paper 69. Paris: Institute for Security Studies, 2004.

"Long Term Vision: Preparing the Future." *European Defence Agency Bulletin* 2 (July 2006): 9.

Luvaas, Jay. "The Great Military Historians and Philosophers." In *A Guide to the Study and Use of Military History,* ed. John E. Jessup and Robert W. Coakley, 59–88. Washington, DC: U.S. Government Printing Office, 1979.

Manners, Ian. "Normative Power Europe: A Contradiction in Terms?" *Journal of Common Market Studies* 40 (2002): 235–58.

Martenczuk, Bernd. "Visa Policy and EU External Relations." In *Justice, Liberty, Security: New Challenges for EU External Relations,* ed. Bernd Martenczuk and Servaas van Theil, 21–52. Brussels: Brussels University Press, 2008.

Martenczuk, Bernd, and Servaas van Thiel. "The External Dimension of EU Justice and Home Affairs: Evolution, Challenges, and Outlook." In *Justice, Liberty, Security: New Challenges for EU External Relations,* ed. Bernd Martenczuk and Servaas van Theil, 9–20. Brussels: Brussels University Press, 2008.

Mattingly, Garrett. *Renaissance Diplomacy.* London: Butler and Tanner, 1955.

McCormick, John. *Understanding the European Union.* New York: Palgrave, 2005.

Meijer, Guus, and Anna Mateeva. *Training on Civilian Aspects of Crisis Management.* Utrecht: Human European Consultancy, January 2006.

Melissen, Jan, ed. *Innovation in Diplomatic Practice.* London: Macmillan, 1999.

Mérand, Frédéric. "Pierre Bourdieu and the Birth of European Defense." *Security Studies* 19 (2010): 342–74.

Mérand, Frédéric. "Social Representations in the European Security and Defense Policy." *Cooperation and Conflict* 41 (2006): 131–52.

Meyer, Christophe O. *The Quest for a European Strategic Culture: Changing Norms on Security and Defence in the European Union.* Basingstoke: Palgrave, 2006.

Miller, Charles R. "Defense Policy and Doctrinal Insulation." In *Handbook of Military Administration,* ed. Jeffrey A. Weber and Johan Eliasson, 191–220. Boca Raton, FL: CRC, 2008.

Missiroli, Antonio. "ESDP—How It Works." In *EU Security and Defence Policy: The First Five Years (1999–2004)*, ed. Nicole Gnesotto, 55–72. Paris: EU Institute for Security Studies, 2004.

Mitsilegas, Valsamis, Jörg Monar, and Wyn Rees. *The European Union and Internal Security: Guardian of the People? (One Europe or Several?)*. Basingstoke: Palgrave, 2003.

Moravcsik, Andrew. "Europe, the Second Superpower." *Current History* 109 (March 2010): 91–98.

Moravcsik, Andrew. "A New Statecraft? Supranational Entrepreneurs and International Cooperation." *International Organization* 53 (1999): 267–303.

Moravcsik, Andrew. "The Quiet Superpower." *Newsweek*, June 17, 2002.

Nilsson, Hans. "Judicial Cooperation in Europe against Terrorism." In *The European Union and Terrorism*, ed. David Spence, 71–87. London: Harper, 2007.

Nye, Joseph. *Soft Power: The Means to Success in World Politics*. New York: Public Affairs, 2005.

Official Journal of the European Communities. "Council Decision of 22 January 2001 Setting Up the Military Committee of the European Union." Document 2001/79/CFSP.

Official Journal of the European Communities. "Council Decision of 22 January 2001 Setting Up the Political and Security Committee." Document 2001/78/CFSP.

Official Journal of the European Communities. "Council Decision of 22 May 2000 Setting Up a Committee for Civilian Aspects of Crisis Management." Document 2000/354/CFSP.

Official Journal of the European Communities. "Treaty of Nice Article 25." Document 2001/C 80/01.

Official Journal of the European Union. "Council's Rules of Procedure, Article 12." Document L285/47, October 16, 2006.

Osiander, Andreas. *The States System of Europe, 1640–1990: Peacemaking and the Conditions of International Stability*. Oxford: Clarendon, 1994.

Outcome of Proceedings. Document 7997/1/05. Brussels: Council of the European Union, 2005.

Parker, Geoffrey. *The Military Revolution: Military Innovation and the Rise of the West, 1500–1800*. Cambridge: Cambridge University Press, 1988.

Pastore, Ferruccio. "Reconciling the Prince's Two 'Arms': Internal-External Security Policy Coordination." *Institute for Security Studies—Western European Union* 30 (2001): 1–21.

Peers, Steven. "EU Migration Law and Association Agreements." In *Justice, Liberty, Security: New Challenges for EU External Relations*, ed. Bernd Martenczuk and Servaas van Thiel, 53–88. Brussels: Brussels University Press, 2008.

Peterson, John. "Decision-Making in the European Union: Towards a Framework for Analysis." *Journal of European Public Policy* 2 (1995): 69–93.

Peterson, John, and Elizabeth Bomberg. *Decision-Making in the European Union*. Basingstoke: Macmillan, 1999.

Pierson, Paul. "Increasing Returns, Path Dependence, and the Study of Politics." *American Political Science Review* 92 (2000): 251–67.

Pistone, Sergio. "Altiero Spinelli and a Strategy for the United States of Europe." In *The Federal Idea: The History of Federalism from the Enlightenment to 1945,* ed. Andrea Bosco, 1:351–57. London: Lothian, 1991.

Pollack, Mark A. "Theorizing the European Union: International Organization, Domestic Polity, or Experiment in New Governance?" In *American Review of Political Science* 8 (2005): 357–98.

Pop, Valentina. "No 'Big Bang' for EU Foreign Service, Says Solana." *EUObserver,* June 23, 2009. http://euobserver.com/9/28355.

Posen, Barry. *The Sources of Military Doctrine: France, Britain, and Germany between the World Wars.* Ithaca: Cornell University Press, 1984.

Pouliot, Vincent. "The Logic of Practicality: A Theory of Practice of Security Communities." *International Organization* 62 (2008): 257–88.

Pouliot, Vincent. "'Sobjectivism': Toward a Constructivist Methodology." *International Studies Quarterly* 51 (2007): 359–84.

Radaelli, Claudio M. "The Public Policy of the European Union: Whither Politics of Expertise?" *Journal of European Public Policy* 6 (1999): 757–74.

Radaelli, Claudio M. *Technocracy in the European Union.* London: Longman, 1999.

Rathbun, Brian C. "Interviewing and Qualitative Field Methods: Pragmatism and Practicalities." In *Oxford Handbook of Political Methodology,* ed. Janet M. Box-Steffensmeier, Henry E. Brady, and David Collier, 685–701. Oxford: Oxford University Press, 2008.

Raustiala, Kal. "Domestic Institutions and International Regulatory Cooperation: Comparative Responses to the Convention on Biological Diversity." *World Politics* 49 (1997): 482–509.

Rees, Wyn. "Inside Out: The External Face of EU Internal Security Policy." *European Integration* 30 (2008): 97–111.

Rees, Wyn. *Transatlantic Counter-Terrorism Cooperation: A New Imperative.* London: Routledge, 2006.

Report by the Head of the European Defence Agency to the Council. Document 8967/05. Brussels: Council of the European Union, 2005.

Report by the Head of the European Defence Agency to the Council. Document 14421/05. Brussels: Council of the European Union, 2005.

Research for a Secure Europe: Report of the Group of Personalities in the Field of Security Research. Luxembourg: Office for Official Publications of the European Communities, 2004.

Rhinard, Mark, Arjen Boin, and Magnus Ekengren. "Managing Terrorism: Institutional Capacities and Counter-Terrorism Policy in the EU." In *The European Union and Terrorism,* ed. David Spence, 88–104. London: Harper, 2007.

Richardson, Jeremy. "Actor-Based Models of National and EU Policy Making." In *The European Union and National Industrial Policy,* ed. Hussein Kassim and Anand Menon, 26–51. London: Routledge, 1996.

Risse, Thomas. *A Community of Europeans? Transnational Identities and Public Spheres*. Ithaca: Cornell University Press, 2010.

Risse, Thomas. "The Euro between National and European Identity." *Journal of European Public Policy* 10 (2003): 487–503.

Risse, Thomas. "'Let's Argue!' Communicative Action in World Politics." *International Organization* 54 (2000): 1–39.

Risse, Thomas. "Transnational Actors and World Politics." In *Handbook of International Relations,* ed. Walter Carlsnaes, Thomas Risse, and Beth A. Simmons, 255–74. London: Sage, 2002.

Risse, Thomas, Stephen C. Ropp, and Kathryn Sikkink. *The Power of Human Rights: International Norms and Domestic Change*. Cambridge: Cambridge University Press, 1999.

Rosamond, Ben. *Theories of European Integration*. New York: Palgrave, 2000.

Ruggie, John Gerard. "International Responses to Technology: Concepts and Trends." *International Organization* 29 (1975): 557–83.

Ruggie, John Gerard. "What Makes the World Hang Together? Neo-Utilitarianism and the Social Constructivist Challenge." *International Organization* 52 (1998): 855–85.

Sabatier, Paul A. "The Advocacy Coalition Framework: Revisions and Relevance for Europe." *Journal of European Public Policy* 5 (1998): 98–130.

Sabatier, Paul A., and Hank C. Jenkins-Smith. "The Advocacy Coalition Framework: An Assessment." In *Theories of the Policy Process,* ed. Paul A. Sabatier, 117–68. Boulder: Westview, 1999.

Sagan, Scott, and Kenneth Waltz. *The Spread of Nuclear Weapons: A Debate*. New York: Norton, 1995.

Salmon, Trevor. "The European Union: Just an Alliance or a Military Alliance?" *Journal of Strategic Studies* 29 (2006): 814–42.

Schimmelfennig, Frank, and Ulrich Sedelmeier. *The Europeanization of Central and Eastern Europe*. Ithaca: Cornell University Press, 2005.

Schmitt, Burkard. *From Cooperation to Integration: Defence and Aerospace Industries in Europe*. Chaillot Paper 40. Paris: Institute for Security Studies, 2000.

Sebenius, James K. "Challenging Conventional Explanations of International Cooperation: Negotiation Analysis and the Case of Epistemic Communities." *International Organization* 46 (1992): 323–65.

A Secure Europe in a Better World: European Security Strategy. Brussels: Council of the European Union, 2003.

Security and Defence Agenda. *Europe's Long-Term Vision of the Defence Environment in 2025: Sharp or Fuzzy?* Summary of an expert seminar organized with the European Defence Agency, Brussels, June 13, 2006.

Security and Defence Agenda. *Shaping Europe's Defence Debate*. Expert workshop, Brussels, March 2007.

Security Research: The Next Steps. Document COM(2004) 590 Final. Brussels: Commission of the European Communities, 2004.

Sharp, Paul. *Diplomatic Theory of International Relations.* Cambridge: Cambridge University Press, 2009.

Slaughter, Anne-Marie. *A New World Order.* Princeton: Princeton University Press, 2004.

Smith, Michael E. *Europe's Foreign and Security Policy.* Cambridge: Cambridge University Press, 2004.

Snyder, Jack. *The Ideology of the Offensive: Military Decision Making and the Disasters of 1914.* Ithaca: Cornell University Press, 1984.

Snyder, Jack. *The Soviet Strategic Culture: Implications for Nuclear Options.* Santa Monica, CA: Rand, 1977.

Spence, David, ed. *The European Union and Terrorism.* London: Harper, 2007.

Spence, David. "The Evolving Role of Foreign Ministries in the Conduct of European Union Affairs." In *Foreign Ministries in the European Union,* ed. Brian Hocking and David Spence, 18–36. Basingstoke: Palgrave, 2005.

Stockholm International Peace Research Institute. *SIPRI Yearbook 2008: Armaments, Disarmament, and International Security.* New York: Oxford University Press, 2008.

Stumbaum, May-Britt U. *Risky Business? The EU, China, and Dual-Use Technology.* Occasional Paper 80. Paris: EU Institute for Security Studies, 2009.

Tardy, Thierry. *European Security in a Global Context: Internal and External Dynamics.* London: Routledge, 2009.

Telò, Mario. *Europe: A Civilian Power?* New York: Palgrave Macmillan, 2007.

Tertrais, Bruno. "The Changing Nature of Military Alliances." *Washington Quarterly* 27 (2004): 135–50.

Thomas, Craig. "Public Management as Interagency Cooperation: Testing Epistemic Community Theory at the Domestic Level." *Journal of Public Management Research and Theory* 7 (1997): 221–46.

Thornhill, John. "EU Struggles to Establish New Economic Order." *Financial Times,* March 28, 2010.

Thucydides. *The History of the Peloponnesian War.* New York: Penguin, 1954.

Thurner, Paul W., and Martin Binder. "European Union Transgovernmental Networks: The Emergence of a New Political Space beyond the Nation State?" *European Journal of Political Research* 48 (2009): 80–106.

Toke, David. "Epistemic Communities and Environmental Groups." *Politics* 19 (1999): 97–102.

U.K. House of Commons. "Select Committee on European Scrutiny Fourth Report, 19 MOD (28077) (28078) European Defence Agency." December 14, 2006.

U.S. General Accounting Office. *Combating Terrorism: Selected Challenges and Related Recommendations.* Washington, DC: U.S. General Accounting Office, 2001.

Valls, Raquel. "Origin and Development of Coreper." *European Navigator.* Translated by Centre Virtuel de la Connaissance sur l'Europe. http://www.ena.lu/.

Verdun, Amy. "The Role of the Delors Committee in the Creation of EMU: An Epistemic Community?" *Journal of European Public Policy* 6 (1999): 308–28.

Wallstrom, Margot. "Public Diplomacy and Its Role in the EU's External Relations." Speech given at the Mortara Center for International Studies, Georgetown University, Washington, DC, October 2, 2008.

Watson, Adam. *Diplomacy: The Dialogue between States.* London: Eyre Methuen, 1982.

Weber, Max. *Politics as a Vocation.* Indianapolis: Hackett, 2004.

Wendt, Alexander. "Anarchy Is What States Make of It: The Social Construction of Power Politics." *International Organization* 46 (1992): 391–425.

Zito, Anthony. "Epistemic Communities, Collective Entrepreneurship, and European Integration." *Journal of European Public Policy* 8 (2001): 585–603.

Zürn, Michael, and Jeffrey T. Checkel. "Getting Socialized to Build Bridges: Constructivism and Rationalism, Europe and the Nation-State." *International Organization* 59 (2005): 1045–79.

Index

Acharya, Amitav, 35
Action Plan on Combating Terrorism, 55
  Coreper's influence, 110, 114–16, 120
  third country initiatives, 57
Adler, Emanuel, 17
AEROBACTICS (PASR research project), 196
aerospace industry, 65–66
Afghanistan
  civilian/police missions, 142, 203, 204
  military missions, 70
  PSC and, 135
African Union, EU relationship, 69
aging populations, 74, 180, 181
agriculture, 83, 85
air transportation, 56, 58, 73, 191
Albania, 176
Alliance of Civilizations, 119–20
alliances, 17, 67
  diffusion of military ideas and, 148, 149–50, 151–52
al-Qaeda, 109–10
Altana, Gabriele, 208–9
Amsterdam Treaty (1997), 48, 58, 59
Anna Lindh Foundation, 118
Antici working group, 90, 129
Antoniades, Andreas, 31
Antunes, João Pedro, 138–39, 172, 184
Article 296 of EU Treaty, 65, 66
ASEAN Regional Forum, 119
Ashton, Catherine, 10
Asia, 119
ASTRO (PASR research project), 194
asylum procedures, 57, 225, 233n20
  as first pillar issue, 48

hard integration of, 59–60, 73
  as internal security, 7
  supranational control over, 58
  See also immigration control
Athena Mechanism, 70–71, 162
Austria
  ambassadorial nominations, 108
  Civcom and, 210
  civilian missions and, 202
  NATO and, 170
  SRR and, 119
availability principle, 54–55
Avant, Deborah, 156

Barnett, Michael, 17
battle groups
  description of, 64
  EUMC and, 167–68
  future of, 226
  hard integration and, 50, 64, 70, 73
  PSC and, 137
  See also military force/capabilities
Békési, István, 159, 164–65, 173, 182
Belgium
  civilian missions and, 202
  CSDP and, 53, 64
  EUMC/NATO representation, 170
  terrorism definition, 55
Benelux countries, European Coal and Steel Community and, 3
Bentinck, Marc, 209
Berlusconi, Silvio, 108
Best, Edward, 91
bilateral diplomacy, 87, 128
Bill, David, 156, 167
BIO3R (PASR research project), 196

biological attacks. *See* chemical, biological, radiological and nuclear (CBRN) attacks/weapons
biometric identifiers, 57, 60, 196
BioTesting Europe (PASR research project), 196, 197
Blair, Tony, 46
BODE (PASR research project), 196
Bomberg, Elizabeth, 23
border control
    Coreper and, 224
    Frontex, 57–58, 85
    Hague Programme (2005–10), 233–34n26
    hard integration in, 57–58, 73, 225
    harmonization, 226
    PASR research and, 195, 197
    as point of vulnerability, 191, 192
    sovereignty and, 150
    as supranational issue, 48, 49
    visa policy and, 59
    See also external security; Schengen zone
Bosnia, military operations in, 70
Braun, Christian, 85, 90
Britain. *See* United Kingdom
BSUAV (PASR research project), 195
Bulgaria, 118, 202–3
Burrell, Sidney A., 17
Busquin, Philippe, 190

Canada, EU relationship, 69
candidate countries, 129
Capability Development Plan, 184, 185
causal beliefs, shared
    common culture and, 88, 100, 101–3
    Coreper, 78, 109, 110–13, 116–17, 120, 131, 143, 217
    EUMC, 131, 166–69, 181–83
    GofP, 190–91, 192–93, 198, 200
    importance of, 25–26
    Long-Term Vision, 180–81
    in NGOs, 15
    vs. professional norms, 28
    PSC, 124, 131, 134–35
    roots in expert knowledge, 19–20, 78, 231n42
CBRN attacks. *See* chemical, biological, radiological, and nuclear attacks/weapons
Central African Republic, 175

Central and Eastern European Countries (CEECs), 210
CFSP (Common Foreign and Security Policy)
    cooperation under, 51–52, 69
    Coreper and, 83, 86, 224
    future of, 226
    historical background, 45–47
    intergovernmentalism, 7
    PSC's role, 125–26, 132
    as soft integration, 51–52
    SRR and, 55
Chabert, Didier, 138, 141
Chad operation, 64, 141, 154, 162, 175–76
Charter of Fundamental Rights of the European Union (2009), 62
Checkel, Jeffrey, 14, 35
Check the Web program, 117, 118, 119
chemical, biological, radiological, and nuclear (CBRN) attacks/weapons
    as key threat to Europe, 8, 191, 192–93
    PASR research and, 194, 195, 196
    protections against, 56
chiefs of defense, 152, 160, 172–73
China, 66, 174
Chirac, Jacques, 46
chlorofluorocarbons, 33
Christiansen, Thomas, 91
Cigler, Mirko, 137
CITRINE (PASR research project), 196
Civilian Crisis Management Committee (Civcom), 11–12, 187–88, 202–13
    common culture, 202, 208–10, 212, 220
    Coreper and, 93
    expert knowledge lack, 203–4, 213, 220
    future of, 226
    heterogeneity, 209–10
    influence, 40, 138, 139, 140, 210–13, 221
    internal/external security links, 144
    meeting frequency and quality, 205–8, 220
    as nascent epistemic community, 186, 203, 220–21
    professional norms, 202, 206–7, 212, 220
    PSC and, 86, 131, 187, 202, 207
    role, 249n35
    selection and training, 203–5
    status, 129, 166
Civilian Headline Goals (2008, 2010), 202
civilian missions, 1, 43, 46, 69

Afghanistan, 142, 203, 204
capacity management, 71–72, 202, 213
Civcom and, 187, 202
classification of documentation about, 124
Coreper and, 240n105
external security and, 188
future of, 226
hard integration in, 73
humanitarian intervention, 155, 175–76
member state willingness to support, 202–3
shortfalls in, 142
supranational oversight of, 50
See also names of missions
Civilian Planning and Conduct Capability (CPCC), 204
civil liberties. *See* human rights/civil liberties
civil-military missions/relations, 67, 155, 185, 191, 226
Civil-Military Planning Directorate, 167
Civil Protection Unit, 56
Civil Protection Working Party of the Council, 56
Clemenceau, Georges, 80
Clemens, Elisabeth, 10
climate change policy, 84
coalitions, 16
codecision procedure, 84
Coelmont, Jo, 145, 155, 168, 169
cohesiveness
  Coreper, 101, 103, 120
  epistemic community strength and, 27, 216
  EUMC, 185
  GofP, 186–87
  meeting frequency and, 159
  PSC, 136
Cold War, 2, 13, 44–45, 47
Combined Maritime Forces, 175
Commission. *See* European Commission
Commission's Monitoring and Information Centre, 56
Committee of Permanent Representatives. *See* Coreper I; Coreper II
committees, defined, 16
common culture
  Civcom, 202, 208–10, 212, 220
  Coreper, 100–103, 120

defined, 28–29
epistemic community strength and, 213, 216
vs. esprit de corps, 29, 208
EUMC, 145–46, 162–71, 185, 202, 218
meeting frequency and quality and, 28, 88
PSC, 123–24, 133–36, 219
Common Emergency and Communication and Information System, 56
Common European Asylum System, 59
Common Foreign and Security Policy. *See* CFSP (Common Foreign and Security Policy)
common market, 8
Common Security and Defence Policy. *See* CSDP (Common Security and Defence Policy)
Commonwealth of Independent States, 49–50
communities of practice, 28
Community Mechanism for Civil Protection, 56
Community Method, 7, 48, 230n16
Concert of Europe, 49
Conference on Security and Cooperation in Europe, 45
Congo, Kivu province, 157
Congress of Berlin (1878), 80
consensus, 10
  Civcom, 206, 207
  Coreper, 84, 91, 96–97
  EUMC, 146, 160, 162
  PSC, 131–32, 134–35, 136, 143
  qualified majority voting and, 9–10, 96–97, 120
  silence procedure and, 161–62
Constitutional Treaty. *See* Lisbon Treaty (2007)
consultation reflex, 68, 134–35. *See also* united voice of EU
contact hypothesis, 28
Convention on the Prevention of Terrorism (2006), 118
Cook, James, 10
Cook, Robin, 125
cooperation, 72
  defined, 49–50
  vs. integration, 51–52, 234n29
  Long-Term Vision and, 184
  PSC and, 142–43

coordination, 72
  defined, 49
  EUMC and, 174–75
  PSC and, 133
COPS. *See* Political and Security Committee (PSC)
Coreper I (Committee of Permanent Representatives), 83–85, 90
Coreper II (Committee of Permanent Representatives), 88–109, 110–17, 221
  causal beliefs, 78, 109, 110–13, 116–17, 120, 131, 143, 217
  common culture, 100–103, 120
  Counterterrorism Strategy and, 55
  as epistemic community, 77–78
  EUMC and, 93, 173
  history/evolution of, 82–84
  increasing workload, 48, 233n20
  influence, 40, 77, 104–9, 110–15, 117–21, 217, 224, 240n112
  instructions and, 91, 107–9
  meeting frequency and quality, 92–93, 103, 120
  military integration and, 240n105
  professional norms, 93–100, 109, 120
  PSC and, 86, 93, 122–24, 126–27, 131–32, 143–44, 166
  selection and training, 88–92, 103, 120
  SRR and, 11, 110–15, 116–17, 217–18, 240n112
  as strong epistemic community, 122–24, 144, 217–18
  verbal negotiations, 238n43
Cornish, Paul, 146
corruption, 43
Cortell, Andrew, 4, 29, 35
Council of Europe, 49–50
Council of the European Union, 7, 94, 99, 230n16, 236–37n8
counterterrorism, 7, 8, 53–57
  CFSP working group on, 110
  ESS (2003), 243n17
  integration and, 42–43, 216
  intelligence/information sharing, 114, 117–18, 119
  internal/external security links, 49, 56–57, 216
  United States, 192, 248n22
  See also Action Plan on Combating Terrorism; Strategy on Radicalization and Recruitment (SRR)

Counterterrorism Strategy, 55
Counterterrorist Group, 54
Court of Justice, 230n16
CRIMSON (PASR research project), 194, 197
crisis response, 2
  EUMC and, 155
  PSC and, 86, 123, 126, 127, 136, 140, 142
  See also civilian missions; military-civil missions/relations
Croatia, 129, 174, 176
CSDP (Common Security and Defence Policy), 7, 11–12
  Civcom and, 187
  civilian crisis management, 71–72, 203, 206–8, 221
  cooperation/integration under, 67–68, 69–72
  decision-making under, 161–62
  EUMC and, 156
  future of, 226
  growth of, 129, 217
  Lisbon treaty, 47
  member states and, 9, 53, 63–65, 135, 184–85, 211
  NATO and, 152
  Petersberg Tasks and, 243n16
  PSC and, 86, 123, 125–28, 132–33, 134–35, 140–42, 219, 221
  as soft integration, 50–52
cyberattack/security, 118, 193, 195
Cyprus, 53, 170, 202–3, 207
Czech Republic, 202–3

Darfur, Sudan, 175
Dassen, Koenraad, 207
Davis, James, 4, 29, 35
decision making in EU, 7, 21–22, 48, 94, 230n16. *See also* consensus; qualified majority voting; silence procedure
Declaration on Combating Terrorism (2004), 43
defense spending, 1, 62
  Athena mechanism, 70–71, 162
  defense fund, 198–99, 200
  sovereignty and, 9
  U.S. comparison, 74, 199
Delbrück, Hans, 149
delegation of tasks, 95–96, 120
Delors Committee, 20
democratic values, 191, 217, 222–23

demographics, 74, 180, 181
Denmark
    ambassadorial instructions, 108–9
    civilian missions and, 202
    defense cooperation and, 74
    selection of Coreper ambassador, 89
    SRR and, 119
Deutsch, Karl W., 17
DG E9 (directorate on civilian crisis man-
    agement), 204
dialogue, intercultural, 117, 118, 119, 120
Dimitrios, Kourkoulis, 162
diplomats/diplomacy, history of, 78–82
Drake, William, 23
dual-application security technology, 188,
    190, 199
Duarte Lopes, Francisco, 98
Duke, Simon, 130
Dunivin, Karen, 146
Dunlop, Claire, 22, 38

economies of scale, 2, 180, 225
EDA. See European Defence Agency
education, 83, 118
Edwards, Geoffrey, 146
EEAS. See European External Action Ser-
    vice
Ekengren, Markus, 44
employment, 83
energy policy, 84
Engdahl, Stefan, 167, 170, 183
England. See United Kingdom
environmental policy
    Coreper I and, 83, 85
    epistemic communities and, 21–22, 33,
        232n64
    integration of, 46
Environment Directorate General, 56
epistemic coalitions, 178–79, 188–89
epistemic communities
    competition between, 19, 24, 28, 39,
        223–24
    defined, 6, 18–20, 24, 75
    democratic values and, 222–23
    difficulties in studying, 37–39
    diplomats as, 89, 147
    importance for integration, 221–22
    loose/nascent, 186–87, 201, 202, 203,
        212–13, 219–20
    vs. other transnational actors, 15–18
    recognizing, 16–17, 154

scientists and, 188–89, 219
socialization mechanisms, 33–35
think tanks and, 39–40
See also Civilian Crisis Management
    Committee (Civcom); Coreper II
    (Committee of Permanent Represen-
    tatives); epistemic community
    strength; EU Military Committee
    (EUMC); Group of Personalities in
    the Field of Security Research (GofP);
    influence of epistemic communities;
    military epistemic community; Politi-
    cal and Security Committee (PSC);
    status of epistemic communities
epistemic community concept, criticism
    of, 22–24, 39
epistemic community strength, 25
    causal variables of, 26–30, 79, 158, 213
    Coreper, 122–24, 144, 217–18
    disbanding of communities, 201
    EUMC, 146, 217, 218
    loose/nascent communities, 186–87
    measurement of, 88, 215–16, 218–19
    PSC, 12, 122–24, 142, 144, 219
    See also influence of epistemic commu-
        nities; status of epistemic communi-
        ties
Erasmus program, 118
escalation to higher levels, 97–100, 104,
    120, 131–32, 172–73
esprit de corps, 16
    Civcom, 207, 208–10, 220
    common background and, 163
    vs. common culture, 29, 208
    Coreper, 100
    GofP, 220
    meeting frequency and, 158
    PSC, 133–34
ESRAB. See European Security Research
    Advisory Board
ESRP. See European Security Research Pro-
    gram
ESS. See European Security Strategy (2003)
ESSRT (PASR research project), 194
Estonia
    ambassadorial instructions, 107, 108
    civilian missions and, 202–3
    external security goals, 135
    military weakness, 53
    radicalization and, 116
EUFOR Chad, 64, 141, 154, 162, 175–76

EU Institute for Security Studies (EUISS), 178, 181, 246n115, 247n23
EULEX Kosovo, 70, 207–8, 221
EUMC Working Group, 153
EU Military Committee (EUMC), 152–77
  causal beliefs, 131, 166–69, 181–83
  Civcom comparison, 187
  common culture, 145–46, 162–71, 185, 202, 218
  Coreper and, 93, 173
  divisions within, 169–71
  double-hattedness, 128, 153, 158–59, 165–66, 169–70, 185, 218
  establishment/description, 152–54
  expert knowledge, 154–55, 157–58, 244n25
  influence of, 40, 70, 145, 171–77, 201, 218
  instructions and, 146, 160–61, 171–72, 218
  internal/external security links, 144, 185
  Long-Term Vision and, 178–79, 181–83
  meeting frequency and quality, 145–46, 158–62
  professional norms, 145–46, 160–62, 165, 185, 202, 206
  PSC and, 86, 131, 135, 152–53, 166, 177
  selection and training, 145–46, 154–58
  socialization, 164–65
  as strong epistemic community, 146, 217, 218
  underutilization of, 221
  working groups and, 244n18
EU Military Staff, 70, 153, 163
EUPOL Afghanistan, 142, 203, 204
Euro-Arab Dialogue (1973), 45
EUROCOP (PASR research project), 196, 197
Eurocorps, 70, 73
Euro Forces, 70, 73
Eurojust (European Judicial Cooperation Unit), 55, 61
EuroMed, 119
European Arrest Warrant, 53–54, 62, 73, 120
European Automated Fingerprints Identification System (EURODAC), 57
European Coal and Steel Community, 3, 44–45, 52

European Commission, 7, 68, 230n16, 236–37n8
European Council, 99, 104
European Council on Foreign Relations (ECFR), 140–41
European Court of Justice (ECJ), 60
European Defence Agency (EDA), 225, 247n125
  communication facilitation, 247n117
  Coreper and, 240n105
  creation, 2
  defense fund, 198–99, 200
  EUMC and, 153, 157
  external security focus, 201
  integration of military research and procurement, 66, 67
  Long-Term Vision and, 178–79, 184
  strengthening of CSDP, 64
European Defence Community (EDC), 45
European Defence R&T Strategy, 184
European Evidence Warrant, 54, 73
European External Action Service (EEAS), 7, 77, 87–88, 229n15
European Gendarmerie Force, 70, 73
European Judicial Network, 61
European Monetary Union (EMU), 20
European Neighborhood Policy, 66–67
European Parliament, 94, 230n16, 236–37n8
European Police College, 119
European Political Community (EPC), 45
European Political Cooperation (EPC), 45
European Security and Defence Policy (ESDP, 1999), 46, 187. *See also* CSDP (Common Security and Defence Policy)
European Security Research Advisory Board (ESRAB), 191, 199–200
European Security Research and Innovation Forum, 200
European Security Research Program (ESRP)
  creation of, 187
  GofP and, 190, 191, 198, 200, 220
European Security Strategy (ESS) (2003), 76, 243n17
  EUMC and, 153
  internal/external security links, 8, 47, 56–57, 67–68
  terrorist attacks and, 42–43
European Space Agency, 66

European Union, Treaty on. *See* Maastricht Treaty (1992)
Europol, 54, 55, 61, 117, 118
Evangelista, Matthew, 35
Evans, Gareth, 131
expert knowledge, 17, 18, 19–20, 201
  civilian crisis management, 203–4, 213, 220
  consensual knowledge building, 33
  democratic governance and, 222
  diplomatic, 81–82, 89, 90–91, 103, 128–29, 204–5, 217
  epistemic community strength and, 218
  EU issues, 90, 91–92, 105, 203–4
  influence of epistemic communities and, 20, 24, 36, 75, 92, 105, 216, 231n42
  military, 155–58, 177, 185, 218, 244n25
  as power, 40, 77–78
  scientific/technological, 30–31, 190
external security, 1–2, 135
  civilian crisis missions and, 188
  counterterrorism and organized crime, 56–57
  defined, 7
  EDA focus, 201
  EUMC and, 145
  future of, 226
  groups influencing, 40
  history of European cooperation/integration, 44–47
  PSC focus, 103, 123, 126, 143
  as second pillar, 46
  use of internal security tools, 43–44
  See also battle groups; border control; civilian missions; internal/external security links; military-civil missions/relations; military force/capabilities; third countries

Faden, Rita, 106
federalism, 5, 6
Finland
  ambassadorial instructions, 107
  Civcom and, 210
  civilian missions and, 202
  CSDP emphasis, 53
  integration support, 116
  NATO and, 170
first pillar, 46, 54, 73, 230n16
  border control, 58

counterterrorism, 57
decision-making, 96
  JHA and, 48
  See also hard integration; supranational governance
Foucault, Michel, 18–19
Fouchet Plan, 45
Framework Program on Security and Safeguarding Liberties, 198
France, 135
  ambassadorial instructions, 137, 138
  Chad operation, 162, 175
  Civcom and, 210
  civilian missions and, 202
  CSDP and, 53, 211
  defense fund and, 199
  EUMC/NATO representation, 170
  EU military headquarters and, 69
  European Coal and Steel Community and, 3
  foreign policy traditions, 52
  Iraq war and, 123
  military strength, 53
  military technology integration, 189
  political will for third-country military operations, 63
  PSC ambassadors and, 128
  rejection of 2005 Constitutional Treaty, 68
  SRR and, 119
  support for EU military capability, 46
  terrorism definition, 55
  terrorist threats in, 113
free movement, 58–59, 62. *See also* Schengen zone
Frontex (European Agency for Management of External Borders), 57–58, 85

Galileo program, 65–66
Gang of Four, 80
GATE (PASR research project), 196
gender issues, 68
The General (Strategicus) (Onasander), 149
General Affairs Council, 99–100
Geneva Refugee Convention (1954), 59
GEOCREW (PASR research project), 194
George, David Lloyd, 80
Georgia-Russia crisis (2008–9), 140
Germany
  ambassadorial instructions, 108
  Civcom and, 210

Germany (*continued*)
  civilian missions and, 202
  counterterrorism in, 117
  CSDP and, 53, 211
  defense fund and, 199
  EUMC and, 170–71
  EU military headquarters and, 69
  European Coal and Steel Community
    and, 3
  military strength, 53
  military technology integration, 189
  SRR and, 119
  terrorist threats in, 113
Gibbons, Emma, 105
global financial crisis, 71, 74
globalization, 14, 75, 180
GofP. *See* Group of Personalities in the
    Field of Security Research
Gough, Clair, 30
Gowan, Richard, 202
grand strategy, 155, 156, 157–58
grassroots participation, 16, 36
Graube, Raimonds, 159–60, 164, 165, 166,
    182–83
Greece
  ambassadorial instructions, 108
  civilian missions and, 162, 202–3
  EU military headquarters and, 69
  financial crisis, 68
  Kosovo mission and, 207
Greece, ancient, 148, 149
Greenway, John, 23
Grevi, Giovanni, 63
Group of Personalities in the Field of Se-
    curity Research (GofP)
  causal beliefs, 190–91, 192–93, 198, 200
  influence of, 40, 190, 197–201, 213,
    220
  as loose epistemic community, 186–87,
    219–20
  PASR impact, 193–97
  professional norms, 186–87, 190, 220
Grube, Claus, 85, 97, 99

Haas, Peter
  definition of epistemic community, 6,
    19–20, 24, 25
  on ecological epistemic community, 33
  on expert knowledge, 31, 231n42
  influence of epistemic communities,
    20–21, 23, 36

scholarly acceptance of epistemic com-
    munity definition, 22
  scientific knowledge focus, 30
Hague Programme (2005–10), 49, 229n14,
    233–34n26
Hall, Peter, 23
HAMLeT (PASR research project), 196, 197
harbor security, 58, 191
hard integration
  asylum policies, 59–60, 73
  border control, 57–58, 73, 225
  defined, 50
  definition of terrorist offenses, 55–56
  EUMC and, 145
  external counterterrorism measures, 57
  first pillar issues, 54
  human rights, 68, 73
  military capabilities, 50, 64, 70, 73
  vs. soft integration, 234n29
  See also supranational governance
harmonization
  border control, 226
  defined, 50–51
  European Arrest Warrant, 54
  immigration control, 59
  justice systems, 72
  military technology licensing, 66
  shortcomings in, 55
  See also soft integration
Harrington, Tim, 205
Headline Goal (1999), 63, 137
Headline Goal (2010), 64
Health Security Committee, 56
Health Security Program, 73
Helicopter Initiative Seminar (2009),
    141
Helsinki European Council (1999), 83–84
High Representative (CFSP), 7, 10
historical process tracing, 11, 34, 36–37
HiTS/ISAC (PASR research project), 195
Hooghe, Liesbet, 34–35
Howorth, Jolyon
  consensus in PSC, 136
  interviews of PSC members, 124
  Petersberg tasks, 46
  PSC and integration, 128, 134, 144
  supranational-intergovernmentalism,
    125–26
Human Rights, European Convention of
    (1950), 61
human rights/civil liberties

biometric identifiers and/privacy rights, 57
cooperation/integration, 60–62
Coreper and, 103
future of, 225
GofP and, 191
Hague Programme (2005–10), 233–34n26
hard integration, 68, 73
harmonization, 72
as internal security, 7
PASR research and, 195, 196, 197
SRR and, 113, 117, 120
Hungary, 53, 202–3

Iceland, 69, 129
immigration, illegal, 8, 43, 61
immigration control
future of, 225
Hague Programme (2005–10), 233–34n26
integration, 57, 58–60, 72, 73
as internal security, 7
SRR and, 120
as supranational issue, 48, 49, 58–60
IMPACT (PASR research project), 194
India, 174
influence of epistemic communities, 40, 49
Civcom, 138, 139, 140, 210–13, 221
cohesiveness and, 27
conditions required, 19, 23, 186, 215–17
Coreper, 77, 104–9, 110–15, 117–21, 217, 224, 240n112
EUMC, 70, 145, 171–77, 201, 218
expert knowledge and, 20, 24, 36, 75, 92, 105, 216, 231n42
GofP, 190, 197–201, 213, 220
nation-state structure and, 35
PSC, 136–40, 142–44, 219, 221
target audience and, 35–36, 37
uncertainty and, 20–22, 23, 31–33
See also epistemic communities; epistemic community strength; status of epistemic communities
informal networks, 15
information sharing. See intelligence/information sharing
infrastructure threats, 191, 192, 195
instructions
Civcom and, 205, 207, 210–12

Coreper and, 91, 107–9
EUMC and, 146, 160–61, 171–72, 218
length of EU membership and, 105
PSC and, 128, 129, 136, 137–40, 219
integration
Coreper and, 101–3, 110–13, 116–17, 120, 217, 224
counterterrorism and, 42–43, 216
future of, 225–27
GofP and, 193, 194–97
obstacles to, 143–44
progress in, 214–15
PSC and, 127–28
stages of, 4–5, 50–51, 52, 72
See also cooperation; coordination; hard integration; intelligence/information sharing; intergovernmentalism; interoperability; soft integration; supranational governance
intelligence/information sharing
as coordination, 72
Coreper and, 233n20
counterterrorism, 114, 117–18, 119
GofP and, 199
Hague Programme (2005–10), 233–34n26
Joint Situation Centre, 49, 117, 236n112
PASR research and, 114, 195, 196, 197
intercultural dialogue, 117, 118, 119, 120
intergovernmentalism
cooperation as example of, 50
CSDP and, 135
decisions to engage in military action, 70
external security as, 7
JHA and, 47–48
PoCo and, 125
police and judicial cooperation, 49
PSC and, 125–26
internal/external security links, 42, 215
Coreper belief in, 103, 143, 144, 224
counterterrorism and, 49, 56–57, 216
EU borderlessness and, 7–8, 43
EUMC and, 144, 185
future of security integration, 225–26
GofP belief in, 191
historical background, 44–49
PSC and, 135, 143
supranationalism and, 67–68
internal security, 2
Coreper and, 103, 126, 221

internal security (*continued*)
  counterterrorism, 53–56
  defined, 7
  future of, 226–27
  growing integration of, 77–78, 225–26
  historical background, 47–49
  influences on, 40
  Ireland, 43
  Netherlands, 105–6
  technology research and, 188
  as third pillar, 46
  tools of, 43–44
  See also Strategy on Radicalization and
    Recruitment (SRR)
International Atomic Energy Agency, 8
International Crisis Group, 131
Internationally Recommended Transit
    Corridor, 175
internet. *See* Check the Web program;
    cyberattack/security
interoperability
  Coreper and, 224
  EDA and, 179, 182, 184
  ESRAB and, 200
  EUMC and, 168, 183, 221
  future of, 225, 226
  GofP and, 193, 198
  internal/external security links and, 225
  military CSDP missions and, 64
  military technology research and, 66,
    67, 182, 189
  PASR research and, 195, 196, 197
  PSC and, 135, 137
  vs. sovereignty, 214
Ioan, Sorin, 159, 168, 181–82
Iran, 69
Iraq War (2003), 68, 123
Ireland
  civilian missions and, 202
  CSDP and, 211
  internal security, 43
  NATO and, 170
  Schengen zone and, 47
ISCAPS (PASR research project), 193–94
Islam, 111, 112, 114, 115, 118, 119
ISOTREX (PASR research project), 196, 197
issue networks, 15, 17
Italy
  ambassadorial instructions, 108
  Civcom and, 210
  civilian missions and, 202

EU military headquarters and, 69
European Coal and Steel Community
    and, 3
  military strength, 53
  military technology integration, 189
  terrorist threats in, 113
i-TRACS (PASR research project), 196, 197

Jäärats, Klen, 95, 102, 107, 134
Jenkins-Smith, Hank C., 23
JHA. *See* Justice and Home Affairs
Joint Investigation Teams, 120
Joint Situation Center (Sitcen), 117,
    236n112
Joint Situation Centre (Sitcen), 49
Jones, Seth G., 47
Jordan, Andrew, 23
judicial cooperation, 53
  hard integration, 54
  harmonization, 72
  intergovernmental nature, 49
  as soft integration, 73
Juncos, Ana E., 130, 133, 137, 140
Justice and Home Affairs (JHA)
  communitarization of, 47–48
  Coreper I and, 85
  Coreper II and, 83, 126, 221
  integration progress, 78
  member state reluctance to support, 104

Kääriänen, Seppo, 179
Kahn, Robert A., 17
Kallert, Peter, 162, 171, 172, 173
Keck, Margaret, 15
Kennedy, John F., 77
Keohane, Robert, 16, 227
Kerchove, Gilles de, 42
Keukeleire, Stephen, 235n94
Kleiweg, Pieter Jan, 106
knowledge-based networks. *See* epistemic
    communities
Kok, Rogier, 105, 106
Korski, Daniel, 202
Kosovo crises (1998, 2007–8), 46, 68, 70,
    140, 207–8, 221
Krebs, Ronald, 28
Kuhn, Thomas, 18

language use in meetings, 131, 159
larger member states
  EUMC decision making, 170–71

influence on decisions, 218
instructions and, 137, 211
military grand strategy, 157
PSC decision making, 132–33, 135–36
Larsson, Ulrika, 85
Latvia, 53, 202–3
League of Nations, 49
legal culture differences, 52, 61. *See also*
    judicial cooperation
Legro, Jeffrey, 35
Liikanen, Erkki, 190
Linnenkamp, Hilmar, 180–81
Lisbon Agenda (March 2000), 197–98
Lisbon Treaty (2007), 68
    civil liberties, 62
    dissolution of pillarization, 48, 72
    EEAS, 87–88
    external security integration, 47
    internal/external security links, 7
    internal security integration, 78
    qualified majority voting, 97
    Solidarity Clause, 43, 56
Lithuania, 139, 202–3
London terrorist attack (2005), 42
Long-Term Vision for European Defence,
    11, 177–85, 218
    causal beliefs, 180–81
    epistemic coalition, 178–79
    implementation, 183–85
    internal/external security links, 225
Luxembourg, 53, 202–3

Maastricht Treaty (1992)
    Coreper I and II roles, 83, 86
    defense equipment market, 65
    influence of diplomats on, 80–81
    monetary experts and, 20
    pillar structure, 72
    PoCo, 124–25
    policy fragmentation, 224
    security integration and, 3, 45–46,
        47–48
Macedonia, 64, 129, 142
Madrid attacks (2004), 42, 192
Mälk, Raul, 116
Malta, 53, 170, 202–3
MARIUS (PASR research project), 195
Mavroyiannis, Andreas, 89, 98–99, 102
media, 93, 97–98, 99, 118, 119, 120
meeting frequency and quality
    among 19th century diplomats, 79–80

Civcom, 205–8, 220
common culture and, 28, 88
Coreper, 92–93, 103, 120
epistemic community strength and, 216
EUMC, 145–46, 158–62
PSC, 123, 129–31, 219
socialization and, 35
*Meeting the Challenge: The European Secu-
    rity Research Agenda* (ESRAB), 199
member states of EU
    ambassadorial instructions, 107–8
    civilian mission support, 202–3
    CSDP and, 9, 53, 63–65, 135, 184–85, 211
    differences among, 5, 52–53, 105–6
    enlargement of, 13
    JHA and, 104
    military integration commitment, 63
    norm of collective action, 50–51
    power/influence of, 9–11
    PSC and, 123
    size disparities and voices of, 64–65, 101
    See also larger member states; newer
        member states; smaller member
        states; united voice of EU; *individual
        states*
Mertens working group, 90, 129
methodology, 36–41
    case selection, 39–41
    framework for analysis of epistemic
        communities, 27–30
    historical process tracing, 11, 34, 36–37
    interviews, 36, 38, 110, 178, 236n3,
        243n3
    limitations, 124, 187
    primary documents, 36, 39
Meyer, Christophe O., 132, 136
Milders, Robert, 134, 135
military-civil missions/relations, 67, 155,
    185, 191, 226
military culture, 146–47, 148–52, 162,
    163–64
military doctrine, 155–58, 163
military epistemic community, 11,
    145–47, 157–59. *See also* EU Military
    Committee
military force/capabilities, 2
    cooperation/integration of, 62–65,
        69–70, 240n105
    difference in member states' capabili-
        ties, 53
    hard integration, 50, 64, 70, 73

military force/capabilities (*continued*)
 multinational military formations, 168
 Petersberg tasks and, 46
 PSC and, 135, 141
 as security, 43
 technology, 66, 149, 150
 See also battle groups
military missions, 1, 63, 69, 70, 226
military technology research and procurement, 221
 dual-application security technology,
   188, 190, 199
 influences on, 189–90
 integration of, 46–47, 50, 178–79,
   181–83
 internal/external security links and, 225
 soft integration, 65–66, 67, 73
 United States, 182–83, 190
 See also Preparatory Action on Security
   Research (PASR)
Mitsilegas, Valsamis, 75
Monar, Jörg, 75
monetary union, 83
money laundering, 43, 54, 73, 196
Monitoring and Information Centre, 56
Moravcsik, Andrew, 13–14
Motoc, Mihnea, 100, 102
multilateralism, 80, 165. *See also* North
   Atlantic Treaty Organization (NATO)
Mutual Legal Assistance Convention,
   61–62

NATO. *See* North Atlantic Treaty Organization (NATO)
NATO Advisory Council (NAC), 166
NATO Response Force (NRF), 167–68
natural disasters, 68, 73
NAVFOR Atalanta, 69, 154, 166–67, 173–75
neorealist theory, 43
Netherlands
 civilian missions and, 202
 instructions, 108, 139, 172
 internal security in, 105–6
 Long-Term Vision and, 184–85
 radicalism in, 116
 rejection of 2005 Constitutional Treaty,
   68
 SRR and, 119
 terrorism definition, 55
networks, defined, 10
newer member states

bilateral diplomacy, 87
Coreper socialization, 100–101
EU expertise and, 90, 91
instructions and, 105
NATO focus, 53
Nice, Treaty of (2001), 125, 142, 219
Nicolaïdis, Kalypso, 23
Nicolaidis Group, 129
nongovernmental organizations (NGOs)
 Coreper and, 93
 PSC and, 131
 SRR and, 111, 112, 117
 as transnational networks, 14, 15–16
nonstate actors
 as global threats, 1, 62
 importance of, 9, 14
 soft integration and, 50
 soft power and, 215
 SRR and, 111
North Atlantic Treaty Organization
   (NATO)
 anti-piracy mission, 174, 175
 Eastern countries' focus, 169
 EU comparison, 2, 64, 167
 EUMC double-hattedness, 128, 153,
   158–59, 165–66, 169–70, 185, 218
 EU relationship, 69, 168
 Helicopter Initiative Seminar, 141
 Lithuania's focus, 139
 multilateralism and, 151–52
 newer member states focus on, 53
 NRF, 167–68
 permanent headquarters, 69
 PSC and, 128, 130–31
 as security cooperation example, 49
Norway, 69, 174, 210
nuclear attacks. *See* chemical, biological,
   radiological, and nuclear (CBRN) at-
   tacks/weapons
nuclear proliferation, 8, 69
Nye, Joseph S., 16

oil transport, 174
old boy's networks, 15
Onasander, 149
organizational theory, 156
Organization for Security and Cooperation in Europe, 49–50
Organization of the Islamic Conference,
   119
organized crime

EU response to, 53–57
piracy, 69, 166–67, 173–75
as security threat, 43, 233–34n26
Orlando, Vittorio, 80

Padeanu, Alina, 98, 105, 144, 224
PALMA (PASR research project), 195
paradigm concept, 18
Parliament. *See* European Parliament
PASR. *See* Preparatory Action on Security
    Research
Pastore, Ferrucio, 72
PATIN (PASR research project), 195
Petersberg Tasks (1992), 46, 153, 243n16
Peterson, John, 23
PETRA.NET (PASR research project), 195
pillarization, 45–46
    cross-pillarization, 73, 225–26
    dismantling of, 48–49, 72
    See also first pillar; second pillar; third
        pillar
piracy, 69, 166–67, 173–75
Poland, 53, 199, 202–3
police
    Civcom and, 187, 209
    cooperation and soft integration,
        53–55, 72, 73, 117, 119
    expert knowledge, 203, 204
    influence on security technologies, 189
    intergovernmental cooperation, 49
    as internal security tool, 43
    PASR research and, 196
    role in civilian crisis management,
        71–72
    supranational forces, 70
    See also civilian missions
Police Chiefs Operational Task Force, 54
Police College, European, 54
policy goals, shared, 37
    causal beliefs and, 28, 33, 192
    diplomatic expertise and, 93–94
    epistemic coalitions and, 178
    as epistemic community characteristics,
        15, 20, 25–26, 33, 34, 216, 221
    epistemic community influence and,
        23, 29, 104, 120–21, 194, 197, 200
    expert knowledge and, 100, 103, 134,
        188
    loose epistemic communities and, 186
    PSC, 142–43
    think tanks and, 40

Political and Security Committee (PSC),
    122–44
    causal beliefs, 124, 131, 134–35
    Civcom and, 86, 131, 187, 202, 207
    common culture, 123–24, 133–36, 219
    Coreper and, 86, 93, 122–24, 126–27,
        131–32, 143–44, 166
    creation, 82, 86, 124–26
    CSDP operations, 140–42
    EUMC and, 86, 131, 135, 152–53, 166,
        177
    external security focus, 103
    influence of, 40, 136–40, 142–44, 219,
        221
    meeting frequency and quality, 123,
        129–31, 219
    as moderate strength epistemic com-
        munity, 12, 122–24, 142, 144, 219
    professional norms, 123–24, 131–33,
        219
    selection and training, 123, 128–29
Political Committee (PoCo), 86, 124–25
Political Military Group, 138
Polybius, 149
Popens, Normunds, 87, 99, 101, 104
Portugal
    civilian missions and, 202–3
    EU internal security and, 106
    EUMC and, 172
    external security goals, 135
    instructions, 108, 138
    terrorism definition, 55
    terrorist threats in, 113
Posen, Barry, 244n30
power
    civilian/soft, 2, 40, 203, 215, 216
    EU as quiet superpower, 13–14
    hard, 157, 167–68, 168–69, 170
    knowledge and, 77–78
    normative, 66–67, 69, 72
    See also united voice of EU
Preparatory Action on Security Research
    (PASR), 11, 114, 187
    description, 191–92
    importance, 190
    projects funded, 193–97
    success/impact, 197–98, 200, 220
PRISE (PASR research project), 195–96
privacy rights, 60–61
PROBANT (PASR research project), 195
Prodi, Romano, 108

professional norms
  Civcom, 202, 206–7, 212, 220
  Coreper, 93–100, 109, 120
  defined, 28
  democratic values and, 223
  of diplomats, 79, 81, 91
  epistemic community strength and, 88,
    201, 216
  EUMC, 145–46, 160–62, 165, 185, 202,
    206
  GofP, 186–87, 190, 220
  meeting quality and, 158
  PSC, 123–24, 131–33, 219
Pronk, Rochus, 127, 132, 139, 184
PSC. *See* Political and Security Committee
  (PSC)
public relations, 87

Qaeda, al-, 109–10
qualified majority voting
  Community Method and, 230n16
  consensus and, 9–10, 96–97, 120
  Coreper I, 84

Radaelli, Claudio, 21, 23
radiological attacks. *See* chemical, biologi-
  cal, radiological, and nuclear (CBRN)
  attacks/weapons
Rathbun, Brian, 38
rationalism, 14
Raustiala, Kal, 23
realist theory, 156
Rees, Wyn, 46, 75
research, security. *See also* military tech-
  nology research and procurement;
  Preparatory Action on Security Re-
  search (PASR); Seventh Research
  Framework Program (FP7)
Research for a Secure Europe (GofP), 191,
  198
Research Framework Program, 58
Reynolds, Christopher, 130, 133, 137, 140
Richardson, Jeremy, 23
Risse, Thomas, 35, 39
ROBIN (PASR research project), 195
Roman Empire, 148, 149
Romania, 118, 202, 207
Rousiers, Patrick de, 158, 161, 168, 169
Ruggie, John Gerard, 18–19, 20, 223
rule of law, 1
  Civcom and, 204

as internal security tool, 43
  Kosovo mission, 207–8, 221
Russia
  Chad mission, 141, 176
  EU energy dependence, 232n79
  EU relationship, 69
  Georgia-Russia crisis (2008–9), 140
  NAVFOR Atalanta, 174

Sabatier, Paul, 23
Sambrook, Adam, 138, 171–72
sanctions, international, 1, 7, 46–47
Sarkozy, Nicolas, 170
Saxe, Maurice de, 149
Schengen Borders Code (2006), 61
Schengen Information System, 54, 57, 61
Schengen zone, 8, 46, 47
Schlieffen, Alfred von, 149
Schmitt, Burkhard, 50
Schweisgut, Hans-Dietmar, 104, 109, 127,
  144
SDA. *See* Security and Defence Agenda
SECCOND (PASR research project), 195
second pillar, 46, 69, 70, 96, 110. *See also*
  intergovernmentalism
SECURESME (PASR research project), 196
security, defined, 43
Security and Defence Agenda (SDA), 178,
  180
security communities, 17, 67
security research. *See* military technology
  research and procurement; Prepara-
  tory Action on Security Research
  (PASR); Seventh Research Framework
  Program (FP7)
Security Research: The Next Steps (European
  Commission), 198
Šefovi, Maroš, 93, 96, 97–98, 109
selection and training
  Civcom, 203–5
  Coreper, 88–92, 103, 120
  of diplomats, 79, 80–81
  epistemic community status and,
    27–28, 88
  epistemic community strength and, 216
  EUMC, 145–46, 154–58
  PSC, 123, 128–29
Semaška, Darius Jonas, 133, 139
Senar, Igor, 101
SeNTRE (PASR research project), 194
September 11 terrorist attacks, 42

Settembri, Pierpaolo, 91
Seventh Research Framework Program
     (FP7)
   funding for security research, 191–92,
      197–98
   GofP and, 200, 220
   internal/external security links, 225
Shackley, Simon, 30
Sikkink, Kathryn, 15
silence procedure
   Civcom and, 206, 212
   described, 70, 161
   EUMC and, 161–62, 176
   PSC and, 142
single market, 46
Sipiläinen, Anne, 128, 134–35, 135–36
Six, the, 3
Slovakia, 109, 116, 202–3, 207
Slovenia, 53, 137, 202–3
smaller member states
   EUMC and, 171, 218
   instructions and, 137, 211
   military grand strategy, 157
Smith, Michael E., 225
Snyder, Glynn, 17
SOBCAH (PASR research project), 195
social context, 13–14, 31, 35, 216–17
socialization, 33–35, 232n67
   Civcom, 204, 209
   Coreper, 100–101
   EUMC, 164–65
soft integration
   defined, 50–52
   EUMC and, 145
   vs. hard integration, 234n29
   military operations decisions, 70
   military technology research and pro-
      curement, 65–66, 67, 73
   police/investigative activity, 54, 61–62,
      73
   PSC and, 141
   third country relationships, 68, 73
   See also harmonization
Solana, Javier, 88, 125, 178–79, 183
Solana document. See European Security
      Strategy (2003)
Solidarity Clause of Lisbon Treaty (2007),
      43, 56
Somalia, 69, 174, 236n97
Soone, Sander, 126–27, 133, 135
Southeast Asia, 119

sovereignty, 1–2
   defense procurement, 183
   vs. efficiency, 180–81
   global challenges to, 75–76
   member states' influence towards, 9
   military secrecy and, 150
   redefining, 214, 227
   vs. supranational governance, 5
space industry, 194, 225
Spain
   ambassadorial instructions, 108
   civilian missions and, 202–3
   Kosovo mission and, 207
   military strength, 53
   military technology integration, 189
   SRR and, 119
   terrorism definition, 55
   terrorist threats in, 113
Spence, David, 76
SRR. See Strategy on Radicalization and
      Recruitment (SRR)
STABORSEC (PASR research project), 196,
      197
STACCATO (PASR research project), 196,
      197
status of epistemic communities, 23, 216
   Coreper, 92, 173
   diplomats, 79–81
   EUMC, 153, 166, 173, 177
   selection and training and, 27–28, 88
   See also epistemic community strength;
      influence of epistemic communities
St. Malo Declaration (1998), 46, 76
Store, Jan, 77, 97, 102, 116
Storr, Peter, 106
strategic culture, 146, 156, 163
Strategy on Radicalization and Recruit-
      ment (SRR), 55, 109–21
   Coreper's influence, 11, 110–15, 217–18,
      240n112
   Coreper's motivations, 116–17
   outcomes and implementation, 117–21
structural realism, 14
The Structure of Scientific Revolutions
      (Kuhn), 18
substantive norms. See causal beliefs
Sudan, 175
summitry, 80
SUPHICE (PASR research project), 194
supranational governance
   civilian crisis funding, 69

supranational governance (*continued*)
  Europol and, 54
  as hard integration, 50
  immigration and border control, 48,
    49, 58–60
  internal/external security link and,
    67–68
  vs. PoCo, 125
  police/military forces, 70
  PSC and, 125–26
  vs. sovereignty, 5
  SRR and, 110
  See also first pillar; hard integration
Supreme War Council, 80
surveillance, 193, 194, 195, 225
Sweden
  Civcom and, 210
  civilian missions and, 202
  CSDP emphasis, 53
  military technology integration, 189
  NATO and, 170
  SRR and, 119

tactical expertise, 155–56, 157, 185, 218,
    244n25
technology epistemic community, 11,
    188–89, 221. *See also* Group of Person-
    alities in the Field of Security Re-
    search (GofP)
technology/security link, 192, 198
telecommunications, 85
Tempus program, 118
TERASEC (PASR research project), 193,
    194
terrorism. *See* counterterrorism
Terrorism Working Group, 55, 110
think tanks, 39–40, 93, 180
third countries
  counterterrorism and, 57
  CSDP and reform in, 67
  development assistance, 1, 192
  EUMC and, 153
  external security and, 7, 188
  immigration control and, 59
  military operations in, 1, 63, 69, 70
  police operations, 118
  PSC and, 140
  sanctions, 1, 7, 46–47
  soft integration in EU relations with,
    68, 73
  weapons procurement and, 65

See also civilian missions; military-civil
    missions/relations; *individual countries*
third pillar, 46, 47–48, 49, 96, 110. *See also*
    intergovernmentalism
Thirty Years' War, 149
Thomas, Craig, 21
TIARA (PASR research project), 194
Tilly, Charles, 17
trafficking of humans, drugs, and
    weapons, 8, 43
transnational advocacy networks, 15–16,
    17
transnational crime, 75–76
transnationalism, 14–15, 15–18, 150–52
transport, 83, 85
Treviño-Ruiz, José, 167–68, 182
TRIPS (PASR research project), 195
Turkey, 69, 129, 232n79

Ukraine, 69
United Kingdom
  Chad operation, 64
  Civcom and, 210
  civilian missions and, 202
  CSDP and, 211
  EUMC and, 170, 171–72
  EU military capability support, 46, 199
  EU military headquarters and, 69, 168
  instructions, 107–8, 138
  internal security, 43, 106
  Iraq war and, 123
  Long-Term Vision and, 184
  military strength, 53
  military technology integration, 189
  political will for third-country military
    operations, 63
  PSC and, 125, 128
  Schengen zone and, 47
  SRR and, 119
  terrorism definition, 55
  terrorist threats in, 113, 197
  U.S. foreign policy support, 52
United Nations, 69, 80, 119, 176
United States
  ambassador selection, 90–91
  anti-piracy operation, 175
  British customary support for, 52
  counterterrorism strategy, 192, 248n22
  defense spending, 74, 199
  EU relationship, 49, 69, 169
  information sharing with, 54, 60

military procurement/technology,
    182–83, 190
NATO and, 2
think tanks and, 180
worldview differences with Europe, 42
united voice of EU, 1
    external security and, 7, 72, 140
    integration and, 12, 52, 68
    limitations in, 51, 68
    as norm, 68, 69, 134–35, 143
USE IT (PASR research project), 195

validity, shared notions of, 25
van Asch, Henrick, 139, 172
van Osch, A. G. D., 160–61, 162, 163,
    165–66, 176, 177
Verdun, Amy, 20–21
Visa Information System, 57
visas, 225
    Hague Programme (2005–10),
        233–34n26
    harmonization in, 72
    information sharing, 57
    supranational control over, 48, 58, 59

See also immigration control
VITA (PASR research project), 194
voice of EU. See united voice of EU
Vrailas, Joannis, 132

WATERSAFE (PASR research project), 196
weapons of mass destruction, 8, 57
weapons research. See military technology
    research and procurement
Weiler, Quentin, 143, 166
Western European Union, 49–50
Westphalia, Treaty of (1648), 43, 79
Wilson, Woodrow, 80
WINTSEC (PASR research project), 196,
    197
Witney, Nick, 180
working groups, 95–96, 106, 110
World Food Program, 174
World War I, 80, 151
World War II, 151

Yugoslavia, collapse of, 46

Zito, Anthony, 21–22, 23, 232n64, 232n80